DO THE CLEARING

A Step-by-Step Guide to Living a Happy Life and Getting What You Want

DO
THE
CLEARING

*A Step-by-Step Guide to Living a Happy Life
and Getting What You Want*

BY

JOHN BENZ

ONE TEN PRESS 110 PRESS TULSA

Copyright © 2015, John Benz LLC.

All rights reserved. The use of any part of this publication, reproduced, transmitted in any form or by any means, electronic, mechanical, photocopying, recording or otherwise stored in a retrieval system, without the prior consent of the publisher is an infringement of the copyright law. For information, go to www.JohnBenz.com.

Yurly Zhuravov, cover photo
Nathan Harmon, author's photo
Derek Murphy, cover design
David Moratto, interior design

First edition.
Published by 110 Press, Inc.
PO Box 52014
Tulsa, OK 74152

Many of my clients went out of their way to recount their experiences for this project, and their generosity has helped make this a better book. While there is tremendous value in these experiences for you, my reader, there is also tremendous value for my clients in moving on from them. With this in mind and to maintain anonymity, I've changed names and specific details for the client quotes and experiences. Any resemblance to persons living or deceased is entirely coincidental and unintentional.

The contents herein are not intended to treat, diagnose, or in any part offer professional counseling for any physical or psychological disorders. The author and publisher do not dispense medical advice or prescribe the use of any technique as a form of treatment for physical, emotional, or medical problems without the advice of a physician, in any instance. The author and publisher are not responsible or liable for any loss or damage, emotional, physical, or otherwise, allegedly arising from any information or suggestions contained within this book.

LCCN: 2014951561
ISBN: 978-1502385529

AUTHOR'S NOTE

The Clearing has two parts. Part 1 is Clearing your possessions. Part 2 is Clearing your residual thoughts. The parts follow a natural progression, so I recommend completing Part 1 before moving on to Part 2. You can read the entire book before you begin, or you can read Part 1 first, complete the steps for Clearing your possessions, and then read Part 2 and complete the steps for Clearing your residual thoughts. Whatever approach you use, the Clearing will be effective.

to Kara

CONTENTS

Introduction *1*

PART I CLEARING YOUR POSSESSIONS

1. Finding the Secret to Weight Loss in My Clients' Homes . . *9*
2. Doing What Your Possessions Are Telling You to Do . . . *13*
3. Introducing the Clearing to My Clients *17*
4. Doing Part 1 of the Clearing with My Clients *23*
5. No Matter What the Issue Is, It's About Power *29*
6. Choosing from the Millions of Moments in Your Past . . *35*
7. Your Possessions and the Current of Your Life *39*
8. Resistance, Happiness, and the
   Craziness of Clearing Your Possessions *43*
9. To Get What You Want, I Want You to Follow *49*
10. The Seven Steps to Clearing Your Possessions *51*
11. Outside Support Partners:
    Working with Others During Your Clearing . . . *63*
12. Being an Outside Support Partner *65*
13. Working with an Outside Support Partner *67*
14. Choosing Outside Support Partners *71*
15. Clearing Your Possessions: The Do's *73*
16. Clearing Your Possessions: The Don'ts *85*
17. Q&A *101*
18. Your Home After Your Clearing:
    Creating a House of Power *127*

ix

PART II CLEARING YOUR RESIDUAL THOUGHTS

19. Taking Care of What's Left Behind *137*
20. The Seven Steps to Clearing Residual Thoughts . . . *149*
21. Doing the Seven Steps : Taking Action *189*
22. Clearing Your Residual Thoughts: The Do's . . . *233*
23. Clearing Your Residual Thoughts: The Don'ts . . . *249*
24. Q&A *257*
25. Your Clearing and After *287*
26. Moving Forward, Setting Goals, and Taking Action . . *297*
27. Conclusion *303*

INTRODUCTION

I WENT TO my first Weight Watchers meeting when I was five years old. I can still picture it perfectly. Back then the center was set up like a church, with two rows of folding chairs and an aisle down the middle leading to an enormous old-fashioned scale. I remember the other women would smile and wave at me as my mother and I made our way to the front so she could weigh in. I'd wave back like I was a celebrity walking the red carpet. They loved it, and I guess in some way I did too. By the time I was ten, I had logged more hours there than most people do in a lifetime.

At home it was Diet Central. My mother would organize meetings and invite her friends over. Everyone sat in the living room, talking about their struggles and discussing what worked and what didn't. They went on different programs together, trying diet shakes and packaged meal plans. They bought books, watched videos, joined gyms, and attended seminars. Some would gain weight. Some would go up and down. Some would lose weight, go away for a while, and then come back twice as big as when they left.

It was always changing; the activities, the approaches, and the weight fluctuations never stopped. Outside of school, I was with my mother for much of the day, and for a good part of that time I was her sounding board, confidant, and partner during her daily pursuit of weight loss.

While I was growing up, this was all just a normal part of my life: diet centers and food stores, programs and plans, therapy and group meetings. That didn't change until I left for college.

I went to film school at NYU, and while I was there, my life was very different. I was going to concerts and galleries. I was out at night, dancing in the clubs, smoking joints in the back of taxis on the way to movies, and going to fashion shows and art openings with my friends. I did an internship at Universal Studios in Los Angeles one summer. I worked on films, and I was busy creating a portfolio of my paintings. At that point it seemed like dieting, weight loss, and that whole part of my life was over. Then one day during my senior year, a voice spoke to me.

I know how that sounds, and I spent some time debating whether even to mention it, but this is what happened: I was standing on the sidewalk near my dorm on the corner of 15th St. and Union Square, and I saw this woman. She was fifty-to-sixty pounds overweight, just like my mother had been for most of her life. I wasn't thinking about anything in particular while I was looking at her. I was just noticing her, and that's when the voice popped in my head and started talking to me. It told me I was going to write a book that would help people, especially people like her. Right out of the blue, just like that, and I thought it was the most ridiculous thing I'd ever heard. Forget for a moment that a voice was talking to me in my head; I wanted to paint and make films. Writing a book that was going to help people, especially with their weight, seemed insane.

I wasn't crazy. I knew the voice was my own, but it was different somehow. I guess that's why I never discussed it with anyone. That, and writing a book like this was just about the last thing I wanted to do. Even with the way I grew up, I never thought of it as a possibility. Still, the voice was talking like it was a done deal, and as crazy as I thought it was I remember agreeing to it. Before I was even conscious of the words forming in my mind, I heard them come out of my mouth: "OK, I'll do it, but not now."

It happened so quickly that it felt as if it were all going on without me. I was about to finish film school and there I was, committing to write some kind of self-help book. What twenty-one-year-old has a voice telling him to do something like this anyway? What would I even write about if I did?

After that day I moved on with my life. I told myself that it was just me talking, that there was no voice, and the whole thing was silly. The years went by. I showed my art, had a design company in New York, and eventually opened a second office in Los Angeles. I played guitar and sang in a band that performed in the clubs downtown, and I was busy having fun with my life. I tried to forget about the book, and what had happened on the street that day, but it was always there in the back of my mind. Eventually I had to admit that this was what I thought about the most.

I like helping people with their problems. I knew that those who were struggling with their weight could have different lives and that making the changes they needed to make wasn't as awful as they might believe. From watching my mother and her friends all those years, I knew the torture they were going through. I knew that somehow I could help, and it was almost painful not to. Once I accepted what was really going on inside me, things began to fall into place.

I discovered a school about fifteen minutes away from where I lived in Los Angeles founded by Dr. John Kappas, a renowned therapist many would consider one of the fathers of hypnotherapy. They had a one-year clinical hypnotherapy program, and I was completely intrigued. I had no idea a school like this even existed. I signed up, started going to classes, and I loved it. The teachers, the students, the curriculum: I enjoyed every part, and it ended up being one of best times in my life.

Dr. Kappas' techniques went well beyond hypnosis, and at school we learned all of them. We did dream interpretation and handwriting analysis. We studied Milton Ericson, Virginia Satir, Fritz Pearls, and others. Mornings and evenings, I watched hours of Dr. Kappas' taped therapy sessions. In the afternoons I attended classes and practiced what I learned with my classmates, and on the weekends I went to any seminar I could that would help me master my new skills. By the end of the year I could hypnotize a room full of people in seconds. I could look at a sentence or two of handwriting and have a good idea of what was going on in someone's life, and using the skills I had developed through my many hours of practice and studying the masters, I could figure out the best way to help someone before any mention was even made of what was wrong.

Before I finished the program, I opened my office. Not long after, the Clearing came to me, and my life changed forever.

More than twenty years have passed since the day I heard that voice, and when I look back now I can see how my life experiences all have led to this book. The voice was right about me. I did want to help. I think I've felt that way ever since I was a little kid going to those Weight Watchers meetings. I wanted an answer, and I knew that I would never feel like I had done what I was meant to do until I found it.

This book is about weight loss, but it's also about something bigger. In the chapters that follow, you will see that the Clearing doesn't affect just one thing; it affects everything. By helping to free you from the negative thoughts and feelings from your past that are hindering your life today, the Clearing can create changes in a very short period of time, not only with your weight, but in all areas of your life.

The realm of the Clearing is a wonderful world, and you are standing at its threshold. I believe in what it can do. I've seen it many times, and I've felt it for myself. You are about to discover what you're truly capable of and just how powerful you actually are. Understand that the Clearing should not be entered into lightly. If you commit to this, you are going to have to accept some changes. You will have to accept being thinner and happier than you've ever been in your life. You will have to accept your relationships working out and getting promotions at work. You will have to accept the respect and love of your family and friends, feeling good about yourself, and having a truly wonderful life. If you devote yourself to the Clearing and make it a part of how you live each day, there will be no way around these changes.

INTRODUCTION

I decided to call this book *Do the Clearing* because the Clearing is about taking action. It's not about talking about changing or contemplating the idea of change. By doing the Clearing, you actually are changing. You have the choice to lie down and accept the things that are happening in your life that you wish were different or to recognize the power inside of you to have what you want and to move toward it. You have to do something different for your life to be different. Welcome to something different.

PART I

CLEARING YOUR POSSESSIONS

1
FINDING THE SECRET TO WEIGHT LOSS IN MY CLIENTS' HOMES

FROM THE START, people came to see me for help with a full range of issues, but no matter what those issues were, almost everyone wanted to lose weight. What I was doing at the time to help my clients shed their extra pounds was working, but it was harder and slower than I felt it had to be, and I was frustrated. I wanted more for my clients. I wanted bigger changes. I wanted them to feel confident and in full command of their bodies, and I was determined to find a way to make that happen.

I knew something was missing, and whatever it was, I started to think that I wasn't going to find it in my office. There, I was taking people out of their lives and out of their normal environment. While this worked great for some issues, for weight loss it didn't seem to fit. I knew I had to do something different. I got the idea to meet with my clients in their homes, and that's when things really started to change.

At first, my plan was to talk in the kitchen. I thought that if we spoke where they prepared their food, my clients would remember the things we talked about when it came time to eat. That was the idea at least, but as it turns out many times during these sessions we never actually made it to the kitchen. In fact, things ended up going in a very different direction.

When I arrived for these appointments, my clients usually offered to show me around. As we stopped off in various rooms, they would tell me about their homes, their families, their lives, and they would also tell me about their possessions: a crystal vase from a favorite aunt, a Persian rug bought at an estate sale in Santa Barbara, a bureau from the in-laws, a porcelain weenie dog from a neighbor who was transferred to Colorado.

As they spoke about their things, I started to notice some of my clients were having strong emotional reactions. I remember one client bursting into tears when I asked about a jewelry box she had on her nightstand. Another appeared shaken after I complimented a sculpture that stood on top of her fireplace mantel. Some showed genuine anger when they recalled the memories their possessions inspired. Even items as innocuous and mundane as a coffee mug or an old blanket seemed to hold tremendous emotional weight.

I followed my instincts to hold back on my plans to talk about food in the kitchen, and as I walked through my clients' homes, I took my time, I began asking more questions, and when I did, I started to realize that not only were my clients keeping possessions in their homes that were making them feel bad, but that these possessions all called to mind situations where like with their weight, they felt powerless.

A book from a business associate reminded one client of a missed financial opportunity. An old jacket brought on feelings of regret and sadness over a recent divorce. A family photo triggered memories of a close relative who had died of diabetes. As my clients spoke about their things, I noticed that their facial expressions mirrored those they had back at my office when they told me about the issues they were having in their lives. I started to wonder: Could my clients' possessions be influencing them to feel powerless? Could the things they kept in their homes be contributing to an image they had of themselves that was holding them back? Is this why my clients thought they couldn't do what others with half their skills and experience could? Were they coming up short because of who their possessions were telling them they were?

From what I saw, it made sense. The emotions matched up. Incredible as it seemed, the feelings my clients were experiencing while talking to me about their possessions were the same feelings they had come to see me about, the same feelings they wanted my help removing from their lives.

The more homes I went into, the more I saw that it was true. Whether it was experiences from childhood, events that took place in high school or at work, my clients were surrounding themselves with reminders of the past that were keeping them from having what they wanted and being happy. Not all of their possessions were causing them problems. Some possessions helped them and made them feel good. But others reinforced feelings of powerlessness that were holding them back. My clients felt powerless to make more money, to get better jobs, to lose weight, to move on from bad relationships, or to simply be happy. Inside their homes, I found they had possessions that were influencing them to feel this way. This wasn't something I noticed every once in a while — this was something I saw happening in every home I went into.

2
DOING WHAT YOUR POSSESSIONS ARE TELLING YOU TO DO

HOW COULD MY clients' possessions have such a strong influence? After all, they weren't necessarily looking at their things and then saying to themselves, "I'm overweight. I don't get things done. I'm not someone with a lot of money. This is as far as I'm going to go in life." But if the memories associated with their possessions reinforced that identity, that's exactly what they thought and what ultimately became true.

My clients' possessions spoke to them. They were influencing them to move in certain directions and sometimes leading them to take actions they didn't really want to take. Some of their possessions told them they would give up at work when things got hard or that they were someone who would have a bunch of crummy relationships with people who would treat them badly. Some possessions told them they would always be forty pounds overweight and fail every time they tried to do something about it. Some kept them from reaching their goals or from even having any goals to reach for in the first place.

In my clients' homes, I discovered that possessions are more than just things and that the moments of the past they keep alive are helping to shape your identity. *Your possessions have power because they tell you who you are, how you should feel, and what you can do. They do this with the memories, thoughts, and emotions that are attached to them.*

It can be hard to imagine that your possessions could be playing such an important role in your life or that they could actually be causing problems for you, but they can and they are. The things you see in your home every day, or simply know are there, influence your thoughts and feelings. You may tell yourself that they are just things: just a sofa, a beach towel, a picture, or a scarf, just some odds and ends, but the truth is, they are much more.

Right now, in your closets, under your couches, and on your shelves, there could be possessions that are telling you that you don't have what it takes and that having a better life just isn't in the cards for you. You could have objects that are reinforcing an identity that limits you, that doesn't reflect who you truly are or what you're really capable of doing.

Maybe you're not quite sure what I'm talking about. Maybe you're looking around at what you have in your home right now and thinking, "What's the big deal? How could these things be having any impact on my life?"

Well, maybe for instance you have an old magazine rack sitting next to your sofa. Maybe it was a wedding gift from your first marriage, and the relationship ended badly. Maybe you bought it when you lived in a place you didn't like or at a time in your life when things weren't going so well. Maybe you broke your toe when you rammed your foot into it one night while you were feeling around in the dark for the light switch, and now when you see it, a part of your mind thinks "pain, injury, hidden danger, accident, fear."

Remembering breaking your toe or being reminded of your marriage falling apart or some other event from your past that wasn't particularly positive doesn't give you the kinds of feelings that you want influencing you, and neither do associations like pain and fear. While your magazine rack may not make you feel so depressed you want to jump off a bridge, if it has negative memories and emotions attached to it, it's steering you toward those things and away from how you want to feel. It's influencing the way you see yourself, and this ends up influencing the things you do in your life.

If you haven't already, go ahead and look around your home. Pick out a possession. What memories come to you when you think about it? Who gave it to you? Where did you get it? What was going on in your life at the time? How do those memories and associations make you feel? Who were you as a person when you first owned this possession, and is this truly who you are now?

The things in my clients' homes were influencing them, just as what you have in your home is influencing you right now. Without the reminders of the parts of the past that are slowing you down, I believe that you can lose weight, you can achieve your goals, and you can have a different life. Thanks to some very brave clients, I discovered that what I believe is true.

3

INTRODUCING THE CLEARING TO MY CLIENTS

"IT'S JUST A ten-dollar vase. Do you really think this is what's holding me back?"

"How can I lose weight by throwing away a lamp?"

"What do these pictures have to do with my marriage not working out?"

Even to me, there are times when what I do sounds eccentric. I haven't been taking any polls, but I'm pretty sure that I'm the only one around helping people lose weight and move on with their lives by walking through their homes, asking a few questions, and then pointing at what doesn't belong and having it hauled away. I was out on a limb with my approach and I knew it, but no matter how different it was, it worked and that's all that mattered.

With each day and each new client, I became more focused on the process. As my clients spoke about their possessions, we talked about the memories that came up. I noticed their reactions, their tone of voice, and their body language. I found questions that connected them to the truth about their things. The process developed and became more effective. I was so convinced about what I was doing that I took everyone through what I started calling the Clearing no matter what they had come to see me for, and always the connection between their possessions and what was going on in their lives was undeniable.

The Clearing quickly became all I was interested in doing. I thought, *Why work with clients in my office only to have them return home to surroundings that reinforce what we were working so hard to change?* So I didn't. My approach and the results I was getting—everything was different after I started doing the Clearing. With my weight loss clients I stopped even mentioning food or exercise. They didn't need my help to figure out how to eat right and exercise. They needed my help to see themselves as people who did eat right and exercise, and that's what the Clearing did. After going through the process they were less inclined to run out and frantically pursue some extreme lose-it-all-in-a-week diet. The panic was gone. I didn't have to talk anyone down off a ledge like I used to. It was as if they had graduated from that life. The drama, the angst—they just weren't there anymore.

Even those whose issues didn't involve losing weight started exercising and getting in better shape after their Clearings. Without the old ideas of who they were, without the negative reminders of the past limiting them and making them feel bad, my clients started to see that they were wasting time hurting themselves and that they could do things differently. They understood why certain events had them thinking and feeling the way they did. As the confusion faded the desperation went with it. Instead of fighting what needed to be done, they accepted it and started making changes.

Now, all of this sounds great, and even though my clients were having these truly wonderful reactions, I don't want to give the impression that they threw open the doors of their homes, I walked in, told them to throw everything out, it started raining diamonds, and everyone got rich, skinny, and had fabulous relationships. Sometimes there was resistance, and I understood why. Today, most of the people who come to see me already know about what I do, but when I started, many had no idea about my approach. People would show up at my office wanting to lose weight, expecting to discuss the issues they were having with their diets and eating habits and I didn't do any of that. Instead, I talked to them about doing the Clearing.

Some were excited and ready to jump right in while others would hurry out of my office as if they were escaping an asylum they'd stumbled upon in the woods. But the same people who left in a rush always ended up coming back; by the time I had finished talking, it was too late. They would go home and see the truth of what they had heard. They'd be sitting in their living room watching TV or in the kitchen eating a bowl of cereal, look at something across the room they'd seen thousands of times before, and a memory would come to them. They would make the connection between that object and their life and never look at their surroundings the same way again.

This is how it was for my client Emily. I discussed doing the Clearing during her initial consultation, and at the end of our time together she told me outright, "That doesn't sound like something I'd be interested in doing." She thanked me for my time and left without making a follow-up appointment. One week later she returned to my office, and here's what she had to say:

Emily: We have this antique mirror hanging on the wall just inside the front door of the house. My parents gave it to us when we got married. That day, after our session, I went home, and when I walked through the front door and saw it, what you were saying popped into my mind and I knew in an instant the mirror was making me feel bad.

I talked to my husband about it, and he said that it's a gift and maybe we should keep it. Up until we spoke about this in your office, I would have agreed. But now that I knew how it was really making me feel. I knew it didn't belong in the house. All it made me think about was how my parents tried to ruin our wedding, plus a few less-than-stellar moments from childhood.

The next morning I drove to a nearby town and put the mirror in a donation bin by this church I knew. I actually cried about it in the car afterward. That really surprised me. I ended up buying a new one from a store in town. My daughters and I painted the frame together and mounted it on the wall. My youngest glued her glass unicorn on the corner "to protect the family," she said. Now I melt every time I picture her saying that to me or when I see that little unicorn on the corner of the frame. I like coming in and out of the house and seeing the mirror there. It makes me feel lucky to have my daughters and my husband. I thought that old mirror was such a little thing. Now I know it really wasn't.

Many times, those who have had the worst initial reaction to Clearing their possessions became the most passionate about the process in the end. My client Brad left my office in an agitated state after I suggested the Clearing. He told me he could see how Clearing residual thoughts (Part 2 of the process) "might make sense." But he said, "Throwing away my things seems ridiculous and kind of a waste." I assured him that he didn't have to do anything he didn't want to do, but he was incensed by the idea of it and abruptly ended our session.

A few weeks later I received a call from Brad, apologizing for the way he had acted. He explained that since he left my office, he had tried to forget about what we had talked about, but he couldn't.

Brad: To be honest, I thought you were full of it. I thought it was stupid, or that's what I told myself anyway. What I kept thinking about though, was how angry I was. I was mad at you. Then I said to myself, "Wait a minute, this guy is just trying to help me. Why am I so angry?" I thought about it, looked around at a few of the things I had in my place, and realized I was mad at you because you were right.

Brad told me that his ex-girlfriend had moved out of their apartment two years earlier, but he'd never removed the things she'd left behind. He realized that he hadn't fully let go of her yet, and it wasn't making him feel particularly good about himself. I thanked Brad and told him that calling me like that took a lot of courage, because it did. We made another appointment, and Brad started getting ready for his Clearing—both parts: the "ridiculous" part and the part that "made sense."

Like Brad, many of my clients didn't feel right because the identities they were living with didn't match who they really were. The things they had in their homes that they thought made them feel good were actually doing the opposite. They were trying to grow, trying to be happy, trying to move on, and all the while their possessions were distracting them, dragging them back, and slowing them down.

Once they had time to think about it, once they really looked at what they kept around themselves, no matter what their initial reaction was, they saw the truth, and when they did, we went to work.

4

DOING PART 1 OF THE CLEARING WITH MY CLIENTS

AS WE WALKED through their homes, some of my clients looked at their possessions and started making connections right away. For others, the answers came more gradually. Either way, the Clearing helped them see their surroundings in a new light. Things they never considered important before began to reveal their power and show their relationship to what was going on in their lives.

During one of my first home visits, my client Jill was showing me around her living room when I remarked about a large painting she had of herself on the wall above her fireplace. She said that a previous husband had it commissioned, and then went on to tell me what a "bastard" he was and how she had "suffered for twelve long years" being married to him. She continued with a few stories of their "epic fights" and ended by saying how happy she was to have finally moved on.

Later I noticed an ornate bowl Jill had on her kitchen counter.

"This is quite a bowl," I said.

"Oh, that," Jill responded. "My sister is keeping some of her stuff here. Next time she's looking for it, she'll probably forget she left it here and accuse me of taking it."

I asked what things were like between her and her sister, and Jill presented a very positive description of their lives together. Before she finished though, she paused, and after a few moments she looked at me and said, "I know it's silly because it's so long ago, but we had this thing over a boyfriend of mine back in high school. She always had to have whatever I did. I caught them together. We're fine now, but that has always bothered me about her."

We moved through a few of the other rooms in Jill's home, and as we talked a clock with an unusual chime started to sound. Before I could ask, Jill remarked, "My grandfather actually built that." I told her how wonderful it was that she had something like that from a close relative. She agreed, but then said, "He was a bit of a drinker, and he used to hit my grandmother. But those were different times."

By this point, I was feeling the effects of Jill's home myself. In room after room, negative thoughts and emotions were coming from her possessions. She genuinely appeared to care for her things, but what was going on was undeniable. Each time she talked about her possessions, she looked miserable; the stories she told were never pleasant or inspiring, and none had happy endings. Jill had come to me feeling depressed. She was sixty pounds overweight and felt powerless to do anything about it. In each room of her home, that same feeling of powerlessness radiated from her things, and whether she was aware of what was happening or not, what came off them was seeping in. Her home was like a place where good feelings went to die. Jill didn't smile once as she showed me her house, and I didn't get the impression that she would be dancing around tossing wildflowers into the air after I left.

The identity Jill was creating with her surroundings made her feel stuck, made her look at life in a way that didn't allow her to have the things she wanted. Each day when she walked into her living room, the portrait from her ex-husband would trigger thoughts and feelings of the twelve years she spent in an unhappy marriage. When the clock chimed, it would remind her of her grandmother being hit by her alcoholic grandfather. When she saw her sister's bowl on the kitchen counter, it would bring back the memories of what took place between them and the damage that they were never quite able to repair. These events, and the thoughts and emotions that went with them, didn't necessarily register with Jill consciously, but her senses took them in and this reinforced her identity as someone who these things happen to, who thinks and feels this way. They would register inside her and tell her who she was, whether she wanted them to or not.

As I walked through Jill's home, the relationship between her life and her surroundings became impossible to deny. Around each corner was an object with a terrible memory attached. Jill's house had become a shrine to the parts of her past that were holding her back. Things she never imagined having an impact on her life were influencing the way she thought, the actions she took, and the success of what she wanted to accomplish. How could she feel good, how could she even attempt to lose weight or move on with her life, when everywhere she looked in her home the reminders of her past were maintaining her identity as someone who didn't feel good, who people mistreated, who suffered for long periods of time, and who was overweight and felt powerless to do anything about it? How could she succeed when her surroundings were telling her she couldn't?

When I looked at Jill's situation, there was no mystery to what was happening—any effort she made to feel different or to create a new identity for herself was continually interrupted by the feelings her things were triggering in her and who they were telling her she was. With the help of possessions she saw every day, possessions she was convinced she loved and were wonderful, Jill was making herself feel powerless and keeping herself from the life she truly wanted.

I started talking to Jill about possessions and how they can influence us with the thoughts and emotions attached to them. I asked her about the memories that came to her when she looked at some of her things and how they made her feel. We talked about her life, what she wanted it to be like, and what kind of person she wanted to be, and then I asked if this person would have some of the things she was keeping in her home. She answered my questions, and the next day I went back and whatever didn't make her feel good or didn't fit in her life anymore, whatever made her feel powerless or even think of powerlessness, we took out of her house and put in her backyard.

As we went through her home, I watched Jill come to terms with feelings of obligation and wrestle with what she thought she should do and the truth about the identity she had been creating for herself. Little by little, her backyard began to fill up. It was simple: it didn't make sense for her to keep objects in her home that made her feel bad. Jill understood this, and by the end of the day she was renting a truck and hiring a crew to take away the things she had Cleared.

A few months after we finished Part 2 of her Clearing, Jill walked into my office, and until that day, I hadn't truly realized to what extent our feelings shape our appearance. She was immaculately dressed, with her hair done and her jewelry and makeup perfect, but it was her face that struck me the most. It just seemed so different. Wrinkles were less pronounced somehow, her eyes sparkled, her cheeks glowed. I knew who she was, but looking at her that day, it was like I was seeing her for the first time.

When I met Jill, her focus was on her past and being unhappy. This was who she thought she was, and even though she was obviously miserable, she seemed defiantly proud of it. Before we started, her shoulders hunched forward, the corners of her mouth drooped, and her eyebrows seemed as if they were balancing heavy weights. Now Jill was in my office standing tall, telling me about a trip she was taking and how she was having her house painted. It felt as if I was talking to her peppy twin sister, the one with hundreds of friends and a booked social calendar. It sounds like an exaggeration, but it was really bizarre how different she was. It was almost as if she was coming back into her body after years of being away.

Like Jill, many of my clients expressed deep love for their possessions, yet when I asked what their things made them think about, I heard stories filled with sadness, guilt, anger, frustration, and regret. Many didn't want to believe that their surroundings were making them feel bad or that they could be doing so to the extent that it was actually causing problems in their lives. Most thought that their possessions were wonderful or that they were simply functional and didn't have any effect on how they felt or the choices they made each day.

My client Beth had vintage issues of *Vogue* magazine on display in her library. When I asked about them, she told me that her mother wanted her to be a model when she was growing up. "But she always said my hips were too wide and my arms were too chubby. I couldn't wear short sleeves because it irritated her." Beth didn't consciously think about those magazines each time she walked past them, but because she knew they were there, the thoughts she had about herself that were attached to them, thoughts like "I can't wear what I want," "I'm not good enough," and "I'm unattractive" were reinforced and ended up playing a more prominent role in her life.

Another client, David, had a beautiful oak table just off the kitchen in his home that he and his family used for pretty much everything. Several years before, he'd had a friend who was out of work refinish it, and David wasn't satisfied with the results. He remarked that his friend hadn't sanded between coats of varnish and the finish turned out "bumpy." David could afford to have the table redone—he could afford a thousand different tables—yet he kept this one and used it every day even though he admitted that it bothered him.

Initially, neither Beth or David saw their possessions as problems, but when they stopped to think about it, they realized that these things were affecting the way they felt and that it didn't make sense to keep possessions around that were working against them.

Powerful memories and feelings were coming from what my clients kept in their homes. The photo album put together with a best friend from high school, a stuffed animal won on a trip to the amusement park, the vanity chair purchased on a summer vacation, an antique broach received as a gift from a relative: all brought the thoughts and emotions attached to them back into my clients' lives. Whether they paid attention to them or not, my clients' things influenced their moods, their decisions, their actions, everything. They were making themselves more like these memories because that's who their memories were telling them they were.

No matter what is happening in your life, understand that when your senses take in your surroundings, you are influenced. The things around you affect your mood, your attitude, your energy, ambition, and willpower. Whether a possession is prominently displayed or hidden somewhere in your home, your office, or wherever you keep your things, if a part of you is consciously or subconsciously aware of it, it's having an effect on you.

Think of it this way: if you are sitting in the middle of Yankee Stadium surrounded by bleachers, the baseball diamond, the scoreboard, and the smell of hotdogs in the air, it's hard not to think of baseball and everything you associate with it. Just like if you have the coffeemaker you bought with your old boyfriend on your kitchen counter, the calendar from your last job where you felt belittled by your tyrannical boss hanging on your refrigerator, or the T-shirt you used to wear at the summer camp where everyone called you "Fatty McDougal" in your bottom dresser drawer, it will be equally hard not to recall the memories and associations you have with these possessions and not to think of yourself as the person you were during these different periods of your life.

How can you notice new opportunities if you're thinking about the ones you missed? How can you avoid making mistakes today if you're distracted by those you've made in the past or if your thoughts are telling you that you're the kind of person who makes them? How can you make sure that your new relationship is working if you're still focused on the old one that didn't? How can you be who you truly are if your surroundings are always influencing you to see yourself as who you used to be?

The past can define you, but only the parts that you let define you, only the parts that you focus on. I knew that if I was going to help my clients, I had to change their focus. I had to get them past the thoughts and beliefs that were stopping them. I started with their possessions, and Part 1 of the Clearing was born.

5

NO MATTER WHAT THE ISSUE IS, IT'S ABOUT POWER

FROM THE MARRIED couple fighting over money to the model struggling with an extra ten pounds, my clients came to see me because they felt powerless, and they didn't want to feel that way anymore. Who could blame them? Feeling powerless is terrible, and feeling powerful is fantastic. When you're feeling powerful, you step around distractions, you steer away from quitting and giving in, and you avoid excuses and complaining. What happens when you're not feeling powerful? You yell, you get irritated, you withdraw, you gain weight, you have bad relationships and you stay in them, you work at unsatisfying jobs, and you spend your days dealing with problems and disappointments and your nights not sleeping well because of them. Confusion, frustration, anger, and sadness can take over. After a while, you can end up forgetting who you are or that you have the ability to feel different. You can even start believing that a few ingredients mixed together in a bowl and baked in an oven have more power than you.

It sucks when you can't do what you want and when you aren't able to get those around you to see things your way or treat you how you want to be treated. *When things aren't going well, when you keep making mistakes or stepping back before you cross the finish line, it's because you're feeling powerless.* It's because something has you thinking that this is who you are, that you are someone who's supposed to do these things and feel this way.

The clients who came to me for weight loss thought that what was going on with their bodies was different from the other problems they were experiencing, but it wasn't. They had trouble with their weight for the same reason they had trouble with relationships or money. It wasn't about food or exercise like everyone thought. Eating the wrong food and not exercising were only symptoms. Whatever their situations were, my clients perceived themselves as powerless. I needed to change this perception and reconnect them with the truth. They were powerful, and I knew it. Anything that was telling them different had to go.

My client Tina was making progress Clearing her home, but she was on the fence as to whether to keep a few of her things. She wasn't sure how they were making her feel, and she was second-guessing herself. We talked about the problems she was having in her life, and I asked her if any of them made her feel powerful.

She replied, "No, not in the least."

I said, "Then you need to feel the opposite way in order to change your life. If you want something different, you need to feel different. If these problems make you feel powerless, you need to make yourself feel powerful. Go home and take away anything that doesn't make you feel this way. Look at each individual object you own. See what memories and thoughts pop in your head when you do. Notice the emotions you feel and then ask yourself, 'Does this make me feel powerful?'"

Tina returned to her apartment and began doing what I had suggested. Two weeks later, half her furniture was on sale at a consignment shop and several carloads of her belongings had been donated to Goodwill. She even moved out of her old apartment and into a new place.

Tina: I had just ended a four-year relationship that had never really been satisfying. I wasn't feeling positive about much of anything in my life. There was very little that made me feel good in my apartment. At first, my furniture and the things on my shelves and around my home all just seemed like things that were there, but when I really thought about them and asked if they made me feel powerful, the memories and disappointments came up and I realized I needed to make some changes. I ended up letting go of most of my things and moving out of my apartment. Not living there made it easier to break out of my negative patterns. It would have taken a great deal more effort to break them staying in my old apartment with the memories built into the walls, doors, cabinets, etc. Locations have an energy, and the energy there was not good.

My clients and I would go through their possessions, and I'd ask, "Do the clothes you wear to work make you feel powerful? What does your nightstand or bedspread make you think about, and does that make you feel powerful? What memories come to you when you look at your high school yearbook, your lamp, your luggage, or your collection of Raymond Weil watches, and do these memories make you feel powerful?"

If there were several memories or a string of different thoughts coming to them from a possession, I'd ask, "When you think of this possession, what stands out in your mind the most? What memory or thought is coming to you the strongest?" Once they answered, I'd ask, "Does this make you feel powerful?" If they looked at a possession and had no idea how it was making them feel, I'd ask, "Who gave it to you? Where were you when you got it? What was happening during the time period when this possession came into your life? What do those memories make you think of, and how do those thoughts make you feel?" Once they connected with what was attached, I'd ask the Power Question, "Does this make you feel powerful?" and then we'd move on to their next possession.

A few of my clients had trouble with the idea of feeling powerful or even with thinking of themselves as being powerful. Some thought of power as a negative thing, as something used to force others to do what they didn't want to do. Some believed they had never felt powerful and, thinking they didn't know how it felt, had difficulty answering the Power Question. For these clients, instead of focusing on power, I had them look at whatever memory or thought came at them the strongest from a possession and determine if it was creating good feelings in them or bad ones. I asked if their possessions or the thoughts attached to them made them feel disappointed, jealous, or angry or gave them any other negative feelings. I asked how their possessions made them see themselves, what part of their lives they recalled, and if they liked the way that made them feel. Power was just a word. What it came down to in the end was simple: any object that was causing negative feelings wasn't making my clients feel powerful and didn't belong in their lives.

Tracy: I had this coffee mug with the phrase, *If I'm not bitching, check my pulse*, printed on it. I was literally telling myself to be a complaining bitch every time I took a sip. That's what I used to think was powerful: being aggressive and abrasive and bullying people until I got what I wanted. Really, people were giving in so they could get away from me as quickly as possible. I didn't feel powerful. I felt lonely, angry, and frustrated. I never learned how to get what I wanted by making other people and myself feel good. John had to teach me that. And that mug didn't survive my Clearing. It didn't get donated either; it got trashed. I figured that's not a message anyone should be sending.

Rene: With my weight, I was constantly moving up and down twenty pounds. I bought a treadmill for the house thinking it would help me be more consistent with my exercise, and I used it for a while, but that tapered off quickly. Eventually I stopped doing anything physical, and my weight skyrocketed.

During my Clearing, John asked me if the treadmill was making me feel powerful. I knew it wasn't. It was torturing me. When it was delivered, it was such a big deal for me, and the kids were excited and climbing all over it, but soon after, they saw that I wasn't using it, and I didn't like the message it was sending them. It was in my bedroom, so every morning I'd wake up and it would be the first thing I'd see. I'd say something to myself like, "I don't have the time today," or, "Maybe I'll start back up again tonight or on the weekend." I can't imagine how many times I said that to myself.

Sometimes I'd just look at it and feel weak. Other times, when I knew I was lying to myself about my plans to use it, I'd say, "You are such a lazy turd," and then go take my shower. At night I'd see it out of the corner of my eye while I watched TV. The thing was so huge it was impossible not to notice.

The day after John left, I had it hauled away, and it felt really good because I really hated that thing. Before my Clearing, I never thought about feeling powerful. I used to think that was just for people I read about or saw on TV. I never considered that I should have those feelings or that I could create them myself.

If you are upset, if you are having trouble, if you are failing, giving up, or going around and around doing things that hurt you over and over again, it's because you feel powerless. Somewhere inside, you have a perception of yourself as a powerless person, as someone who can only go so far, who fails, or who can't get things to work out. In your home, your office, the trunk of your car, even your gym locker, your possessions are helping to keep this perception in place.

This is what I saw happening to my clients. Asking the Power Question and removing objects that were having a negative influence helped them get off their old path and onto a new one. It changed their view, and when their view changed they were able to connect with the parts of themselves that allowed them to do things differently.

Some of the situations you've been involved in may have knocked you off track. The objects in your home can act as reminders of these events. They take the past, place it prominently in your life today, and help define who you are with their presence. My clients didn't need their surroundings dragging them down, telling them to be who they didn't want to be and subtly draining their feelings of power. Neither do you. If you don't feel right, it's because the identity you've been living with doesn't match the person you actually are inside. When my clients started asking the Power

Question and Clearing their possessions, they discovered that they weren't the people their things were making them out to be and that they were capable of much more than they originally thought.

You are powerful. No one has been able to convince me otherwise about any of the people who have come to me for help, and no one will be able to convince me otherwise about you. Give yourself a chance to realize that this is true. Give yourself a chance to grow, to redefine yourself, and to make room for what comes next. When the time comes, Clear what doesn't make you feel the way you want to feel. Clear what doesn't make you feel powerful. It's up to you to make sure what your possessions are telling you is what you need to hear.

6

CHOOSING FROM THE MILLIONS OF MOMENTS IN YOUR PAST

I REMEMBER ONE night I was out with some friends in Los Angeles when one of our group bumped into a friend of his named Andy. Andy had his cousin's name and the date of his death tattooed on his right arm. While we were out that night, I ended up hearing the story of Andy's cousin's death four times as various people came up and commented on his tattoo. The story just kept repeating. People came over, Andy recounted the details of his cousin's demise, and anyone who happened to be within earshot ended up having to say goodbye to their good time.

Andy's death story affected everyone, and not in a good way. People weren't saying, "Oh, your cousin's dead. Let's party! Bartender, another round for everyone!" Most of the people who came over had to say how sorry they were and tell their own stories of death. Andy and his tattoo ended up influencing what we talked about, the thoughts that came into our minds, and the actions each of us took. Instead of all the great things I was thinking about before Andy joined us, I was thinking about death and accidents and loss.

And how about Andy? Was his life as good as it had been before he got his tattoo and had to tell the story of his cousin's death every time he left his apartment in a short-sleeved shirt? When he got out of the shower in the morning, did he look in the mirror, see his tattoo, and say to himself, "All right, my cousin's dead. This is going to be an awesome day"? Probably not.

I didn't know Andy well, but I'm guessing that like most of us he had many positive experiences and people he cared for in his life, but because of the physical presence of this tattoo on his body, this one aspect of his past started to dominate and crowd out the others. Andy may not have seen it this way. He may have become so used to the tattoo that he didn't consciously get the same pull of emotion as he did when he first got it, but if he asked himself the Power Question he may have been surprised by the feelings and thoughts that were still there and how they were playing a role in his life and the things he did each day.

The point is that things like this affect us whether we are paying attention or not. What you see, what you take in through your senses, whether it's a tattoo, a table, or your collection of vintage records, can change your focus and crowd out other parts of your life and aspects of your personality that could be making you happy and producing the feelings you need to create success.

Maybe you have a tattoo like Andy's or a photo of a deceased loved one prominently displayed in your home. Maybe you have a relative's name spelled out in vinyl letters on the back windshield of your car along with the dates of his or her birth and death, and maybe you're having a bad reaction right now to what you're reading because of this. That bad reaction is because what I'm saying is pushing you to see things differently.

Keeping mementos can be a part of the grieving process, but there's a reason people stopped having the family burial plot in their backyards. Thinking about negative things for long periods of time, being reminded of them, seeing them or simply knowing they are there, whether you make the move to consider them consciously or not, changes your focus and influences the actions you take.

There is no judgment here. I've done things like this many times. I've taken actions that have ended up making me feel bad because I thought they were the right thing to do, because I loved someone, or because I just didn't realize what I was doing. I made excuses to justify these actions, but that only made me feel worse. When I started to understand what was happening, I began to pay more attention to the way my things were making me feel. Now I feel a lot better, and so do my clients. When you Clear away the possessions that don't belong in your life, so will you.

Possessions you keep because you think you should, because you've gotten used to having them around, or just because that's what other people do may be playing a significant role in the way you're feeling and what you are able to accomplish. While negative emotions are part of the richness of life, surrounding yourself with possessions that are causing these feelings or putting what inspires them on your body can have a very damaging effect, one that can last for decades.

Sometimes people say, "Well, that's my past. That's me. That's who I am." But the truth is that there are millions of moments from your past that help create who you are. It's the moments you surround yourself with and focus on that have the greatest impact on the way you see yourself and the things you do.

What memories are attached to the objects you're surrounding yourself with? How do they truly make you feel? Instead of being around possessions that have you feeling sad, guilty, or depressed, even neutral, you could be surrounded by ones that have you excited about your life, that make you feel confident and free, and that have you seeing yourself as someone who could be in a relationship that makes you happy, as someone who can meet new people, find a better job, and even make more money.

Maybe there have been times when you behaved as less than the person you are. Maybe people got hurt. Maybe you got hurt. These parts of the past are over now, but the problem is your surroundings could be telling you they aren't. Some of your possessions could be making you believe that these moments are you in your entirety, when the truth is that they are only a small part. There have been plenty of times when you succeeded, when you helped others, when you were kind and brilliant, when good things happened, and when you felt great about yourself. You can choose from these moments what will create the thoughts and feelings that will benefit your life the most, and you can let go of what is defining you as someone you don't want to be.

Do you remember the feeling of freedom you experienced when you were at summer camp, when you went off to college, moved to a new town, or perhaps just went on vacation? When your surroundings change, it can clear your vision to see things differently, to see yourself differently, and to do things you might never have thought of doing before or believed you could ever do. You have the choice right now to create this same situation in your own home and to become someone you are happier being.

You may have been thinking you're trapped, but that's only what your surroundings have been influencing you to believe. You are free to do this. This is your life, and these are your possessions. It's not necessary to deny the past, but you don't have to take commitment vows to it either. You get to decide what to place around you. You get to choose from the millions of moments in your past which events you will represent and use to influence the actions you take, so make decisions that will help you focus on what you want for your life today and for your future.

You might think that success is a complicated mystery, but it isn't. It's about the way you feel. Take the most joy, the most inspiration, the most good feelings you possibly can from what's around you, and it will help you make the most of your life.

7

YOUR POSSESSIONS AND THE CURRENT OF YOUR LIFE

If YOU'VE EVER been swimming in the ocean, you understand the pull of the current. One minute you're floating along, and the next you're looking up to find that you've drifted halfway down the beach. You may not have been aware of it, but while you were splashing around on the surface doing your thing, the current was working beneath you the whole time, gradually pulling you away.

No matter where you're trying to go in your life, your possessions are creating a constant force moving you in a direction that the memories, thoughts, and emotions that are attached to them are inspiring you to go. You may believe that you can't make lasting changes, when the truth is more likely that when you tried to make them in the past, you were being pulled by a current that was working against you the whole time.

Maybe you find yourself giving up or acting in ways that don't make sense to you. Maybe you keep repeating mistakes and feeling frustrated, and you don't understand why. One minute you're treading water, and the next you're nowhere near where you wanted to be. You're overweight or in debt and your life isn't anything like you imagined. What you're experiencing is the pull of your current. What creates this current are the moments from your past that are most prominent in your life today. One of the ways certain moments achieve this prominence is through your possessions.

Look at your possessions. What do you see? Maybe you have an electric razor that makes you think of when you sprained your wrist waterskiing. Maybe when you look at your bed you think of your spouse cheating on you with your neighbor right before your divorce. Maybe there's a movie in your collection that brings to mind a time in your life when you made a bad decision and ended up struggling financially. Maybe there's a picture hanging in your hallway that's just plain ugly and that you never really liked. Are these the kinds of things you want contributing to the current you're flowing in now?

Maybe your life is much different from the one you had hoped for. Maybe you're unhappy and dissatisfied. Maybe it's been like this for a while and you're thinking this is it, this is all you can expect, this is just who you are and what your life is supposed to be like, and things aren't going to get any better. If these are the kinds of thoughts you're having consistently, they are a part of the current you've created and that you're moving in right now.

What you need to know is that thoughts that make you feel powerless are not true. They are lies your surroundings are helping to keep in your focus and maintain in your life.

Old boyfriends, old girlfriends, things you said that you shouldn't have said, missed opportunities and mistakes — your life is filled with experiences, both good and bad. *We all fail, and we all succeed. It's what we choose to focus on out of those experiences that tells us who we are and influences the life we ultimately have.*

You can keep your surroundings the way they are and continue to focus on what has you flowing in the wrong direction. You can drift away from the relationships, the lifestyle, and the body you want. Or, you can use what's around you to help create a current that moves you toward the destination you decide.

If you are trying to make improvements, trying to get ahead when what's around you is telling you that you can't, you're going to find it more difficult than it has to be to make changes. Why make it hard on yourself? Why protect your old life if it isn't working, if it isn't making you happy, or if you just want something more? Why be stubborn or come up with excuses for keeping things the way they are? Why spend your time fighting a current that is pulling you away from the things you want?

You control this. You create the current, so why not use what's around you to influence the thoughts and feelings that benefit the things you do today? Why not do everything possible to surround yourself with what tells you that you can and with what helps you see yourself as successful?

If you are feeling powerless, swept along by the current, then remember that possessions have power. Your life and what you have inside of you are too important to waste struggling with a current that's pulling you in a direction you don't want to go. Use what's around you to your advantage. Clear what isn't powerful, and create a current that steers you toward the life you want.

8

RESISTANCE, HAPPINESS, AND THE CRAZINESS OF CLEARING YOUR POSSESSIONS

I KNOW THERE will be some who will hear about the Clearing and say, "Come on. This guy wants me to throw everything out and it will make me skinny and all my dreams will come true?"

I understand this reaction, but once you see the connections and realize that *only the things that are making you unhappy and holding you back need to go*, Clearing your possessions seems less crazy and begins to make a lot of sense.

Regardless of how much sense it makes, moving on from the past can be a strenuous exercise for some, while for others it can be a more fluid experience. You may be at a point in your life where you are ready to breeze through Part 1 of your Clearing. You may also experience a little apprehension when it comes to letting go of your old things. If that happens, it's OK. Understand that this is natural. The changes you're making are threatening your old way of life. There's a part of you that has become used to how things are, and this part may be afraid of what you're planning. The Clearing will reveal possibilities and lead you toward a life that could be very different from the one you are living now. Some will feel this potential and get excited, while others will wonder what their future will be like and resist the unknown. The truth is, you can become so accustomed to being unhappy and going around and around with the same problems that you could experience resistance to the Clearing or to anything that presents an opportunity for change.

Why does resistance take hold? Why do so many people quit or fall short of their goals? Many who try to make changes do so while carrying the weight of past mistakes, memories of bad relationships, missed opportunities, disappointments, and regrets. They run into difficulty because who they want to be doesn't fit what they believe about themselves and who their surroundings are telling them they are.

In the past you may have attempted to move forward when what was around you was telling you that you couldn't, and you didn't get the results you wanted. Maybe you fell back into old patterns after convincing yourself that the changes you were trying to make weren't worth it. Maybe you told yourself that it's safer to continue being unhappy, and less painful to accept your life the way it is. And maybe because of this, good things like falling in love, living where you want to live, getting the new house or car, watching the numbers on the scale go down, feeling good in your clothes again, seeing the reactions on the faces of the people you know as they notice the changes in your appearance and your life may not even enter your realm of possibilities.

Maybe you've gotten so used to feeling bad that you've forgotten what feeling good can actually be like. But the love and admiration, the recognition and appreciation, the lifestyle you want—they're all waiting for you. Give yourself this chance. Allow yourself to create something new. Objects can be replaced, but your life and the way you feel are precious.

Maybe you're on the fence about taking this step. Maybe you think that Clearing your possessions sounds crazy. Maybe you believe that you're not the kind of person who does something like this, and maybe this belief has been stopping you all along. If you understand that your surroundings are influencing you, or even if you believe that they're having only a small impact on your life, why not make sure that everything you own is working for you? You want to feel as powerful as you possibly can. If you were Superman, you wouldn't have a bunch of Kryptonite sculptures and furniture inside your Fortress of Solitude, so why have anything in your home that could be slowing you down, even if it's just a little bit?

Nadine: I knew I needed a change because I was so unhappy. A couple of months before I did my Clearing, my boyfriend and I adopted a puppy. A few weeks later, we broke up and he moved out.

He used to work out of our apartment, so the plan was that he'd be around for the puppy, but when he left, it was up to me. I felt stupid because I should have seen this breakup coming, and I was totally unprepared to care for this little dog. After a few days I realized that if I kept him, he would end up spending most of his life alone in my apartment or in a kennel every time I went on a business trip, and it broke my heart.

I love animals, and this was no life for one to have. I didn't want this beautiful dog to suffer for my mistakes. Without my boyfriend around, it just wasn't fair, so I found the puppy a new home with a great family that fell in love with him instantly. After that, I went back to my life, but I was depressed about my job and my weight. I was also depressed about everything that had happened. Nothing was going right and I didn't really feel like I had much to look forward to, so I started spending quite a bit of time thinking about the past and all the things that had gone wrong. I wanted a house. I wanted a family, and I wanted to be married. But there I was, no boyfriend, no dog, nothing.

I had a few pictures of the puppy on my camera that I started looking at every day to make myself feel better, or at least that's what I thought. He was so sweet and cute that at first when I looked at the photos I would feel good, but always at the end of these memories I would start thinking about my ex and end up feeling bad. There were pictures of him on my camera as well, but I never looked at those. Still, I would think about him. I fooled myself into believing that we could work things out and that we were building something, but the truth was that we were fighting a lot and I was stuck.

I didn't realize it, but each time I even looked at my camera, I would feel kind of weak in my body. I would reach into my purse, sometimes several times a day, and sneak a quick look. It's weird, but I think making myself feel bad became some kind of crutch for me, like I had to punish myself for giving my puppy away and for things not working out with my boyfriend.

When I was doing my Clearing, I realized that my camera and the pictures were affecting the way I felt about myself. At first I thought the pictures made me feel good, and I was going to keep them, but when I asked if they made me feel powerful, I started thinking about it more. I realized that the camera and the photos made me feel powerless and were keeping me stuck feeling that way. I kept thinking about it and going back and forth. It was time to let them go, and I knew it. My boyfriend wasn't really right for me, and my dog was living with a wonderful family. The truth was that I wasn't as upset about the puppy and my boyfriend as I thought I was. I think I was just scared about the future and being alone.

When I asked Nadine why she kept these pictures, she responded, "When I get sad I look at them to remember a better time. They make me feel better." Without the Power Question, that's what she believed. She wasn't aware of how she was actually making herself feel. For Nadine the photos had become a trap. By looking at them and seeing the camera in her bag several times a day, she was creating an environment of powerlessness. In this state she was unable to see how she was really making herself feel. Through repetition, she became used to these feelings and started thinking this was who she was and the way someone like her should feel.

We tell ourselves things like, "They're just some photos," and that "It's no big deal." But when there are emotional connections and memories, those things aren't just photos and they are a big deal.

I asked Nadine, "Does looking in your bag, seeing the camera, and knowing it contains those pictures make you feel powerful? Does turning the camera on and seeing them make you feel powerful?"

The answer she discovered was no.

The Clearing is about letting go of what doesn't belong and moving forward. If what you're surrounding yourself with is influencing you to feel powerless, you are creating an environment that leads to immobility. You can't get what you want if you are busy holding on to what makes you unhappy. Nadine's camera contained more than simple photos of a puppy. The memories and the feelings of that period of her life, her ex-boyfriend, their breakup, and the emotions they entailed were all attached to it. Because she was seeing her camera and taking a break to view the pictures several times a day, she was living in a depleted state and making this part of her past and the powerlessness she felt over those events an even bigger part of her life.

The photos on Nadine's camera told her that she was someone who doesn't move forward, someone who is alone and who has relationships that don't work out. The photos spoke to her every time she even glanced at the bag the camera was in, steering her to think things about herself that made her unhappy and caused her to struggle. The Power Question showed her a different perspective and allowed her to change the pattern. She had found a good home for her dog and left a relationship that was making her unhappy. Nadine was right: It was time for her to move on.

You decide what clothes you wear, the style of your hair, the food you eat, the movies you watch, the music you listen to. You also get to decide what kind of person you are and what you will bring into your life. By Clearing your possessions you are making this choice and saying, "These are the aspects of me I will focus on. These are the thoughts and emotions I want behind me, making me feel good, backing me up and helping me to have a great life."

You can resist this, but what for? What is it you would want to resist? Removing possessions from your life that are weakening you? Letting go of what is taking your focus away from getting the things you want? Being happy? Joining those who know how to live successfully? These aren't scary things. These are awesome things.

Don't let the fear of the unknown stop you. Summon your desire for the life you want, for the people you love now and will love in the future, and devote yourself to what you are about to do. Put your passion into what's coming next. You can make today the start of something incredible. There's no reason to resist being happy. There's no reason to hold on to bad feelings. Let them go. Clear, and be who you are without them.

9

TO GET WHAT YOU WANT, I WANT YOU TO FOLLOW

BEFORE WE GO any further, I'm going to do something that I know from experience will ensure your success. I'm going to ask you to follow. That's right, I want you to abandon your old way of thinking, forget about all the better ways you may have of doing things, and follow. If you commit to this, if you devote yourself to what you're learning now, you can move past the tricks your old identity uses to hold you back; you can move past all the distractions and negative influences around you and begin to change the things you want to change about your life.

You think you know yourself. You think this frustrated, dissatisfied, struggling person is you. Well, it isn't. You are creating this person because of who you believe you are, and your belief that this person is you is what's preventing you from changing. That's all. If you follow what is written here, you can bypass these beliefs and start to see things in a new way. You're not a victim, and you're not an unhappy person or a failure. You're not someone who gives up or gives in. You can make yourself happy and create happiness in others. You really can. Will it always be comfortable to do the things I'm suggesting in this book? Probably not, and that's OK. Change is exciting and different; it's not supposed to feel comfortable. Take any sensations of discomfort or momentary anxiety as a sign that you're on the right track and keep going.

You are worth making a change for. You're worth letting go of things that are standing in your way and keeping you from what you want. Fall in love with your life. Why not? Your life is the greatest thing there is. If you haven't recognized that, it's time you did. Clear away what's keeping you from seeing the truth. Give yourself the space to discover something new about yourself and a chance to realize that you are more than you thought you were.

I don't believe we exist on this earth to repeat what doesn't work until we die. If your life isn't working out the way you want it to, then it's time to do something about it. Great relationships, the respect and love of your family and friends, feeling good about yourself, having the body you've always dreamed of: If you truly want something different, if you can accept giving up what makes you unhappy and devote yourself to what you are about to do, then, just as it did for my clients, the Clearing will work for you.

To allow your body and life to assume their true form, you need to know the truth about yourself. To get to the truth, you need to Clear what's keeping you from seeing it. Devote yourself to being the best follower you can be, and the Clearing will show you parts of yourself you didn't know you had, parts that will help you get past the hurdles and lead your own life successfully.

Moving forward doesn't mean making a bunch of halfhearted attempts, quitting, and then living in denial about the way you feel; it means stepping away from the place where you are now and continuing on. Put your energy into the steps you will take. Forget about how you used to do things. Devote yourself to following, and when the time comes you will lead with confidence. What you put into your Clearing, you will get back many times over. Prepare yourself. Give everything you can to what is about to happen. From here there's only one thing left to do. Are you ready? Let's do the Clearing.

10

THE SEVEN STEPS TO CLEARING YOUR POSSESSIONS

I'M THERE WHEN it happens. I walk my clients through the process, and we talk about it afterward. I've seen the boxes get hauled away, and I've watched the Clearing take a wasteland of a life and turn it into a continually blooming garden. I've witnessed what works and what doesn't, and these experiences have created a path that the Seven Steps will help you follow.

> Step 1: Realize you can do this, and tell yourself you can.
> Step 2: List the places you will Clear.
> Step 3: Gather your supplies and prepare.
> Step 4: Make your Power Question sign.
> Step 5: Write your commitment statement.
> Step 6: Begin, and go until you're finished.
> Step 7: Complete your closing ceremony.

Set time aside to do steps 1–5 all on the same day, one after the other. Then begin completing steps 6 and 7 either the next day or within a few days after. Once you commit, it's time to Clear. Focus and let nothing stand in your way.

STEP 1: REALIZE YOU CAN DO THIS, AND TELL YOURSELF YOU CAN

You can do this. You have the power to follow the Seven Steps. You are perfectly capable of Clearing your possessions. The way you've been seeing yourself, the person you've been believing you are, and the thoughts you've been having about yourself have been blocking you from making the changes you want. Forget what your things have you thinking about yourself and what your old identity may be trying to tell you is true. You can change your surroundings and use them to realize the life you want.

You've made all sorts of changes before. Maybe you gave up something that was hurting you or learned a new sport. Maybe you got some training and switched jobs. Maybe you changed a few of your relationships, your brand of toothpaste, or how you speak to people at work. Maybe you changed the way you treat yourself and your friends and family.

Some changes are difficult, and they test your strength and persistence. For some, you have to endure great hardships. Smoking is a good example. Maybe at some point in your past you decided to become a smoker. You bought some cigarettes, you inhaled hot smoke into your lungs, and even though it burned your throat, even though it hurt, you kept going; you did it anyway. Every day you inhaled until tears came to your eyes, until you were seized with fits of coughing, and instead of stopping and giving up, you continued and did it again. You didn't quit. Even though it made your mouth taste like soot, even though it made you dizzy and feel like you might throw up, you kept going. You weren't even addicted yet, but you wanted what you believed cigarettes could give you, and you didn't stop until you got it.

People who smoke are strong, just like the people who resist starting or who quit along the way are strong. Smokers think they are weak because of what their behavior has done to them, but they're still the same inside. The strength that caused them to endure all the hardships and physical pain it took to become a smoker is still there. The problem is that some of them don't believe it's there. They've become so used to their new identity and to feeling bad that they have trouble believing that they have any power, so it stops them.

It's the same with weight. People who gain weight are just as strong as those who maintain a healthy weight. Think about it. People who gain weight have to endure eating food that has them feeling good for a few minutes but then puts them at a disadvantage for everything they do afterward. They have to eat certain foods at such quantities that it takes away their energy, changes the way they look, what they're thinking, and their self-esteem. These changes affect every part of their lives, but even when faced with these hardships, even when they notice their bodies growing, their sex life going away, and people they've known for years suddenly having trouble recognizing them, even though they feel tortured when they look in the mirror, they keep going. That's strong. It may be just how you look at it, but to me it's undeniable. If you don't think that these types of actions aren't evidence of your capabilities, that's nuts!

Whether you are hurting yourself or helping yourself, your success at either is a testament to your strength and your power to create. You may think that you don't have what's necessary, that the abilities it takes to make the changes you want simply aren't inside you. But they are. Gaining weight, smoking, graduating from school, buying your first house, starting a business, getting a promotion—they all show your power, your abilities. Where these abilities take you is just a matter of which way your thoughts are directing them to go.

Within you there is tremendous potential, but there are thoughts that are making it hard for you to see it or to believe that it's there. These thoughts have been stopping you from recognizing that you can change your life. They make you believe you can only do things halfway and quit, that you can't, that this is the kind of person you are and all that you are worth.

You need to get past this garbage. To do this, to start to turn things around, sometimes what we need the most, especially at the beginning, is someone telling us we can do it. For Step 1, I want this someone to be you.

Whether or not you believe you have the power to complete your Clearing and make the changes you want, tell yourself you can right now. Say it out loud and in a way that you can really feel it. Summon all your passion. Summon your desire for your new life. Bring up all your energy and enthusiasm and say "I can do this!" and repeat it until you mean it. Even if you have to say it a hundred times. Scream it out loud. Run naked through the woods rubbing mud on yourself if that's what it takes to get your passion up. Go out your back door, raise your head to the sky, and yell to the sun, the moon, the trees, the world, "I can do this!" Go ahead and swear if it helps: "I can fucking do this!" Climb a mountain. Stand on its peak and declare it to the world, "I can do this, and I will!"

You may think this is silly, and maybe it will feel awkward to say this out loud, and maybe it's not such a good idea to go running through the woods naked, and that's OK. The point is to have fun and engage your enthusiasm for your new life. Even if it seems strange and different to do some of what I'm suggesting in the steps, do it because it works.

You need to get on your side, and you need to get passionate about your life. There's no need to waste time defending what isn't working or making you feel good. There's no reason to back away from the things you truly desire. Right now, today, you want to be happy and get the most enjoyment you can out of what you do. It's your life, and you want it to be the best life possible. Forget about attempting to dismiss the possibilities that exist. Get past the old identity and embrace what's really going on. Just as you have the power to do something bad to yourself and hurt your life, you have the power to go in the other direction, to do something good and improve it. Within you is the power to make your life a hundred times better. Believe it's possible. Realize you can do this. Tell yourself that you can (because it's true). Tell yourself with meaning and passion for your new life. Once you have, move immediately to Step 2.

STEP 2: LIST THE PLACES YOU WILL CLEAR

For this step, take a piece of paper and a pen and write down all the places you will Clear. Start with the rooms of your home, and then add the other locations where you keep your possessions. While it's important to Clear your home, and this will probably be where most of your things are, for your Clearing you need to put all your possessions through the process, wherever they may be.

Maybe you have your boat under a tarp at a friend's place, and it's become the new neighborhood beehive. Maybe when you switched jobs and moved, you left your wedding gown from your first marriage at your sister's house and haven't gone back for it yet. Maybe you have a truck full of your things in your brother-in-law's barn in upstate New York, or your parents have been keeping your old bedroom exactly as you left it when you were seventeen. Maybe your things from college have been sitting in boxes in your best friend's basement ever since you moved out of the dorms.

It doesn't matter where they are—your home, your car, your office, your safe deposit box, or a storage unit—if your possessions are there, add that location to your list. When you're finished, continue on to Step 3.

STEP 3: GATHER YOUR SUPPLIES AND PREPARE

Before you begin, think about what you are going to do with the items you're Clearing. If you will be bringing some of your things to donation centers like Goodwill or the Salvation Army, go ahead and get their locations and hours, and find out if they have a free pickup service for your larger items. Take a moment to find the nearest recycling center for your old electronics and computer equipment. If you will be using a consignment shop, be sure to ask about their terms of sale, their payment policies, and the length of time they will display your items.

You can also list items online, but remember, you want what you're Clearing out of your home and out of your life quickly and for good. If you're spending six months trying to sell your ex-wife's skis or every weekend haggling with potential buyers over an old canoe your dad used to spend his two-week vacation each summer yelling at you in, you're making those things an even bigger part of your life. Give yourself a time period to sell what you're Clearing, and if there isn't any interest during the time you've allotted, make arrangements to have what remains taken directly to the nearest donation center or your local shelter, and never look back.

Prepare for what you are about to do by gathering shipping materials and supplies such as tape, scissors, garbage bags, and boxes. Have what you need ready so you can remove what you're Clearing as soon as you've decided it needs to go.

Creating a pile of things that you plan to remove one day isn't doing the Clearing. You need to make sure the possessions you've gathered are out of your home and all the other spaces you're keeping them in and that they are no longer part of your life. You don't want to risk letting the things that make you feel powerless linger and continue to make you feel that way. Avoid this by removing the items you Clear permanently and without delay. You don't have to go running through your house wildly throwing furniture out the window, but there should be some level of urgency to what you are doing.

Next, grab your calendar and schedule your Clearing. Some of my clients have taken a few days off from work to Clear their possessions while their family members were at their own jobs or at school. Others have done theirs on a weekend or over the course of several weekends. Set aside enough time to go through everything: every drawer, every closet, every box and piece of paper, to go up in the attic and down in the basement, into the garage and storage spaces, every place on your list, and remove what doesn't belong.

Once you decide, mark the days on your calendar and continue on to Step 4.

STEP 4: MAKE YOUR POWER QUESTION SIGN

Find a piece of paper or cardboard and make a sign with the Power Question on it. You can use, "Does this make me feel powerful?" or you can modify the question any way you like:

"Do the feelings I get from this possession make me feel powerful?"
"Do the memories attached to this make me feel powerful?"
"Does what this object makes me think of make me feel powerful?"
"When I think of this possession, what stands out in my mind the most, and does it make me feel powerful?"

You can even ask:
"Does this make me feel good?"
"Does this inspire me?"

If a possession isn't doing one of these things, then it isn't making you feel powerful.

You could also turn the Power Question into a statement like "This possession is powerful because _____." or, "This makes me feel powerful because _____." If you can fill in the second half of the sentence and it feels right, you have your answer. Go ahead and make adjustments until you find a version that works for you.

I've created a four-question sequence to help you ask yourself the Power Question with your possessions. For your sign, you can use your own version, you can use the original Power Question, or you can write out the four questions I have below.

1. What does this possession make me think of?
2. How do I feel when I think these thoughts?
3. Is this the way I want to feel?
4. Does this make me feel powerful?

If you like, make your sign big. If you are crafty and want to put some extra effort into the design, go for it. When you begin Clearing your home, prominently display your Power Question sign in each room you are working in.

Once your sign is ready, continue to Step 5.

STEP 5: WRITE YOUR COMMITMENT STATEMENT

Think of what your life would be like today, think of the things you would know and be able to do, think of the successes you would have if those times when you had the choice, you fully committed to what you were doing instead of just trying. Maybe you would be running your own business right now. Maybe you'd be working for your favorite sports team. Maybe you would love the way your body looks when you see yourself in the mirror after your morning shower. Maybe you'd be married to Mr. Right and be happy going to work each day at your dream job.

You may have tried different things in the past to change your life, and maybe *trying* was part of the reason you didn't find the success you were looking for. Do the Clearing differently than you've done those other things and commit. Get a pen and a piece of paper, and in a few short sentences, write out what you are going to do, when you are going to do it, and how long you plan to take. Finish with a promise that you will not stop until you've Cleared each space on your list. Sign the statement and date it. Put it on your nightstand. Fold it up and tape it to the wall next to your bed, or place it wherever you can see it before you go to sleep at night and when you get up in the morning, and keep it there until you've completed Part 1 of your Clearing.

You can use the example below as a guide for writing your own commitment statement.

> *I, _____, will review all my possessions and Clear from my home and all other spaces I use, rent, or own, every object that does not make me feel powerful. I will begin on _____ and finish on _____. I will use the Power Question to help decide what to keep and what to discard. I promise to continue until I've Cleared each space on my list.*
>
> _____
> *Signature & Date*

Your old identity may try to tell you that you're not the kind of person who needs to write down a commitment statement and that a few of these steps don't really apply to you. It may try to tell you that you don't need to commit and that you should just give it a try and see what happens instead. It may attempt to diminish parts of the Clearing and tell you there is a better way, just like it did those times in the past when you found yourself giving up and not getting what you wanted.

Don't be distracted by this crap. You can do this! These are just thoughts your surrounding are helping to influence you to have, the same thoughts that in the past may have been keeping you from making the changes you've wanted to make to your life.

You have to decide who is going to win this time. Focus on finishing what you've started, and you will. Don't let your old life creep back in. Do everything you can to finish by the date you've chosen. If you have to adjust it after you begin, then go ahead. But before you start, consider that if you don't complete this task, or if you decide to go against the answers you receive from asking the Power Question and keep certain objects that you know are affecting you negatively, they will not only have the old memories and feelings attached, but also a new memory of you quitting and breaking your promise to yourself. Avoid this. You need to show yourself you can complete your Clearing, that even if it's hard, you can stick to it and finish.

Bubblegum-flavored ice cream is something you try; the Clearing is something you do. Don't try to have a new life or to make things better. Commit to it. After you've written your commitment statement and signed it, move on to Step 6.

STEP 6: BEGIN, AND GO UNTIL YOU'RE FINISHED

Set up your sign in the first space on your list and begin. Go item by item, room by room. Look at everything from the lamp shades to the paint on the walls. Focus on the feelings you get from the memories and thoughts that come to you. Ask the Power Question for the possessions you might want to keep, and when you receive your answers remove what doesn't belong. Instead of going back and forth, jumping from room to room, doing a bit of work here and then a bit more there, make it easier to focus and to feel like you are accomplishing something by Clearing each space on your list, one at a time. When you've completely Cleared one room, check it off your list, grab your Power Question sign, and move on to the next.

As you walk through your home and the other spaces on your list, you may look around and know right away that you want to remove most of what you see. Maybe when you open the door to your storage space you'll take one look and think, "I don't really want any of this stuff." Maybe you'll immediately notice a feeling of powerlessness and decide that it doesn't make sense to sort through any of it. If that happens, great! Clear it away, and then move on to the next space on your list.

It may be more likely though, that during your Clearing, your enthusiasm for your new life will be battling with the pull of your old one. If you find yourself reminiscing for long periods of time, dwelling on old photos from school, letters from ex-boyfriends, and knickknacks from your travels, if you're spending hours going through every birthday card and piece of paper you've collected since you were six or find yourself reading a half-finished screenplay that's been holding down the lid of your fish tank for the past three years, you're falling back into the patterns your surroundings have helped to create and the life you've been working so hard to change.

Pause to contemplate your possessions for too long and you run the risk of your old life pulling you back in. Do everything in your power to work efficiently and to spend as little time as possible rummaging around in your past. If you devote too much time to going down memory lane, you could end up walking up and down that same street for the rest of your life.

Clearing the spaces on your list could take a day or a few weeks. Move as quickly as you can. Stick to the Power Question and honor your commitment promise. It's OK to be thorough, but move with stealth, knowing that your old patterns are battling for their survival. You may run into a difficult decision and start telling yourself you've done enough, but enough is only when you are finished Clearing everything on your list.

If you need an extra weekend, add it, then change the finish date on your commitment statement, and keep going until the possessions you're Clearing are no longer in your possession. Leaving them in the trunk of your car or moving them into your basement or a storage space won't remove their influence. Until they are completely out of your life, they are still your possessions. It doesn't matter if they are seen or hidden away. If they stay, you will know they are there and they will affect you.

If you've put off finishing things in the past, set a new standard for yourself with the Clearing. Even if it takes longer than you thought it would, stick with it. When you see the finish line, don't pause to take a breath. Put in even more effort, and go until you've stepped across it. Think about it. Is there a reason to hold out? Is there something else you're waiting for? Is there something better going on or that might happen one day that you should save your energy and effort for, instead of changing your life right here and now and committing to a different future? You know that you have to make changes, so do it. Stop putting your energy into fighting yourself about this.

Get on your side and stay there. You want to move on, so move. Create some distance from your old life, and give yourself room to breathe. You're pushing the weight of your past off your shoulders with the Clearing. Don't be afraid of the feeling of lightness. Embrace it. Give yourself a chance to become accustomed to it, and keep going. Forget about housing your old life and setting up displays for what's already happened. Make room for what your life's becoming. Begin and go until you are finished with all the spaces on your list, and then move on to Step 7.

STEP 7: COMPLETE YOUR CLOSING CEREMONY

Once you've Cleared your home and all the spaces on your list, once you've removed your last box, made that final trip to the donation center, and honored your commitment, take out a small piece of paper and a pen and write:

> *I promise to keep myself free of possessions that inspire negative thoughts, encourage feelings of powerlessness in me, or interfere with my efforts to have a wonderful life in any way.*
>
> _____
> Signature & Date

Hold off on signing it for now, and put it aside. Go through each room of your home, throw back the curtains, open the windows and the doors, clear out the old air, and let the new air in. If it's cold out, so be it. Take a stroll, look around at the space you've created for what comes next, and feel good about what you've done. You've made important moves by Clearing your possessions, moves that will have a definite impact on the rest of your life and on what happens in Part 2 of your Clearing.

After you've had time to review what you've done, remain standing and take three deep, long breaths, close your eyes, and then envision yourself in your home, being happy, feeling good, and living the way you want to live. If your living space isn't what you want it to be yet, see it the way you do want it, and once you are smiling and feeling good, open your eyes, and get out the piece of paper with your promise on it. Sign your name underneath what you've written, include the date, fold up your paper, and save it in the money compartment of your wallet. This paper will remind you that whatever you buy, whether it's food, appliances, new sheets for the bed, anything, it should be able to pass the Power Question before it enters your home.

Once your ceremony is complete, move immediately on to Part 2 and to completing your Clearing.

11

OUTSIDE SUPPORT PARTNERS: WORKING WITH OTHERS DURING YOUR CLEARING

MAYBE YOU'RE READING *Do the Clearing* with a few of the people from your job, with your aunt or your sister, or someone from your running club. Maybe you're planning to partner up with someone, to start together and help each other out. Doing the Clearing with other people could work or it could be a disaster, and that all depends on how you go about it.

Let me say this before we go any further: The Clearing is about you. It's about your possessions, your memories, your feelings, your power, and your future. You don't need to work with other people to do the process and in most cases it will be easier and more beneficial for you to simply Clear your possessions without partnering up with anyone.

Let me explain. Working with friends or getting advice from some of the people in your life can introduce their memories and feelings into what you're doing. It makes your Clearing not only about what you think and feel, but also about what your friends think and feel. No matter how strong you are, someone else's view will influence your own and affect your decisions, which is the opposite of what you want for your Clearing.

Realize that when you bring your friends and loved ones into the process, you are bringing in people who see you according to your old identity. They will give you advice that is in line with who they think you are and what they believe is right for the person they see you as. This isn't something to fault anyone for, but if you want to work with other people for your Clearing, you need to establish the roles you will play in supporting each other before you start, so you can prevent any issues like these from interfering with your success.

Coming up, I will describe the best way to go about working with others by being what I call an outside support partner. I follow this with advice on how to work with your partner and how to determine who would be good to work with if you should decide to go this route.

12

BEING AN OUTSIDE SUPPORT PARTNER

IF YOU CHOOSE to do your Clearing with someone you know, you can avoid the pitfalls I've mentioned by being outside support partners (OSPs) for each other. What is an OSP? An OSP is someone who is responsible for helping with what happens outside of the home and any other spaces being Cleared, so the person Clearing can work undisturbed and focus on his or her possessions. This could include things like picking up the kids from school and dropping them off at swimming, ordering take out meals, or running out for supplies like extra boxes and tape.

What an OSP doesn't do (and this is extremely important) is help with what's happening inside the home and the other spaces being Cleared. This means that the OSP doesn't help answer the Power Question or give advice on what possessions to Clear.

It's really as simple as that. Your role as an OSP is outside support only. If you give advice or become involved with helping answer the Power Question, you diminish the experience for the person you are supposed to be supporting. Keep in mind that no one can reach their true identity by applying the answers of others to themselves. Be available, but also avoid any bad feelings that could occur if you were to become directly involved in the process of Clearing your partner's possessions. In other words, don't help others out of having a great experience by stepping out of your role as an OSP. Make it your goal to provide the best outside support you can by giving your partner the time and space he or she needs to focus.

If you find your role as an OSP too confining and you're thinking about having a more hands on approach, or as you're fulfilling your role as an OSP you feel the need to step in and "help" with a few friendly words of advice, consider this: What if the person you are supporting calls you in a moment of weakness and asks you what she should do with some of the possessions she's on the fence about? What if, based on your advice, she goes against the answers she's received from asking the Power Question and keeps a few items that she later realizes she should have Cleared and blames you for all the things that have gone wrong in her life since? What if your friend starts talking about his Clearing and you're tempted to compare it to your own? What if you end up thinking that the person you are working with is having a better, more meaningful experience than you and you become distracted by the effects these thoughts are having?

If you're thinking you're helping your friend out by telling her it's a no-brainer to donate her wedding ring from her last marriage to charity, or that maybe she should keep that summer dress because she looks so hot in it, you'd be interfering and diminishing the potential rewards she could get from having made those choices herself, and you will be influencing her to make decisions that could end up causing problems for her. As good and as kind hearted as your intentions may be, if you get directly involved in the process and stray from your role as an OSP, the things you do will most likely work against the person you are supposed to be helping.

These issues and others can be avoided by following the guidelines I've given here. Always remember, the O in OSP is for "outside." If as an OSP, you commit to helping only with what happens outside of the home, you can be of tremendous benefit to anyone you choose to partner with.

13

WORKING WITH AN OUTSIDE SUPPORT PARTNER

If YOU'VE DECIDED to partner up with one of your friends or family members, be respectful of the role this person plays as your OSP. Bypass creating unnecessary pressure or bad feelings by steering away from any discussion of the process or the possessions you are Clearing. Contact and converse with your OSP only when absolutely necessary, and focus on the Power Question and Clearing the spaces on your list as quickly as you can.

If you're thinking the suggestions I've made so far regarding working with others are for someone else and that your relationship with your OSP is different, and you don't have to be concerned with any of the issues I've mentioned, ask yourself this: What if you bring your OSP around while you are going through your things, and he or she falls in love with something you're letting go of? What if, instead of being free of that possession and its memories, you hand it over and it becomes something you see every time you go to his or her place? You're feeling great, you go to your friend's house one day, and *blam!* There it is—your old sweater, end table, crystal vase—saying things to you that you don't want to hear, telling you who you are, and bringing you back again into the moments that you worked so hard to remove from your life.

What are you going to tell your girlfriend who has always had her eye on those Louboutin heels or that Coach purse you're Clearing while she's helping you ship them off to a charity? What are you going to say to your buddy who would really love the pool table he just helped you pull out of your basement? What if when it's your turn to be the OSP, you go to your partner's home and feel the urge to make a few exceptions of your own? What if you see some things you want for yourself? (For more on why this is a bad idea, see "Don't #1: Don't Give Your Things to Your Neighbors, Relatives, or Friends" later in the book.)

An important thing to remember as well is to never mistake having an outside support partner for having a dumping partner. That isn't what "support" means when it comes to the Clearing. If your relationship with your OSP is based on sharing your problems, this habit could end up interfering with your Clearing and changing your focus. You may find yourself giving in to the temptation to say things like, "This is too hard," or, "It's taking longer than I thought," or, "I didn't realize I had so much stuff; maybe I should do this another time." (Your old identity can have you coming up with all kinds of excuses to distract and delay you.) If your OSP tries to comfort you by telling you it's OK when you say these things or when you try to skip some of the spaces on your list or keep possessions you know you should Clear, your OSP isn't being supportive, she is standing in your way, and you will have been the one who put her in a position to do it. Besides, doing the Clearing is about taking action. Save the discussion for later, and get busy with what you need to do to complete the Seven Steps.

Instead of seeking advice from your OSP or some of the people in your life, seek advice from these pages and look inside of yourself. If you rely on your OSP for outside help only, you will avoid sabotaging your Clearing, you will protect both you and your OSP from taking on any negative feelings that could result if you were to elicit his or her opinion, and you will increase your chances of Clearing the possessions that need to be removed from your life.

If you and your spouse, domestic partner, boyfriend, or girlfriend are Clearing at the same time, consider that you both have the same goal: You want to complete your Clearings and have the best lives possible. The person you're working with is your partner.

When you share the same mindset, you can create an incredible life together. Give each other room to Clear on your own and to go through the process without interference. Then, help each other out during those times when you come together to discuss shared items. Be honest. Talk about what you want your lives to be like, focus on creating your future with each other, and use this opportunity to leave the past behind.

14

CHOOSING OUTSIDE SUPPORT PARTNERS

BRINGING OTHER PEOPLE into your Clearing, even as outside support, can be tricky. If this is the direction you are determined to follow, first make use of the Power Question to decide your best move. If you and your friend Diane are reading *Do the Clearing* together and you want to help each other, ask the Power Question and see if it's a powerful thing to do. Maybe a vision of Diane flirting with your boyfriend at your birthday party last year will spring into your mind, or maybe you'll remember all the times she's dumped her marital problems on you without ever asking about your own life.

Or maybe it's not like that. Maybe the first thing you think of is Diane helping you with the kids that time you had to visit your mom in the hospital or the surprise party she threw for you on your twenty-seventh birthday the year you got divorced and weren't feeling so good about yourself.

The Power Question could tell you that having one of your friends be your OSP is a powerful idea, or it could tell you that you shouldn't do your Clearing with certain people. When these same people ask the Power Question about doing their Clearing with you, they could get an answer telling them that partnering with you isn't powerful, something you may want to think about before you consider asking certain people to join you.

If the Power Question is telling you not to have someone as an outside support partner and you decide to go ahead with it anyway, you're sabotaging yourself and probably doing the same sort of thing you've done in the past to stop yourself from losing weight, making more money, getting a better job, or having great relationships.

Before you go ahead and start asking some of the people from your life to join you, ask yourself why you want to do Part 1 of the Clearing with other people instead of by yourself. Is it because you think it will be fun? Or is it because you don't have faith in yourself to follow through?

Be honest with yourself from the start. If you follow the suggestions provided here, an OSP could be an asset during your Clearing. At the same time, I must emphasize that as much as you love them and want them around you, you don't need your friends or family to help you with this. All you need is this book and your desire to have a better life.

Ultimately, the Clearing is a time for you to recognize your strength and power, to stand on your own, and to see for yourself that you can do it. I encourage you to Clear your possessions on your own and to organize your time before you begin so that you can do so quickly and thoroughly. At the same time, I realize that having children, a job, and many other responsibilities can interfere with your efforts and that along with your preparations, having an OSP can be a big help. In these cases, and if you've found the right person, and you've determined that it's powerful to do, go ahead and Clear with the assistance of your OSP. After you've Cleared the spaces on your list, and it comes time for you to fulfill your role as the OSP, be the exceptional person you are, and give your support to your partner in the manner described here.

Remember, and tell yourself out loud, that you are powerful, that you are capable of accomplishing the Clearing and so much more. Tell yourself this now and then give yourself a chance to show yourself that it's true. Whether you work with outside support or not, what is most important is that you start and you finish and you use what you've learned here to take the actions you need to take to have an amazing Clearing and a sweet life.

15

CLEARING YOUR POSSESSIONS: THE DO'S

#1: DO DETERMINE IF YOU ARE READY TO START YOUR NEW LIFE

Start when you are ready. Start when you really feel the truth of what you are reading and you know you are going to give one hundred percent to your Clearing. If you're unsure or you're struggling with the idea of letting go, read Part 1 again and then see if you feel different about your things. You don't have to pressure yourself. Give yourself a chance to live with the ideas that are here and to see the truth. In order to have a successful Clearing, you have to really believe it's time to let go of your old life and the way you've been living. You have to really *want* something different. You have to feel not just that it would be nice, but that changing your life is the only thing that's acceptable to you. When you feel this way, you are ready.

Maybe you didn't complete some of the things you started in the past. Maybe you made some mistakes or were embarrassed, and you retreated into a shell because of it. Maybe you stood on the sidelines and watched everyone else have a good time, or maybe you've never really fully committed. Make this time different. First, determine whether you are ready to begin. Be honest with yourself about what you want and what you are willing to do. If you recognize the effects of your possessions and their ability to influence you, if what you are reading in this book makes sense to you, if you see yourself and your life in the words written here, then give yourself this chance at something new. Make *this* the time you jump in with both feet, with no reservations and no holding back.

You may have come to believe that what's been happening in your life is just the way it is, that it's supposed to be hard, frustrating, and filled with disappointment, but if you allow it, if you give yourself a chance, you can get used to believing different things and to feeling the way you want to feel. You can get used to being happy. You can have an amazing life, and you can put the pieces in place that make it happen. Be honest about how things have been turning out in your life and how you want them to be, and then be kind to yourself by letting go and moving forward.

If you really want something new, something different, something better, if you really want change, let nothing stand in your way. Determine if you are ready to start your new life, and if you are, get started, keep going, and don't stop until you have it. Stick to the Seven Steps and the guidelines I've laid out for you here.

#2: DO FACE DENIAL HEAD ON

If you're looking around your home thinking that everything you see is wonderful and power-inducing and that there isn't anything off about the identity you've been living with even though you are overweight, struggling with different areas of your life, and not feeling too powerful about anything, if you're thinking that I must be talking about someone else here in *Do the Clearing* and that your problems are different and that's why nothing seems to work out the way you want it to, then you aren't living in the reality you think you are. You are living in denial. You don't think so, and that's what denial does. It keeps you in the dark.

Everyone has spent time in denial. Whenever you don't want to face the truth, it's a tempting place to go. It can seem so much easier to think that a problem is someone else's fault than to admit that it's you causing your own difficulties. But is it actually easier? It can feel that way, and that's why denial is such a trap. When you use denial, things temporarily look better because you leave out what you don't want to see, and it's nice, for the moment. But then one day you get a glimpse of the truth. You wake up and realize that the five or ten pounds you thought you'd gained are actually forty, that you've spent the past three years being unhappy and secretly plotting your divorce, and that nothing you can put on a plate, grab out of a vending machine, or buy from a fast-food drive-through is worth the way you look or how you feel about yourself.

Out in the world, denial puts you at a tremendous disadvantage. You're walking around oblivious, but your kids, your friends from school, your spouse, and the other people around you see what you've decided not to. Denial kicks in to protect you, but if you don't take the next step to deal with what life is giving you, in the end the only thing it protects you from is your own happiness.

We all have to grow in some way; it never stops no matter how old we get. I know that when I'm eighty, I'll still be facing challenges every day, and either I can step up to meet them and enjoy what comes when I do, or I can deny what's happening and pay the price in the way I feel, the way my body looks, and what that ends up doing to those around me. Growing and facing challenges can be upsetting, fun, scary, and exciting, but whatever it is for you at this moment, it's something you will always have to do. You have the choice. You can try to avoid the truth of what's going on around you by ignoring the answers you receive or by giving up before you've honored your commitment. You can try to slip out the back door, as you may have done in the past when you were about to experience real change. You can retreat and start denying that you want your life to be different, or you can decide to step off that ride and start being who you really are instead.

If you want the life you envision, stick with your plan. Why deny your potential just because of something that happened in the past? Why stand in the way of yourself because of something someone once said to you? Why live in denial of what you want and what your life could be because of anything that once was, over a memory that could have you believing things that aren't really true about yourself? You can be unhappy and live in a bubble of denial, or you can embrace, explore, and enjoy all the wonderful things you are and can be by sticking with what you start and the things you know are going to improve your life.

You've been able to change in the past. You've made good decisions. You've been powerful before. Your surroundings need to reflect this part of you. Whatever doesn't define you as someone who can change and who will succeed—someone who recognizes happiness, pursues it, and gets it—is something you don't need. No possession is worth holding yourself back from getting the things you really want or from having a fulfilling life.

#3: DO MAKE THE POWER QUESTION A PART OF YOUR LIFE

The more you think about what is making you feel powerful, the more you'll recognize what is powerful, the more you'll move toward it, the more you'll feel it, and the more you will be able to make the things you want happen in your life. For most successful people, recognizing what makes them feel powerful and what is slowing them down is an automatic response. With practice, you can develop the same skill, and feeling powerful can simply be the way you live your life.

Your power is your ability to create change. You always have that ability, but when it comes to certain parts of your life, you may feel like it isn't there. Maybe your weight is where you feel the most powerless, maybe it's your relationship with your husband, wife, boyfriend, or girlfriend, or maybe you notice your power missing when you are with people from work. The truth is that your power is there in all these situations, but something is blocking you from seeing and using it the way you want to.

Sometimes your old identity pushes you to repeat patterns that don't suit who you truly are. When it tells you to eat more food when you're already full or to make excuses instead of taking the steps you know you need to take to be happy, or when it tells you to give up when you are perfectly capable of continuing on, it ends up making you feel bad. When you feel bad it isn't because of what other people have done. It's your identity limiting you and telling you to respond in this way. You may be aware that what it wants you to do doesn't work, yet you believe you can't do anything else because that's what your identity is telling you. You believe that this is you and that this is the only way. You convince yourself that you have only one choice, while others who have the life you want and an identity that is more suitable see dozens of alternatives.

If you believe that you're someone who doesn't get what he or she wants or who isn't powerful, you're wrong. Believing those things is stopping you, and it's the reason why you aren't as happy as you want to be. Think about it. Feeling weak, helpless, or victimized feels bad because you're not supposed to feel that way. You should feel good and you should feel powerful wherever you are. Why get used to feeling generally dissatisfied or as if you're just getting by? Forget that! If you're having lots of stress and feeling little satisfaction, if your body is expanding all around you, realize that you can feel different. You've just forgotten what it's like, and your thoughts have been keeping you from seeing it.

Diane: I have to say that at first I did feel a little ridiculous answering the Power Question, but I don't think I would have made the changes I did without it. I thought it was silly, but I was just telling myself it was silly because I didn't want to let go. When John asked me the Power Question, I felt like I had to answer, but when I first started doing it on my own, I started trying to back out of it. Then I got mad at myself. I knew I wanted to change. I thought it was me I was fighting with, but it was the old me fighting to hold on, and I wasn't going to let her win anymore.

Practice using the Power Question in different situations and see for yourself. Ask what is the powerful thing to do and experience what can happen when you follow the answers you receive. See the truth about how you've been choosing to make yourself feel, and then choose to feel the way you want. The more comfortable you become with using it, the more the Power Question will help you discover the truth, not only when it comes to your Clearing but with every part of your life.

#4: DO AVOID "GOOD REASONS"

Maybe you feel you should hold on to some of your things because they are expensive or because they're gifts and you are afraid the people who gave them to you will notice they're gone. Maybe you believe you will feel guilty if you let them go. Indulge these "good reasons" for keeping things that are making you feel bad and contributing to feelings of powerlessness, allow them to distract you, roll them around in your mind one too many times, and you will struggle with your Clearing and risk becoming stuck.

"I can't get rid of this. My mom gave me this."

"I got this my senior year in high school. Maybe I should have something to represent that time in my life."

"It's too valuable."

"It's too important."

"It's too hard to sell or get rid of."

"I might need it one day."

No matter what good reasons come to mind, if a possession is making you feel bad in some way, it's putting you at a disadvantage for everything you do. Don't get confused. The Clearing isn't about coming up with "good reasons" for keeping your things. It's about finding out what isn't making you feel powerful and then doing something about it.

Why fight the truth? When has that ever worked out for you? Avoid rationalizations for keeping things you know you should let go of, and stick with the answers the Power Question gives you. You've listened to the "good reasons" before and what did it really get you? Don't be fooled into going down the same road again. *You don't lose weight and move on with your life by continuing to repeat the same thoughts and the same actions.* The truth can get you what you want if you pursue it. Focus on your Seven Steps and your future. Move past the "good reasons" and your old ways of doing things. Get on your side, begin to live under an identity that works, and end your relationship with the power-stealing parts of your past.

#5: DO REALIZE THAT YOUR POSSESSIONS CAN BE REPLACED

If the objects you are Clearing have a function in the day-to-day operation of your life, such as a table fan, kitchen tools, or even a car, you may be tempted to disregard the way they're making you feel and keep them. But it doesn't matter what it is or how much it costs. If what you own is creating or nurturing feelings of powerlessness, it doesn't belong in your life and it will continue to affect you negatively as long as it is in your possession.

While I was discussing the Clearing with a client recently, she was reminded of the new car her husband had bought for her. When it came time to choose what she wanted, she told him which model she liked, and she was excited about it. The only thing she wanted to make sure of was that her new car had leather seats. The car she had been driving had leather seats and she loved them, so she wanted them in her new car. The day her car came, it was exactly what she had picked out, except for the seats. Instead of the leather she had asked for, they were fabric. And instead of saying something to her husband, she kept her disappointment to herself.

Now, she admits she drives around in the car resenting him and feeling irritated about it. "I feel like he didn't love me enough to listen to me. It was the one thing I told him I wanted, and he didn't get it." Every day, this is what her car and the fabric seats are saying. Her car has value because of its function, but that's nothing compared to the way it makes her feel. To her, the car has become a symbol of not being loved. It tells her what her value is. It tells her that the person she counts on the most didn't think her needs and desires were worth remembering. Whether this perception is actually true or not, it's what she believes.

As you do your Clearing, you may be asking yourself, "What if I really need the things that don't make me feel powerful?" If you are, listen to what you're saying. Do you really need things in your life that keep you from feeling powerful? Do you think that you don't deserve to feel powerful, and that's why you are trying to convince yourself that there's no option other than to have objects that have you feeling powerless and unworthy in your life? Do you think if you keep these things and just try really hard to feel powerful instead, you will turn things around? What is it you really need? Are you holding yourself back to make sure you never feel different or experience anything new because you are scared of what will happen and what your life will be like if you do?

You need to feel different. That's what this is about. It's not about feeling the same, doing the same, and keeping everything around you the same so you can continue to have the same life. Are the things you want to keep really worth the way you've been feeling about certain parts of your life? My client was happier with her old car even though it was worth considerably less money. Don't let this happen to you. Entertain the possibility that you can find a way around situations like these. You are capable of finding solutions. To do this, you need to let go of the excuses or any good reasons you have for feeling the way you do and embrace this opportunity to see things differently. Accept what you are doing and move toward being happy by devoting yourself to making this change happen. Place value on your life and the possessions that make it good, not on those things that could be keeping you from having the life you want.

Possessions, even expensive ones like new cars, can be replaced. That may seem radical, but you will be surprised at what alternatives come up when you ask yourself for them. Once you free yourself from what is attached to these objects and the emotions that are depressing your powers, you will find alternatives. When you stop telling yourself that you can't and that you have no options, much of what was standing in your way will disappear.

Think about the life you're going to have and ask yourself if the things you have around you will help you feel the way you want to feel in this new life. If you can look at your possessions and see that they are out of place for what you are becoming, that they are more appropriate for who you thought you were, then there's no need to ask more questions or delay. If the things around you don't belong in your new life, or if they can be replaced with what makes you feel powerful, let them go and make space for what makes you feel the way you want to feel.

When you Clear, you give yourself space to grow. You make room for what your new life brings. Whatever decisions you do make, you will find replacements for what you've Cleared, and you will like these replacements more because they won't have the negative associations that your old things did.

#6: DO FOCUS FORWARD INSTEAD OF ON MISTAKES

As you go through your things and the memories that are attached come up, there are bound to be some recollections of painful missteps. But focusing on the people you hurt, on missed opportunities, on regret about wasted years, or on all the things you did or didn't do because you were afraid isn't going to get you what you want. Focusing on past mistakes or what's going wrong now can create a pattern that has devastating results. I know from personal experience. There was a time in my life when I was at a very low point. I was in a car accident that left me with neurological damage in my legs and on the right side of my face. Around the same time, I ended a long-term personal relationship, I let go of my business, and the art market had withered away to nothing as the economy hit another in a series of downturns. I ended up on public assistance, and at one point I was living out of my car. It just didn't seem like anything in my life was working out. I went to my brother's house one day in tears and told him, "I don't know what's wrong with me. I keep making mistakes."

He looked at me and said, "So what? I make mistakes every day, and big ones, too."

He didn't say anything else. He didn't give me a speech telling me that I had to keep going and that one day I'd find my dream or anything like that. And I thought about it. My brother has a successful business. He is a millionaire many times over, and he makes mistakes every day. As I sat there blowing my nose, a time I was with him a few years earlier flashed into my mind. Noticing his lifestyle, the cars, the drivers, personal chefs, I had asked him if maybe he should save some of his money. He responded, "If I need more money, I'll go out and make it."

And there it was. Not having money wasn't part of my brother's thought process, and neither was dwelling on the past or on any of the mistakes he made every day. It wasn't arrogance that prompted his response; it was his forward focus. My brother wasn't stuck thinking about the things that would bring him down and make him feel powerless, and he wasn't spending all day thinking about the mistakes he had made. He was thinking about the lifestyle he wanted and the things he wanted to do, and those thoughts moved him toward those things. The evidence was all around him. Focusing on a past event or something he did that didn't work out, even if it was something that had happened only a few hours earlier, didn't get him what he wanted, so he wasn't interested in occupying his mind with it.

My brother was doing the opposite of what I was doing, and it was working. I was thinking about the things that weren't working out and what I didn't want. I was picturing these things in my mind and I had started to make them my focus. After I realized what I was doing, I began to consciously pay attention to what I was thinking every day and to replace the old thoughts with better ones about my future. Sure enough, when I started thinking about what I wanted instead of about the mistakes I had made and what I was afraid of, my life got better — much better.

Focusing on what you want to happen creates better outcomes than focusing on mistakes and what you don't want to happen. You are going through your things in part to help break this pattern. As you Clear your home and recall these memories, realize the potential they have to slow you down and create a pattern of living with the feelings they create. The sooner you let go of them, the sooner you get out of this pattern of reviewing your mistakes and living with the feelings they create, the sooner you will have access to all your talents and abilities, and the sooner your life will change.

16

CLEARING YOUR POSSESSIONS: THE DON'TS

#1: DON'T GIVE YOUR THINGS TO YOUR NEIGHBORS, RELATIVES, OR FRIENDS

Don't give the things you are Clearing to your neighbors, relatives, or friends, no matter how much you think they would enjoy them or how good you believe it would make you feel. I know how this sounds, and I realize that what I'm saying may go against all of your natural tendencies, but take a moment and think about it. When an object has a negative memory or emotion attached, when it calls to mind and reinforces an identity that limits you and makes you feel bad, do you really want to have it popping back up in your life again, bringing everything attached along with it, especially after you've gone through the effort of discovering its impact and letting it go? The purpose of Clearing your home is to permanently remove objects that are contributing to your feelings of powerlessness, not to have them become your best friend's dining-room centerpiece or something you see your sister wearing when she visits on the weekends. Even giving the money you earn from the sale of what you Clear to someone you know could backfire because you may not appreciate how it ends up being spent.

Suppose that your mother-in-law comes over every holiday, drinks too much, and treats you like a doormat; now imagine that the plastic bird fountain she gave you one year for Christmas is in your next-door neighbor's front yard, and you have to see it every time you pull into your driveway. Suppose that you join your friend for lunch and she is wearing the bracelet from the weird guy you went out with for three weeks the year you were depressed and forty pounds overweight. Imagine that you visit relatives, and hanging on their wall is the anniversary gift your ex-husband gave you right before he told you about the affair he had with your brother. In all of these situations, you will find yourself experiencing the feelings that are the whole reason why you gave those things away in the first place.

Denise: I gave away some very expensive designer dresses to a friend's daughter during my Clearing. I justified it by telling myself I was doing the right thing because she wasn't directly my friend but was a daughter of a friend. She was also someone who I never saw. Well, I learned that I should follow instructions better. I was warned against going this route, but I thought that I knew better, which I have discovered has been my mistake with my weight and a few other things in my life that have been going wrong.

I always saw myself as a "carve my own path" kind of girl. But the paths I kept carving were going nowhere. When I looked at my life, the times I succeeded seemed to be those where I was forced to get the training or it was required in order to do what I wanted to do in the end. With my weight, there was no requirement, or none that anyone was forcing me to stick to. I never learned how to eat properly because it was never something I felt I had to do to get what I wanted. I never learned how to maintain my body with exercise. I'd join a gym, feel out of place, and quit. I just looked at it all with dread and anger.

With food and exercise I thought I knew better than the people who were in shape and thin, and now it was the same with the Clearing and my dresses. If I had followed the recommendations I was given at the beginning, I wouldn't have been irritated that my friend's daughter didn't acknowledge my gift or send a thank you note. I could have simply been free and moved on. I was all set to let go of negative associations, but I did things my own way and added another one instead.

For a while, every time I saw my friend or he mentioned his daughter, I would think about the thank you note I never received, not even a call, and for a moment it would make me feel bad. I even felt stupid for wanting a thank you note in the first place. I laugh about it now, at how pigheaded I could be. I use this incident as my reminder that directions can get you where you want to go to, and that other people may know some things that I don't. Now I'm more open-minded and determined to stay that way.

Don't #1 is an important one to follow. Make this a smooth transition, and get the most you can out of your efforts by taking this warning to heart: don't give your things to neighbors, relatives, or friends.

Avoid having a garage sale as well. The money you make from spending the day selling your things to your neighbors won't balance out the effects of seeing your old things again and again all over town.

Whatever you decide to do with your possessions, avoid turning the people around you into a billboard for your past. Instead, follow the Seven Steps and let go completely.

#2: DON'T FIGHT THE ANSWERS TO THE POWER QUESTION

When it comes to the Clearing, there is no right or wrong answer to the Power Question, so there is no need for anxiety or apprehension. If your answer is yes, keep the object and move on with your life. If the answer is no, let it go and free yourself from the effects it has on you. Either way, you win.

While you might breeze through your Clearing, tossing things away, feeling moments of fear as you say goodbye to your old identity is normal. Doing something different can be scary, and during the Clearing it can be also a sign that you're on the right track.

You're not doing the same old thing anymore. You're not doing the comfortable thing, so you will feel different. Even if you are a little afraid, give yourself a chance to get used to what is happening and to the new possibilities you're presented with. Think about it: Why be afraid of leaving behind what isn't making you happy? You've been looking for answers, and now you're getting them. If the answer is no, you can take action and move forward with your life without the interference that object created. If the answer is yes, and the object gives you the kinds of feelings you want to continue to experience, keep it and move on.

Carrie: When I asked myself the Power Question, the answer to almost everything I owned was no. Nothing made me feel powerful, so I started to psych myself out, thinking I was answering the question incorrectly. I compare it to taking a multiple-choice test in which your choices are "a" through "d," and for each question every answer you get is the letter "c." After the third or fourth "c" in a row, you start to wonder if maybe you've gotten a few wrong just because of the pattern.

The truth was I had surrounded myself with things that weren't making me feel good. When I realized what I'd been doing, I was devastated in a way, but I also felt relieved, like a mystery had been solved.

Valerie: I was sprucing up the house when I decided to frame some photos of my husband's children from his first marriage and put them on my piano. They're all grown up now, and they don't live with us, but I thought that when they came around it would be nice if they saw they were represented in the home. Really, I wasn't sure how to get them to like me. My husband said they would "warm up" to me, but it didn't feel like that was happening. It wasn't something I was imagining, either, because a few weren't shy about telling me how they felt.

I know it's stupid, but I had this fantasy that they would come by and notice the photos, have a change of heart, and we could start being friends. I wanted my gesture to smooth things out a little, but the truth was, no one noticed, and it didn't make a difference.

When I asked the Power Question about the photos, I didn't want to admit to myself how I felt, but I knew it was true. The pictures were making me miserable. I thought they should be there and that I was being nice, but it didn't feel powerful. When I did the Clearing, I realized that I had actually been avoiding the living room of my house. I wasn't even playing the piano that much anymore.

I wanted to get along with my husband's children, but I knew that making myself feel bad in my own home and slowly giving up the piano wasn't the right way to go about it, so I replaced the photos with new ones of my husband and me and our dog.

It was a little strange at first, and I felt a little guilty about it for a day or two, but then I decided torturing myself didn't make sense. I stopped dwelling on what I thought was right, and I started doing things to make myself feel good instead. You told me that the better I could make myself feel, the more solutions would come my way, and each day I'm finding out how true that is.

I didn't want to do any of this when we started. It seems incredible to me now that I was struggling and arguing with myself, actually making a case for the way I felt, even though I had come to you to help me change that. Before, it seemed normal, but now I realize how far astray my thinking had gone. How could making myself feel bad be normal? It didn't make sense. I used to think that I didn't have a choice and that when I got into a situation like this, there was no other way than to do the things I did and make myself feel bad. Now I stop and think, "Wait a minute, how does this affect how I feel?"

I didn't understand what I was doing to myself with the photos before, but now I see things differently. It was as if someone was asking for volunteers, "Who will donate their time to torturing this woman?" and I was standing up and saying, "Me. I'll do it. I will torture myself." That's what I was doing. No one was asking me to put those photos there. I just took it upon myself. My husband's kids came around once, maybe twice a year, and I was looking at the photos almost every day. I was feeling bad all year long about people

I saw for a few hours around the holidays. I've spent more time with the bagger at my local grocery store than I've spent with those kids.

After the Clearing my perspective changed, and I decided to do things differently in my life. Now I let the feelings I'm experiencing guide me. I used to tell myself I was wrong to feel the way I did, but now I listen and pay attention to how I really feel. I was fighting with myself about it. Now I tell myself I don't have to participate in other people's problems, and I stopped volunteering my energy to fix every negative situation that comes along. I have so many other wonderful places to put my attention. I feel different now, and people are responding to me better, even my husband's children.

Why fight an answer? You are doing this to feel different, so embrace the answers you receive and give yourself a chance to have what the Clearing brings. Allow yourself to become familiar with something new. Before you cruised down your first hill on your bike, there were a few wobbly moments when you struggled, but then you got the hang of it. Keep going with your Clearing. You will get used to asking the Power Question and you will enjoy the new sensations you experience when you follow the answers you receive.

#3: DON'T LET ANYONE TALK YOU OUT OF IT

You could have wonderfully supportive friends and family members, and talking to them about what you are doing could be a great experience, or you could share what you are doing and be disappointed by the reaction you get. It isn't the easiest thing to consider, but some of the people in your life may prefer you the way you are now and might even be having a relationship with you because your life is the way it is. They may like that you are overweight or that you feel powerless. Maybe your failures make a few of your friends feel good about their own lives, or perhaps they enjoy having someone to commiserate with. Maybe some of the people you know feel superior to you because of the way your body looks and the state of your personal life. Maybe their identity is based in part on how your life makes them feel about theirs. How are they going to feel when you get your life together? How are they going to feel when you lose weight and when you aren't complaining about your relationships anymore because you are doing things differently and you're happy?

Yeah, I know it's not pleasant to think about, but the bigger the potential for change, the bigger the potential for backlash from some of the people in your life. I say, why bother? You could be excited about your Clearing, call your best friend or your sister-in-law, tell her about what you are going to do, and end up getting a heavy dose of negativity and discouragement. Why create an issue you don't need to deal with? You're excited about what you are doing, so skip the detour and get to it.

This is not your husband's or wife's life, not your sister's or mother's life, not your coworker's or best friend's life. It's yours. If you feel there is potential for a bad reaction, don't slow down for the experience. You've gone down that road before, and you know where it leads. Devote yourself instead to focusing on the Seven Steps until your Clearing is complete. The people around you don't need the burden of contemplating changes they haven't asked for, so don't place it on them, especially if their reaction might deflate you and wear at your resolve.

Above everything else, this is about you. You are creating changes in your life. Deal with any potential issues or bad reactions from the people who may not be as happy as you are about the changes you're making gently and from a position of strength. There will be plenty of time to talk about your experiences after your Clearing, and when that time comes, if you feel it's something powerful to do, tell whoever you like. Allow the people you decide to speak to to make up their own minds and to do so at their own pace. Be forgiving of those who resist what you are telling them, and continue to focus on your own life. Remember, they haven't had your experiences yet, so they won't have the same knowledge and understanding of the process that you do. There is no reason to keep what you are doing a secret, but, at the same time, the only one who really needs to be in on this is you.

You can try to sabotage yourself by ignoring Don't #3, or you can commit to your Clearing and refuse to let anyone or anything stand in the way of what you are creating. If you have a friend who sees the downside in everything, if you have a parent who has a limiting view of who you are and what you can do, if your ex was never supportive of a single thing you did while you were together or after, why include them? Why open yourself up for disappointment? If there is even the tiniest doubt at this point, why bother? Focus forward and on your Clearing. This is your road. You own it. If you've decided this is right for you, don't let anyone talk you out of what you're doing. Don't even give them a chance.

#4: DON'T MICRO-COMB

If, during your Clearing, you find yourself reading every word of every old letter you've received throughout your life, listening to all your old CDs, and poring over all the videos you've made during the past twenty years before you discard them, you are going to wear yourself out, lose focus, and sabotage the changes you're making with your life.

Spending too long on one item can slow you down; so can going through your things as if they were holy relics. Skip the micro-combing. Start from the right frame of mind. The goal isn't a clean house or an organized past. You're Clearing. You're judging the objects that you own according to their emotional content and the thoughts they trigger. If you want to move on, you have to get in the spirit of your new life. You must begin to think of yourself as already there and act accordingly.

What would the successful you have in your home? Look and see what fits with this identity. When you get rid of the guilt and obligation and "good reasons" and start making this about your future and the person you see yourself as when you are in it, you will be able to put your past in perspective.

Jade: When I started, I had several spaces to go through — my apartment, my car, my office, and my parents' house. I Cleared the first three quickly, but I kept putting off Clearing my possessions at my parents'. Most of my childhood things were there, and I was afraid of how I would react to seeing them. Would I be thrust into a deep depression? Would I have to spend days or weeks working to get back on track, moving forward, and feeling good again?

I was also nervous about seeing my parents. I hadn't spent much time with them since I started the Clearing, and I knew they weren't happy about that. Talking with them brought back so many of the old, bad feelings that I had been working so hard to shed, so I rarely spoke to them. Plus, there were a lot of new things going on in my life since I started the Clearing, and I didn't have nearly as much time for them.

So, with all this fear in my head, I decided to take the advice John gave me, and I saw the destination I wanted. I saw myself driving away from my parents' house with a smile on my face. I focused on that good feeling I would feel. I did this several times over a period of a few days. Then I gathered some boxes and drove to my parents' house.

I had made a few decisions ahead of time. I knew that I would be throwing away the majority of the items I had stored in their home, so I decided it would be best not to share this fact with them. It would bring up too many questions that I didn't want to spend time answering, and it might upset them, and that really wasn't necessary. So, my plan was to pack up everything that was mine and start asking the Power Question with my things when I returned home. However, I would not bring the items into my home. Instead I planned to park my car near a dumpster and go through them in the parking lot of my apartment complex. This way I felt I could quickly go through the process and not get stuck looking through my childhood artifacts. I also knew that this way I wouldn't procrastinate and leave everything piled up in my Cleared home.

When I arrived at my parents' house, I visited with them briefly before I began to gather my possessions. I knew I had to keep moving quickly so that I wouldn't get bogged down in conversation. I kept talking with them as we moved from the living room, where I found videos I had made in college, to my old bedroom, where I found long-abandoned clothing and linens, to the attic, where I found old college papers, high school yearbooks, and scores of items I had forgotten about. As I talked with my parents, I kept the focus on them and other family members so that I would not have to explain the new aspects of my life. I answered questions they asked about me and then followed up with statements or questions that redirected the focus to them, their dogs, their home, and what was new in their lives.

After three hours of packing and talking, I was on the road. I did leave a few things behind. My mother had integrated many of the books I'd bought in high school and college into her library. I removed any books that I had negative reactions to, but left the ones that I had neutral feelings for. They seemed to be her books now, anyway.

I parked near a dumpster, went inside for a snack, and quickly returned to the car. What happened then surprised me—I spent the next few hours smiling and sometimes even laughing as I quickly went through my old things. Cards and notes reminded me of the kind people I had known over the years. Photos reminded me of the fun times we had enjoyed. I laughed at the melodramatic tone of the notes friends had passed to me in junior high and the few journal entries I allowed myself to read.

It could be that months of living and working in Cleared spaces and following John's advice had allowed me to look at my childhood objects differently. I think that without following his program, I would have mourned the friends who were no longer in my life. I would have pored over notes from old boyfriends, looking for what went wrong. I would have focused on all the missed opportunities of my late teens and twenties. And I would have felt terrible.

Instead, I avoided objects that I suspected might upset me. I didn't even open the stack of high school yearbooks. They went right in the dumpster. I only read a few notes and cards before dumping the rest of the lot in the trash. I sifted through photos quickly, and from the photo album and shoebox of photos, I kept only two, both of me as a toddler. I went fast, focused on the nice aspects of what I was reviewing, and avoided what seemed laden with negativity.

After a few hours, my carload had shrunk to one plastic bag with a few mementos of past successes, plus boxes of items that would go straight to Goodwill. I was amazed that when I was done I felt different about my childhood and my college years. I felt good. If I ever choose to look back, there were kind people and successful projects that brought me happiness, and that's what I can remember. I know now that there are so many happy times ahead and too much to do to spend time going back to the past.

Recognize the micro-combing slowdown, laugh if you catch yourself doing it, then take decisive action and increase your speed in the direction of the vision you have of your future. Stay on track with your commitment, follow the Seven Steps, move swiftly through your past and on with the rest of your life.

#5: DON'T SKIP OVER ANY POSSESSIONS

In Don't #4 I've warned against spending too much time, as you go through the process, contemplating each of your possessions. While this is important for your successful Clearing, it is also important to avoid skipping over possessions you may believe don't matter much when it comes to your life and the way you are feeling. You may have never imagined that some of the objects in your home, like a blender, a hairbrush, or even some old luggage, could possess emotional weight, but in many cases they do. Ask the Power Question and be sure of how you are being affected. See what memories and emotions are attached to all of your possessions. You may be surprised at what you find. Avoid skipping over select items, thinking they don't count. Everything that you're keeping counts, and often it's the one thing that you try to convince yourself doesn't that's having the biggest impact on your life.

Ask the Power Question for every possession you are considering keeping, from personal mementos to expensive electronic equipment, from the pile of notes in the binder on your desk to the stack of canned goods on the bottom shelf of your pantry. Leaving things out of your Clearing by telling yourself that they are unimportant is your old life trying to hang on. You've committed yourself to Clearing the spaces on your list entirely, so do them entirely. Take everything you plan to keep through the process.

Tina: During my Clearing, I replaced all of my old silverware except for two spoons. I thought it would be fine because I didn't really have any direct memories or associations attached to them, but every time I used them, cleaned them, or put them back in the silverware drawer, there would be a second of recognition that they were from my old place, and I found that seeing them would take me back there. Silverware should be about as benign as a household object comes, but those two spoons still had an association that would stop me for a moment. Objects do have emotions attached to them, even spoons.

#6: DON'T BE FOOLED BY SEPARATION ANXIETY

As you're Clearing, you might come across possessions you'd forgotten you even had that will suddenly seem very important to you. Don't be fooled into believing the elevated importance some of your things take on once you start thinking about removing them from your life. The old you may desperately want to grasp at anything to stop what you are doing from actually happening. Be aware of this, and if you feel the pull of the old ways, be prepared to step decisively toward the destination you've decided to pursue. You've gotten used to seeing yourself as someone who has the possessions you have around you and who exists with the identity they help create, when the truth is that, if you remove them, you can just as easily get used to something else.

Whatever you encounter, trust the Power Question. Base your actions on the answers you receive. Be honest with yourself. Decide what is more important, your future or your past. Don't be fooled by a sudden burst of emotion. Remember what it is you're separating yourself from, and avoid being taken off-course by a sudden episode of separation anxiety.

You can let go of the things around you that aren't making you feel powerful. You can let go of the identity that's causing you pain and keeping you from the things you want. Finish Clearing your home and discover what those who have gone before you have found—that you really don't miss what you've Cleared, and you can't believe that you once thought you would.

Stacie: The effects of Clearing my home have been very positive. I don't have constant reminders of mistakes I've made or the years I wasted staring at me and pulling me back into the past. I feel lighter, more open now. It is powerful to be able to look back and say I am more powerful than what I was surrounded by. Like what John says about being "more powerful than a cookie"—I am more powerful than my furniture, my towels, my clothing, my computer, the place I lived, etc. I decided that my future is more important than my past and acted on that decision.

#7: DON'T "SORT OF" LET GO

Maybe you're living in the house that your ex-husband built. The rooms are filled with objects from your life together, each with memories, thoughts, and emotions from past events attached to them. Mixed in with these objects are possessions from the time before you met, possessions that helped create and reinforce the identity that had you believing it was OK to stay in a relationship that made you miserable for close to a decade. With all that around you, defining you, telling you who you are and what you are capable of, what do you think is going to happen when you say to yourself, "OK, now lose this weight," or, "Make more money," or, "Find someone to love"? How is that going to work out for you?

When you're Clearing your possessions, realize the potential your things have to work against you, and don't "sort of" let go. Let go completely. Get serious about what you are doing. Forget about renting storage space and stashing things away or putting things in your parents' attic and saying to yourself, "Well, I never really go there anyway." If there are unpleasant memories or emotions attached to an object, or if it doesn't represent who you want to see yourself as, free yourself completely from the extra weight it brings by letting it go permanently.

Diane: When we were married, my ex-husband and I collected antique cookie jars. My kitchen was filled with them. When I did the Clearing, they didn't pass the Power Question, and I felt really bad about the idea of getting rid of them. Without my cookie jars, I thought my kitchen would be empty and cold. I'd had them for so long, and there were so many memories. I struggled with it, and they ended up being one of the last things to go.

After my Clearing, I decided to take a cooking class. That's when I really got into sun-dried tomatoes. I researched seeds and planting techniques and drew up a small business plan, and that year I planted a pretty big garden and grew several varieties of tomatoes. With what I learned from my cooking class, the Internet, and friends, I made my own organic sun-dried tomatoes, and after my first harvest I was supplying a local restaurant with my tomatoes. It happened that fast! I experimented with combining different fresh herbs, oils, and glass displays, and eventually a few local gift shops picked these up as well.

Now I can't believe the cookie jars were so important to me. I guess I didn't want to let them go and admit that part of my life was over. I think what happens is, we resign ourselves to this idea of getting old and think that we're going to sit around and want to stare off into the distance on a porch somewhere and remember things or sit around in our living rooms looking at pictures all day. But that wasn't the way I felt. I wanted to live. I liked doing things, and I wanted to be happy. No matter what those cookie jars made me think of that was good, they always made me think of my ex-husband, the mistakes I had made, and the way that worked out. That was the simple truth of it. What was I going to do? Box them up in the basement so that in another twenty years I could take them out and think about all that again? I thought, "Why should I bother?" I use my basement now to germinate my seeds early in the spring so I'll have only the best plants to harvest from. I think that's a much better use of that space, and yes, John, it makes me feel powerful.

Diane could have kept the cookie jars and said things to herself like, "I just can't bring myself to let them go. They've been a part of my life for so long." She could have told herself, "I spent years building this collection; I should keep it," or, "I love the way they look, and I don't think I could do without them." She could have kept this part of her old identity as a collector of cookie jars, but she took a chance and kept going instead. She created room, and it allowed her to grow. It opened up possibilities, and she discovered it was true. She was much more than she thought she was.

And so are you.

17

Q&A

1. I have gifts from my wedding, birthdays, and anniversaries that I want to Clear, but I feel conflicted about letting them go. Can I really Clear a gift?

Some gifts make you feel great, some fill you with pressure and anxiety, and some are more about the person giving the gift than who's receiving it. The only thing that matters is what you decide after you've asked the Power Question.

My client Karen and her husband Greg had moved into a new house and were in the process of decorating it. On weekends they would go to local shops and auctions looking for antiques. They were having fun picking out new pieces and looking at websites and magazines for ideas. One day, Betty, Greg's mother, showed up unannounced at their home with two deliverymen and a sofa.

Karen was in another part of the house when the truck arrived, and as she walked toward her front door, she overheard her mother-in-law saying to Greg, "Well, Karen's taste could use some help. I'm just happy to do my part." Karen pretended she hadn't heard what Betty said and then spent the next six weeks looking at the sofa and feeling inadequate and angry.

During her Clearing, Karen told me that she didn't like the color of the sofa, but "the fabric was very good quality." I asked her what came into her mind when she thought about the sofa and if the emotions she felt when she thought about it made her feel powerful.

She took a few moments before answering and then said, "Do you know what is coming into my mind? My mother-in-law invited herself along when I went to pick out my wedding dress and talked me into getting one I didn't even like. I think I spent half the wedding thinking about it, and now I keep thinking about this sofa."

Not only were Betty's comments about Karen's taste attached to the sofa, so was what happened with her wedding dress. Karen hated the way she felt about both of these situations, and we ended up spending some time talking about them. Toward the end of our conversation, Karen said, "I think what you are telling me is that I'm giving up my happiness and telling myself it's worth it for a sofa I don't even like." She was smiling as she said it. Karen is smart, funny, and capable. Instead of doing the same thing she had done with her wedding dress all over again, she needed to access her abilities and find a different approach.

Karen wanted to be "nice" and "polite" so people would like her, but then she would secretly resent them when they walked all over her. The sofa was telling her that she didn't set boundaries and that she was the kind of person who always let people get their way. Being "nice" and "polite" had become the crutch Karen used to stay where she was in her life and avoid doing anything different, like standing up for herself and the happiness of her family.

The Clearing peeled away the excuses for Karen because it forced her to look at the sofa in terms of one thing only—her power. Did the sofa make her feel powerful? The answer was either yes or no, and when it came to her sofa, Karen found the answer was no. When she saw the sofa, she didn't think to herself, "Betty is so sweet. I'm the luckiest daughter-in-law in the world. I think I'll go bake her some brownies." Just the opposite: Karen resented Betty and couldn't walk past the sofa without feeling like she was getting taken down a few notches.

Not doing anything with her wedding dress hadn't worked, so this time Karen decided to take action. To honor her commitment to the Clearing, she knew she had to listen to the answer she received from the Power Question and face her feelings. Karen knew she couldn't keep the sofa. She decided the truth was her best option. She called the furniture store and had them pick up the sofa, and they took it over to her mother-in-law's home.

Karen: I knew that if I called Betty, it might have dragged on and I would lose my nerve. I know myself, and I would have started making excuses because I just didn't want to face it. I knew my choice was either doing something to change the way I felt or keeping the sofa. I didn't want to chance having the sofa in the house any longer and having this become a bigger deal than it had to be or another thing I ended up getting used to instead of doing something about. I had to get it out of my house. In the past I wasn't direct. I would let things build and just get sad and frustrated, and I would usually end up making a bad decision. This time I wanted to be different.

When I got to her home, Betty came to the door. She was definitely confused by the sight of the truck. I think it was the last thing she expected to see. I hugged her and thanked her again for the sofa. I explained that even though it was a well-made piece and very nice, it didn't fit in with the rest of the furniture in my home, which was the truth.

I told her what I had overheard her say about my taste and that it hurt me and I was embarrassed by it. I told her that I should have said something earlier but I felt uncomfortable because she is my husband's mother and I want to have a good relationship with her. That's when she did something I never expected: She looked at me kind of funny and then burst into tears. She told me that it was her fault. She said that she was upset because she felt like she was losing her son, and she knew it was silly, but that's why she was pushing her way into our lives. She apologized and promised she'd never do anything like this again. We stood there hugging each other and crying. The poor delivery guys were there with the couch in their hands watching us the whole time. We must have looked ridiculous.

Because she stepped up and went in a different direction from what she usually would, Karen felt better about herself, and Betty was given the choice to accept her daughter-in-law as her own person, with her own will and desires, and she did. Karen and Betty went back to the store together, Karen picked out a sofa she liked, and they ended up having a lot of fun.

Karen's decision to be direct and kind instead of silently resenting Betty gave her a chance to have a real relationship with her mother-in-law. If she hadn't decided to step out of the identity of the quietly suffering "nice" and "polite" person she'd been trapping herself in, the relationship would have stayed the same, perhaps for the rest of their lives.

If you honor your commitment to your Clearing, you will understand; you will see that there are other options available besides the same old way and the same old feelings. This is your life and these are your possessions. Why let other people decide what's going to go on in your home if you don't want them to? On what planet is that acceptable? You can let the people you know direct your life. You can experience resentment and powerlessness, or you can face that you need to change, accept that you want this change to happen now, and then start making it happen.

Doing something like allowing someone to put a sofa you don't like in your living room or keeping a painting from a friend that makes you avoid an entire section of your home or listening to your parents lecture you every Sunday when they come over for dinner about how you've placed the lawn furniture they unloaded on you in the wrong section of your yard isn't the polite thing to do. It's self-defeating and ridiculous, and it makes you feel bad because what you are actually doing is giving your power away.

If you let someone else control what you keep in your home, the sensation of not being in control will spread to other areas of your life. Instead of moving toward the things you want, you will move closer to things like weight gain, resentment, jealousy, apathy, drama, and powerlessness. What you don't want will dominate your thoughts and show up in your life. You will find yourself devoting your time to excuses and denial in order to maintain this life when you could be following your dreams and creating the life you want instead.

The sofa Betty showed up with that day symbolized Karen's old identity. The comments Betty made about Karen's taste and what happened with the wedding dress were attached to it, and seeing it brought to the surface all the times in the past Karen had behaved in a similar fashion. It reinforced an identity for her as someone who silently suffered instead of someone who used her talents and abilities to find solutions and be happy. The sofa that Karen picked out when she and Betty returned to the store together was a symbol of her triumph and of the actions she had taken to change the way she felt. It told Karen that she could stand up for herself and that doing so was actually the kind thing to do. The new sofa told her she could work things out and come up with solutions. It reinforced an identity for Karen as someone who is powerful and who can make good things happen. It was exactly the kind of possession she wanted to have in her home.

You will continue to feel the same way you've always felt, you will have the same life you've always had, and the same types of people will distract you and keep you from feeling the way you want to, unless you take action. Instead of allowing her mother-in-law to direct her power in her own home, Karen took action, made the powerful move, let go of a few old beliefs and a few of her things and along with them went the bad thoughts and feelings that were attached.

Can you Clear a gift? Yes, you certainly can. If it's yours and it doesn't make you feel powerful, it doesn't matter whether it's a gift or something you inherited. It doesn't matter if it cost a ton of money or has "good-quality" fabric. Go with what is powerful and never look back.

2. OK, I can let something go even if it's a gift, but what do I do the next time the people who gave me the gift are over at my place? I don't want them to feel bad when they see that it's gone, and I'm also worried that they might make me feel guilty that I gave their gift away. What should I do?

Remember that the people who have given you gifts have their own homes to decorate. Would you want your friends and family members to feel uncomfortable because they felt obligated to display a gift from you? Besides, a gift is a gift; it isn't a loan. When you receive a gift, it is yours and it's your choice what to do with it.

Realize that this is your life and that living it according to someone else's standards or desires could be the reason you haven't been feeling the way you want to and why things aren't turning out how you planned. You might not want to deal with any fallout that could come when the person who gave you the gift notices that it's gone, but the alternative is worse.

Shelly: My best friend likes to decorate, and she got me these curtains as a housewarming gift. The whole thing was my fault because I suggested we put them up. She was standing there holding them in her arms. She had brought curtain rods, everything. I really didn't know what else to do. After that I was stuck. She was so excited, I didn't have the heart to tell her that I didn't like them and they weren't my taste. What was I going to say: "Your curtains make me feel like I'm in a funeral parlor"?

When it hit me what I had done, that I couldn't find a way out of this, that I was somehow committed to having them up, I got such a sinking feeling in my stomach, and that was the same feeling I got when I asked the Power Question about them during my Clearing. I was lying to my friend, telling her how lovely they were. I was looking at them and hearing a funeral dirge. I was feeling bad because of curtains. I realized how ridiculous that was, and I took them down. Boy, did that feel good. I never really made the connection before, but it was true. I was making myself feel powerless in my own home, and I didn't want to admit it.

It's so simple and doesn't seem like there should be a problem. I mean, they were just curtains, right? When I looked at them and thought about what they represented to me, I started thinking about all these times in the past that I let people push me into doing things I didn't want to do. I did let other people have control, and it wasn't making me happy. In my mind I heard the excuses going off, the ones that would always stop me, and they weren't powerful, either.

There was nothing powerful about what I was doing or who the curtains were telling me I was. They were telling me I was powerless, and so were a lot of the other things in my home.

With the Clearing you are turning your home into a power base, not a giant display case for gifts you don't like. If your friend Teddy comes to your home, sees that the moose head he got you on one of his garage sale adventures is gone, and asks about it, your response could be as simple as:

"I've decided to try something new for a while."

"I'm in the process of changing things around."

"I'm going in a new direction with the place."

"I've decided to donate a few things to charity, and that moose head is going to help feed hungry kids. You're a good man, and I knew you would want it this way."

There are hundreds of responses. Have fun with this. Get creative. Come up with two or three sentences to use if the situation arises. Then prepare something interesting to talk about or to do, so that once the issue of the missing gift has been addressed, you can gracefully move on to something new. You don't have to hide what you are doing, and you don't have to explain yourself to anyone either, especially when it comes to what you put in your home.

None of what you are doing to make these changes has to be painful. When you speak to the person who has given the gift, leave the excuses behind. Be kind, and tell the truth. You will find that this is the most powerful thing you can do. If you love them, tell them you do. You can follow up by letting them know that not everyone likes sushi, Miles Davis solos, or Jeff Koon's sculptures, but even if they don't, that they can still be your friend. If this person has repeatedly pushed his or her will and desires into your life, use this opportunity to change the dynamic of your relationship. You may think you're being kind by ignoring how you are being treated and the way it makes you feel. You may find some comfort in telling yourself that you don't want to hurt anyone's feelings and that's why you don't say anything, but what you are really doing is keeping the bad feelings and what happens because of them around for you, the person who has given you the gift, as well as all the other people in your life.

All the effort it takes to live with these bad feelings is a lot more to deal with, and much less attractive, than a two-minute conversation where you put your thoughts out into the air and experience the relief of no longer holding them inside. Sure, these conversations can be scary prospects, but so can a wasted life full of unsatisfying relationships and swallowing your feelings. Give yourself this opportunity to experience the increase in confidence you will gain from dealing with these situations as they come up and the relief of not having to think about them any longer once you have.

Consider also that there is a good possibility you could be concerned for no reason. Your friend or relative might have completely forgotten about the gift, or it may not be as important to him or her as you think. Why not give yourself this chance to find out? The kind thing to do is to protect your happiness and increase your feelings of power. Do this, and everyone around you will benefit, including the people who've given you the gifts you want to Clear.

3. Will I regret selling or giving away my old things?

You may think you will regret letting go of a few of your possessions, and when I first started doing the Clearing I thought that might happen as well, but so far, I haven't had any clients tell me that they miss their old things. No matter how they felt initially, most felt relief after the possessions they Cleared were finally gone. You're getting rid of what isn't making you happy and what you no longer need—these are things that people usually don't miss when they're gone.

Julie: I'm amazed at how much I had, and I'm also amazed by how much I was able to consolidate. I walk through the rooms of my home and I can't remember half of what was there. That's funny to me now because it seemed like such an ordeal while it was happening. I was upset about a lot of things and struggled with letting go of many of my possessions, and now I can't believe I bothered.

Instead of regretting letting go of your old things or missing them, you end up moving on. Regret is a waste of time anyway. When you look back to regret something, you're taking time out of your life to make yourself feel bad. You take your attention off what is in front of you and put it on what has already gone by. With repetition, regret can become a habit, and feeling bad a way of life. Why bother when you can orient yourself to the future, feel good, and move toward what you want instead?

Once you commit and begin moving in your new direction, you will experience the sensations of being on a different path. Give yourself a chance to get used to these feelings. Be patient and keep going.

Will you regret removing the things from your home that were making you feel bad? If you do, you will be the first.

4. **What do I say when people ask about the changes I've made to my home? How do I respond when friends question me about giving away my things? What do I say if someone I know wants a few of the possessions I'm Clearing?**

If people ask you what you are doing and why, your response can be something as simple as, "I've decided to make some changes." If a friend or acquaintance wants an item you're Clearing, tell the truth and be direct: "These have been donated," or, "Everything is already spoken for," or maybe, "Sorry, I have plans for these."

Before or after your Clearing, make time for the people who aren't involved with it because, once you start, it's go time! It isn't stop what you are doing to tell the story of your Clearing to everyone who comes by time. You want to focus on your things and discover the feelings they're producing with as little interruption or input from those around you as possible. While you're Clearing, Clear! Be too busy for explanations. Plan well and reduce the potential for interruptions and for people to ask if they can have a few of your things. This isn't a Q&A session or some gift-giving holiday. This is your Clearing. Stick to the Seven Steps and avoid any confusion.

If some of your friends or acquaintances do stop by unexpectedly, steer the conversation toward what's happening in their lives and keep it short. During your Clearing it's important to spend less time talking and more time doing. Other people's comments could dampen your resolve and undermine your enthusiasm. Why let that happen? Make plans to catch up at a later date, and focus on moving forward. If you've completed your Clearing and your friends come around and notice that half your stuff seems to be gone, tell them as much or as little as you like. The truth is that people make changes to their homes all the time and for many reasons. You have simply made changes to yours for your own.

Eve: Some of my friends were a little freaked out. Even the people at the consignment store looked at me like I was crazy for getting rid of so many of my things. When they asked me if I was sure that I didn't want to keep certain pieces, I smiled and told them that I wanted to get a fresh start because it was true and it felt good to say it.

If you get a few comments you don't like, it's OK. It isn't your job to sell the Clearing to the people around you or to justify your actions. I understand if you are excited about what you are doing and want to tell people about it, but never let your desire to spread the word interfere with completing what you've started. There will be time enough to talk with friends and acquaintances about what you've been doing once you've honored your commitment.

5. **What do I do if I really like my things or I have a few items I simply feel like I should keep, but the Power Question is telling me to let them go?**

Remember, it's you who's answering the Power Question. It's you who's saying that the object isn't powerful and doesn't belong in your life any longer. You're embracing a new lifestyle philosophy now. Part of this lifestyle is keeping things because they make you feel good and not because you think that you should.

If you find yourself feeling attached to something that isn't making you feel powerful, take a moment and think that through. Why have something in your home that you know is holding you back? Why weigh yourself down with objects that bring fear or guilt into your life or trap you in self-imposed obligation or with an identity you find uncomfortable and that has you repeating the same mistakes over and over again when you are working so hard to be happy and create the life you want? *If you don't like the answer you're getting from the Power Question, ask yourself if you like the way you're living now.* Are you happy, and is this object contributing to this feeling? Do you enjoy the way it makes you feel, what it makes you think of, or the part of your life it represents? Is this possession something that will help you get where you are going, or is it helping to keep you where you are, thinking of yourself as someone you're not? You may think it's difficult to face the truth of the answers you receive, but it's much more difficult to deny the truth and live with the consequences.

The Power Question is pushing away the fog that has risen up around you, and you're seeing things differently. Maybe some of the answers you receive will surprise you. That's good. You're getting at the truth of what is going on. Don't let what's different deter you. Different may be just what you need to have a better life. Why do the same thing over and over if it doesn't work or make you happy? Why experience the same disappointments and negative emotions when it comes to the things you want to change about your life? Why hide or live a certain way just because you've gotten used to it? I don't need to know how old you are to know that you are too young to put an end to learning or to stop changing. *If you've been avoiding change, you are avoiding your life.*

You are doing the Clearing to create something different. Using the Power Question may feel strange in the beginning, but what new process doesn't? Learning to ride a bike or drive a car, even doing basic math probably all felt a little strange at first. How about your first kiss? You weren't the master you are today the first time you tried that, were you? Imagine what your life would be like if you had let some awkwardness, anxiety, or self-consciousness stop you and you had to live without all the skills you take for granted now.

Possessions came into your life. You got used to them, and because they stayed they helped shape your thoughts and your identity. They also helped you become stuck believing that this person you think you are and who you don't feel right being is you. You have a lot of life to live. You can stay where you are, with the things "you really like" that aren't making you feel powerful, or you can move forward, focusing on your future and experiencing your full potential. You may not like the initial answer you receive from asking the Power Question, but if you take the appropriate action, you will like the results.

6. **I'm replacing some of the things I've Cleared. Will the new things I buy remind me of what I'm replacing and cause those old memories and thoughts to come back?**

Do you think about your old TV while you are watching your new one? Do you reminisce about your old toaster oven and all the memories and thoughts that were associated with it when you are heating up a sandwich in the one you have now? Once the old possessions are gone, you will find that you don't really don't think too much about them.

It isn't essential, but why not go in a different direction with the items you're replacing? Buy things in different colors and different brands. Consider whether you even need to replace what you're Clearing in the first place. Streamline your life. Give yourself the room to discover that there are many different things in the world that can make you happy.

7. **I live with other people, my spouse, the kids, and my mother, and some of their things don't make me feel powerful. How do I complete my Clearing?**

Other people's things, even if they are part of your shared environment, are other people's things. You may think that your daughter's surfboard, some of the posters your son has hanging on the walls, your husband's golf clubs, and the entire contents of your mother's bedroom need to be Cleared, but only your possessions are part of your Clearing.

Respect the possessions of others as you Clear, and you will always feel good about what you are doing. Let your kids and your mother have their rooms and their things, and focus on your own. Talk to the people you share items with and come to decisions together. You wouldn't want to come home one day and find that someone had donated your things to charity, so you can imagine what that would be like for someone else.

If your husband has a few possessions around the house that are producing a negative reaction in you, go ahead ask him if it's OK to remove them. Approach him the way you would want someone to approach you about your things. Try out what you want to say on yourself first and see if it feels powerful. Be clever, kind, and maybe offer a few suggestions:

"Would you mind if we donated these to charity?"

"I was thinking of replacing the _____ if that's OK with you."

"What if we took out the _____ and got some _____ instead?"

Maybe your husband has no idea of the effect some of his possessions are having on you. Maybe it doesn't matter to your wife whether something stays or goes. Your significant other may feel the same as you, or he or she may want to keep a few things. You, your spouse, your boyfriend or girlfriend are different people. You like different things, and that's one of the reasons you're attracted to each other. Keep this in mind while you're making decisions, and give each other a chance to speak and room for individual preferences and tastes.

If your husband wants to keep something that you want to let go of, get the good feelings you're looking for from knowing how this object is making him feel. You want to feel strong and powerful, and you want the person you love to feel the same way. If you don't, then you need to ask yourself why you are with someone you care so little about. What helps your partner helps you. Look out for each other during the process, and you will both benefit.

Let your partner know how you feel when it comes to your shared items. Be direct with the people you live with, while being kind and tactful. No one wants to hear that their things aren't powerful or are causing unhappiness. Make your decisions and keep moving forward. Getting caught up in lengthy discussions over your old things could slow you down, drain your enthusiasm, and invite disharmony. Stick with the simplicity of the Power Question. Remember that you love this person and what that means, and move on.

8. I mentioned I was doing the Clearing to my family and a few of my friends. Now everyone keeps coming by my place to help me, but it's more like they're telling me what to do. I'm getting confused. What should I do?

If your family members or friends are telling you what you should do and you're obeying them whether you like their ideas or not, you can begin regaining your self-esteem and reclaiming your living space by going through the Seven Steps on your own. These are your possessions, your past, and your life. You are discovering the way *you* feel. If you include other people in your Clearing or let them push you around, your chances of Clearing what you need to will be in jeopardy.

Maybe in the past you let the people around you manipulate you into paying attention to their life and their problems instead of your life and what you wanted to accomplish. Maybe a few of your dreams died because of this. Take the necessary actions that allow you to focus on your Clearing and break this pattern. Making a list of the places you will Clear, creating your Power Question sign, gathering your supplies, writing your commitment statement, setting aside time so you can be on your own and focus, moving quickly — these actions are all part of the Seven Steps because they work. Don't fight their wisdom; embrace it and they will help you make the most of your Clearing and your life.

Change your identity from someone who lets other people run the show to someone who is in charge and strong. Never use the people around you as an excuse for not doing the things you want with your life. It's your home, and it's your life. If someone is coming over and interfering with your Clearing, you can ask them to leave. You will find a way. Why be who your family or friends think you are and have the life they want you to have when you can be the magnificent person you are and have the fulfilling life you want to have? The people you know have their own lives to live. Don't waste another day letting them live yours as well.

9. I tried the Clearing for a couple of weeks and did a few of the techniques, but I'm not sure it's working for me. What am I doing wrong?

"It didn't work for me."

"It just wasn't my thing."

"I gave it a try, but…"

Are you setting yourself up for failure and regret by not truly committing because failure and regret are what you're used to feeling when it comes to changing your life? Is the old you steering you toward quitting, reinforcing an identity that has you trapped in a lifestyle that isn't making you happy? Is the old you throwing doubt and fear into your focus and doing everything possible to make you say, "I knew this wouldn't work," just so you can feel like you're right about something and that you have control?

Trying is one thing; doing is altogether different. You're not going to get what you are looking for by *trying* the Clearing; you have to *do* it. You can't stick your toe in the water and say you went swimming. If you are going at this halfway, choosing from the process only what suits you and discarding the rest, you are not going to get the same results you would if you actually followed the Seven Steps.

It's time to forget the depressing routine of setting yourself up for failure, time to skip the tried and not-so-true "good reasons" you've used in the past for backing out of the things you know you should do and gather your determination and desire to make your life different. There are benefits, and they are within your reach. They only seem far away because of how you've been living and the way you've been treating yourself.

Dating someone you know is no good, working at a job you hate, getting involved in distractions and problems instead of moving forward—all of that has to stop. You need to move on with your life, and you can begin by doing the Clearing instead of only trying to do it. Find out what is going on with your surroundings. Think about how you want your future to be. Be serious, more serious than you've ever been before. Decide on the life you want and the person you are going to be. Connect with your true identity, practice it, surround yourself with objects that reinforce it, and stick with it. Don't try to make your life different. Do it.

10. **When I look at one of my possessions, I get several memories. Some make me feel powerful, some don't. How can I tell which memory is the important one?**

It's simple really: How do you want to feel? If you are confused about an object, ask yourself if you want the feeling it gives you to be a part of how you react to the people you meet or the different situations you encounter each day. Do you want these feelings to be part of the new business you're starting or your efforts to improve the one you already have? Do you want the feelings inspired by this object to be in the mix when you start to change the way you eat or when you transform yourself into the woman no man in his right mind would ever ignore? Do you want them there when you pop the question or when you start your relationship with the person you've been waiting your whole life to be with?

If you're still having trouble deciding what to do with an object, think about how it came into your life. If it's a gift, ask who gave it to you and what associations you have with that person. If it's something you bought for yourself, ask what was going on in your life at the time and what were the circumstances surrounding the purchase.

What does it make you think about, and how does it make you feel? Does this object make you feel happy or excited about life? Does it fill you with feelings of love? Does it call to mind the best parts of you? Does it remind you of your talents and abilities, your excellent taste, and the person you are taking actions to be? Does this object give you a sense of your power? Once you tap into the various associations your mind has with the object and see which ones emerge as the strongest, you will arrive at your answer.

Your subconscious is on your side. If you ask the Power Question, and you're willing to listen, it will start moving the answers into the conscious part of your mind. It's almost as if it's been waiting for this knowledge to arrive, and now that you understand what is happening with what's around you, it's ready to start talking. You are asking the right question. It is simple and direct, and your subconscious knows how to answer by putting the images in your mind and the feelings in your body that tell you the truth.

Pay attention to the images that come to you and what creates the strongest feelings. If there are several memories, focus on what jumps out at you the most and the dominant feelings you experience. Don't waste time wrestling with the answers. Relax, take a few deep breaths, and allow your mind to reveal the truth. If an object has you feeling a mixture of good and bad feelings, it's your choice: You can keep the level of powerlessness it inspires and maintains in your life, or you can let it go. Always remember that these are material things, and no matter what the old you is saying, they can be replaced.

Daniel: I had a sweatshirt I bought when I was dating a woman a few years ago. She and I didn't have a very good relationship, so I had that thought attached, but it was also the sweatshirt I gave my new girlfriend to wear the night of our first date when we got caught in the rain, which was a really good memory. I thought about it some more, and I realized the sweatshirt made me glad I was no longer with the first girlfriend, and it also reminded me of how lucky I was to be with the woman I'm with now. Then I thought to myself that a ten-dollar sweatshirt wasn't worth any sort of dilemma and that I needed a new one anyway, so I dropped it in the Goodwill box next to my grocery store.

Even if you keep a possession you were on the fence about, or that the Power Question has revealed doesn't belong in your home, if it needs to go, your mind will keep bringing the possession into your focus until you do something about it. It will become an itch that you must scratch. Everyone who has tried to keep a few things they know they shouldn't has had the same experience, and in the end these possessions never last long. No one seems to want to live with the itch, and why should they when they can scratch it and be done with it?

Andrea: After I finished my Clearing, I wanted to keep a teacup and a penholder that were cute and that I thought had no negative memories associated with them. However, when I looked at the big picture, I realized that they did have negative emotions connected to them because every time I used them or looked at them, I was reminded of a period of time when I was depressed and felt like my life wasn't going anywhere. So I got rid of them. Now I rarely have a thought about them. In fact, I hardly ever think about any of my old things anymore, which is surprising me. Some of them I had for over twenty-five years, and I really thought I would miss them. There were so many things I was convinced I needed that I didn't, and it turns out that I am much happier without them.

Explore what is attached to your possessions. If you get several memories, some powerful and some not, gauge what is coming at you the strongest and what emotions are most prominent. Then ask the Power Question again. Instead of relying on what you thought before and making old decisions, rely on what you know now and make new ones. Give yourself a chance to realize the truth and then move on. If you are struggling, you are putting pressure on yourself and that isn't necessary. Take a break. Go for a walk and clear your mind. Stretch out in the grass for a few minutes. Close your eyes.

Think about how you want your life to be and imagine yourself living that life: the way you will look, what you will wear, what your surroundings will be like. Review what has inspired you to come this far, think of your future, and come back strong.

11. **I inherited a few things from my great aunt, and I know this sounds bad, but I don't want to keep what she left me. How can I feel OK about Clearing these things?**

As with a recent divorce or breakup, there could be a lot of strong emotions going on inside of you after someone close to you has died, whether you were fond of the person or not. Allow yourself to get to the point where positive emotions such as love, gratitude, affection, and respect have a chance to play a part, rather than allowing your despair or other negative emotions like sadness, anxiety, and grief to dominate your decisions. When that time comes, deal with what was left behind and Clear what doesn't belong.

My client Malcolm is sharp and articulate. After graduating from an Ivy League school at nineteen, Malcolm went on to spend the next two years working in South America. While he was there, his estranged father passed away from liver failure. During our first session together, we talked about this and a few other things. When I told Malcolm about the Clearing, he said, "You're not going to try to get me to throw away all my things, are you?" I said, "No, of course not." Then I asked, "Do you have something you think needs to be thrown away?" Malcolm quickly responded, "My car. That's a joke, well, not really." Here's some of what Malcolm went on to say:

Malcolm: While you were talking, that's what came to my mind. That, the cigar smell inside of it, and my dad drunk and yelling at my mom.

My father left me the car in his will. He wasn't around much when I was growing up, and the times he was weren't so great. Before I got the car, I hardly ever thought about that part of my life. After I got it, I started thinking about my father and my childhood more. I would drive around remembering some of the awful moments from my past and trying to figure out why they had happened, but the thing was, I already knew why they happened. My dad was an alcoholic. He had a tough childhood and was never quite able to pull it together. I'd already forgiven him for not being around when I was a kid and for not being such a great dad when he was.

I moved on, and things actually worked out because I have a wonderful stepfather, and I consider myself very lucky. Even though that was the case, after I got the car I found myself thinking all over again about what had gone on.

I wasn't really happy about getting the car. Still, I never considered selling it. I felt like I should be glad to have it because it cost so much and was better than the one I had, but I wasn't. I had just accepted it. Selling the car and letting it go seems like such a simple solution. Part of me feels like it isn't right to let it go, but when I ask myself what "isn't right" actually means, I realize it means nothing, and I've been making myself feel bad over nothing.

Possessions come into your life in many different ways. Some are gifts, some you buy, some life hands to you, like the car Malcolm inherited. Whatever your situation, help yourself reach your goals by moving toward them unencumbered. Create the feelings you want with everything you bring into your life. No matter what they are or who they're from, you need your possessions to inspire you to move in the direction you decide. Your obligation is to yourself and the way you feel. You can continue to experience the feelings that items like Malcolm's car can bring, or you can choose to feel powerful. You can honor your life, or you can honor the leftover things from someone else's. It's your choice.

12. Is it OK if I put the things I'm Clearing into a storage space temporarily until I can figure out what to do with them?

No. Remember "Don't #7: Don't 'Sort of' Let Go." You can't move your things to another property or rental space and consider them gone or even out of your focus. The possessions you Clear aren't Cleared until they are no longer in your possession. If you store things, even "temporarily," you will know that they are there and they will continue to affect you.

Whether they are in your field of vision or you're consciously aware of them doesn't matter. The subconscious mind always sees, and your old possessions will continue to bring up thoughts and feelings that shape your identity whether they are neatly tucked away in your storage space or back where they were in your home. You don't even have to see them or think about them for you to be affected. Just knowing they are there will be enough. You could even be doing something as simple as walking down the street or listening to the radio and hear someone say "storage space" or "storage unit" or "I'm going to the store," and a part of your mind will draw an association that will keep you tied to the past.

Why bother? Why continue to keep these feelings around by moving the things you are Clearing to different locations? Why store feelings of powerlessness? What would you even use this powerlessness for?

Putting items in a storage space isn't doing the Clearing—it's moving your things to a storage space. Once you get at the truth of your possessions, don't store your bad feelings. Let them go and move on. Finish what you've started, and get the benefits of truly Clearing your things.

13. **My boyfriend and I broke up a few weeks ago. Is now a good time to do the Clearing?**

A breakup or divorce means that two people who were unhappy and feeling powerless are taking steps to change the way they feel and have better lives, and that's a good thing. If this is what you are doing, you are ready for your Clearing. In fact, your timing couldn't be better.

By doing the Clearing, you're committing to a forward motion. Ask yourself if now is the time by asking the Power Question. Ask yourself if what you are about to do will be powerful today as well as tomorrow or even next year. Look ahead and be sure that you are ready to move on with your life. Focus on what will happen from this point on: who you are going to be, the actions you will take, and the things you will do to feel powerful and create your life.

What is taking place with your Clearing is bigger and more important than the demise of a recent relationship. If it's the right time, you will know, and if it is, let nothing stand in your way. Make your move and begin.

14. **Between the kids and my job, time is tight, and I'm not sure I can do this. How long will the Clearing take to complete?**

How long it takes to Clear your possessions depends on how many you have, your enthusiasm, your determination, and your desire for your future. How excited are you about your life and what you're planning? How badly do you want to move forward? As you begin to Clear, you may feel your enthusiasm growing and find yourself getting things done faster than you thought you would, or you may have underestimated the expanse of your possessions and need extra time.

I believe it's best to go through your things and remove the items you are Clearing in a concentrated effort. Generally speaking, that's a one- to four-week period. However, that doesn't mean that people haven't had successful Clearings that took longer or that took less than a day.

Any step you take to Clear your possessions, no matter how small or large, will benefit you and the people in your life. Do everything you can in the time you have. Forget about settling in for a nice leisurely review of the past. Follow the Seven Steps and keep heading for the finish line. If you need extra time to sell your items, then take it, but maintain your momentum and get things done. Start telling yourself you can do it, and you will.

15. Should I just get rid of all my things?

I wouldn't want anyone to end up on the street from Clearing all their possessions, but by the same token I wouldn't want to limit anyone's experience with the Clearing by deciding for them what they should or shouldn't do with the answers they receive from the Power Question or how far they should go. These are very personal decisions, and only you can decide what to do with your Clearing and with your life.

16. What if an object only makes me feel good, not powerful?

Is feeling good a powerful feeling? Yes, it is! If an object makes you feel good, happy, or even nice, and there isn't any interference from negative emotions or memories, and it doesn't have you seeing yourself in any way that could be holding you back and limiting you, then it's powerful. Keep the objects that make you feel good. This isn't about eliminating your past. It's about achieving a sustained forward motion. It's about having a really great today and an amazing future. Surround yourself with what helps you achieve the things you want to achieve, and let go of the rest.

Austin: When I asked the Power Question on my own, I wasn't sure about the answers I was getting. Looking back, I realize this uncertainty was another way I was telling myself that my possessions weren't powerful. The problem was that I didn't know what being powerful felt like, so to make it easier I decided to ask other questions before I asked the Power Question, questions like, "Will this object help me move forward?" or, "Does this object have any unpleasant memories attached to it?" or, "Is this something the person I want to be would have in his home?" These questions were my training wheels. They helped me begin thinking in this new way, and they were easier to answer, which was a big help when I first started.

I love this "training wheels" reference, and these are great questions to ask. You can ask questions like "Does this object make me feel good?" or, "Is there anything about this object that makes me feel bad?" or, "Are there any unhappy memories attached to this object?" There are many examples throughout the book to choose from (see Step 4). If you find the Power Question daunting to start, put on some training wheels. Make your own list of questions. If there are any bad feelings or unhappy memories attached to an object, then chances are the object isn't making you feel powerful and you have your answer.

17. **My friend has a bunch of his things at my house, and it's taking forever for him to pick them up. I don't want to delay finishing my Clearing. What should I do?**

If a friend or relative is storing his or her belongings at your place and the items don't pass the Power Question, contact the owner and offer to drop the items off at his or her home or office at a certain time. If the item is small, then consider sending it through the mail. As quickly as possible, do whatever you can to remove anything that doesn't pass the Power Question. Don't leave unfinished business lying around your home. Things that are half done or that you have left out because you plan to "get to it one day soon" can subtly shift your energy, distract you, and slow you down. The Clearing is your opportunity to take care of loose ends once and for all and make a fresh start. So take care of these things now and honor your commitment.

18. **I'm done Clearing my possessions, and now I am thinking of telling some friends about it, but I'm afraid of what they might say. What's the best way to do this?**

You're excited about what you've done, you're feeling great, and you're pursuing your future. You're doing new things, even dropped a few pounds. The next day you tell someone close to you about your experiences, and he or she says, "I'm not so sure about all this Clearing business," or, "I know you, and you'll be back to your same old ways by the end of the week," or, "How is this any different from all the other things you've tried?"

Your friends may be excited for you and supportive of the actions you're taking, or you might find that a few of the people in your life aren't so happy about the changes you've made and try to diminish them or make you feel bad about what you've done:

"Oh, you only got $20 for that necklace? I could have got you $500."

"I can't believe you just donated that credenza. Wasn't that custom made?"

"I can totally see why you got rid of that sculpture. I remember how much your ex loved it. I still can't believe he cheated on you."

Why go this way if you think that something like this could happen? You are feeling good from what you're doing, so why deal with negative comments from the people you know are going to make them? How is having someone rub dirty boots all over your exciting new experience going to help you? Skip the trouble and get on to Part 2. You need to do this the right way, and part of doing that is avoiding discussing what you've accomplished with the people who you feel may try to undermine what you've done.

To move forward, you need to feel good and create some distance from your old life, not dive right back into it. Before discussing what you've done during your Clearing, be sure that you're ready and that you feel confident about what you are sharing and the people you are sharing with. Ask yourself if it's a powerful thing to do. It may be best to move on, or it may be good to share with like-minded people.

If you don't think it's a good idea to talk with those around you right now and you still feel the need to share, you can start a journal. You can also email your thoughts to my staff at johnbenz.com, and maybe your experience will get posted on my site and inspire others. Opportunities to share your experiences will most likely come up as you live your life, so share with the people you want to as you go.

The Clearing gives you momentum and a boost to your feeling of power. You want to protect these feelings and increase them, not go back to those who could diminish them and offer them up for sacrifice. When you've Cleared the spaces on your list and completed Step 7, be prepared to make the best use of the forward motion you've created and move immediately to Part 2.

18

YOUR HOME AFTER YOUR CLEARING: CREATING A HOUSE OF POWER

IN SOME WAYS, this chapter may be more appropriate for the end of the book, and I do want you to come back to it and read it again after you've completed Part 2 of your Clearing. (You'll see why.) However, there are things that are important for you to know now, so I've placed them here.

Above all, I don't want you to stop. It's essential that you maintain your momentum and move right on to the second part of the Clearing. After Clearing your possessions, you may find yourself staring at a bunch of half-empty rooms and itching to replace some of what you've Cleared, but hold off. If you've made some purchases already, that's fine, but more important for you at this moment is to move on to Part 2 so you can complete your Clearing. This doesn't mean that you are barred from getting anything new or buying some basic necessities. It just means that getting right to Part 2 tops the list of what's important.

When you've completed Part 2, you will be in the best position to make sure that what you bring into your life suits the person you truly are. Until that time, allow yourself to experience your home as it is and stay focused on moving forward with your Clearing. You might even find that you like the new openness of your surroundings and that very little needs to replaced.

Jennifer: At first I hated it. I thought my house looked like someone had come in during the night and taken what they could. It just looked barren to me, and I planned on redecorating immediately, but I ended up getting busy at work. After a few weeks, when I finally had the time to shop for a few things, I decided I liked the new open feel. Instead of filling my home again, I started to rearrange the furniture I had. I found two chairs and a table for my living room at an estate sale. I had the chairs reupholstered, and now I feel like my house is perfect. I like to walk through the rooms and look at how everything turned out, and I really like having less stuff around. I thought I wouldn't, but now I do. I breathe deeply, and I smile. I used to ignore most of what I had in my home, or at least that's what I thought I was doing. Now I'm aware that my things are making me feel good. I still can't get over how different it feels.

Clearing your home gives you a better understanding of the influence your possessions have on your life. After you've completed Part 2, I want you to use this knowledge to create your house of power. Take what gets you excited about life and hang it on your walls. Find out what puts you in the mood to look and feel the way you want to, and place it on your tables and shelves. Ask yourself what the powerful person you are would have in his or her home, and then have it.

Feeling happy and inspired benefits you and everyone around you, so do everything you can to make yourself feel good in your home. Turn it into a make-me-feel-good-atarium. As you move forward, bring in only what will produce the best feelings in you. You control the space in your home, so use it to create the thoughts and emotions you want to have, and that will help you create the life you want.

Creating a house of power isn't about having expensive things like designer furniture or the latest media equipment. That isn't the point. This is about what your possessions and surroundings say about you, what they are communicating to you, and how they influence you to feel and think about yourself. A picture you cut from a magazine can have you feeling better and contain more potential to influence the direction of your life than something that costs thousands of dollars.

To create your house of power, take whatever gives you the good feelings you want and surround yourself with it. Maybe for you that's having fresh-cut flowers around the house each week or a room with the walls painted yellow. Maybe it's a frame for the first dollar you're going to make with your new business or a letter from someone you admire. Use whatever you bring into your home as a vehicle to foster and maintain the powerful feelings inside you, and then begin to direct those feelings toward what it is you want to achieve.

William: I had Cleared almost everything from my home. I had my bed and a new Apple computer, what was left of my clothes, and that was pretty much it. Everything else was gone. When I had finished my Clearing, I asked myself the questions you suggested. I asked myself who I was and who I wanted to be. I closed my eyes and pictured myself at my best. Then I asked myself how this person would live and what he would do. I started thinking of this "me" in my vision as the ultimate me, so I would ask myself questions like, "What would the ultimate me have in this room?" and, "What would the ultimate me do each day?" The first thing that came to me was that the ultimate me probably does fifty push-ups a day, so, among some other changes I made, I immediately started doing push-ups. Three days later I felt like someone had been beating me with a hammer.

At first I was only able to do twenty push-ups a day, and I had to do them five at a time. By the fourth set of five, I could barely do two at a time, and the ones I was able to do... let's put it this way, I was glad no one was around to see me doing them. Eight weeks later, I did fifty. It took me all day, and they may not have been pretty, but I kept going until I had done fifty total.

I was probably more sore during those first few weeks than I'd ever been in my life. When it was really bad, the voice came into my head telling me that I should just stop, but this time I was ready and I wasn't going to put up with it. When you told me to pounce on these thoughts, I had never considered treating them as something separate from me or something I could attack somehow or just say no to. I just thought they were me. I was sick and tired of being fat though, and thinking about it so much, and I didn't want to hear excuses from myself. I didn't even want them approaching the perimeter of my mind. So I didn't let them. I just kept thinking about my push-ups. I was going to do this, and that was it. There was nothing to ponder or reason my way out of. I was someone who does fifty push-ups a day, period.

I had played some sports in high school, so I knew I'd be sore as my muscles became used to being used again. I thought I was using them a lot because I was always busy, but when I really thought about it I realized I hadn't been using my body for anything other than walking to and from the car and hoisting myself onto the couch, so after those first few days I was like, "Oh, yeah, I remember now. There is going to be a period of adjustment."

I kept it up every day, and gradually the soreness started to lessen and I started to do more push-ups. Seven, nine, then ten push-ups at a time. I approached food the same way. I wanted to eat what the ultimate me eats, not what the person I thought I was before ate. I wanted to eat what could help me do my push-ups. Was I obsessed? Maybe a little, but I figured this was a good thing to be obsessed with. Anyway, I knew I had to give my body what it needed in order to do what I wanted to do, and I knew my old food wasn't going to cut it. So I cleared everything out of my kitchen and started over. I subscribed to a couple health and fitness magazines and began pulling out recipes. I decided I was a "sauce on the side" kind of guy, and I made a few other changes. I ordered bulk spices online from a wholesaler so I wouldn't have to rely on frying everything in oil for flavor. I also bought a good quality water-filtration system. Now my water tastes great, and I drink a lot more of it, which made giving up soda a lot easier.

For my house, I bought a really nice reading lamp with a brushed nickel finish that fit in perfectly with my bed and was definitely something the ultimate me would have. I used to watch TV for hours, but I canceled the cable. I told myself that for now I would focus on other things, and I did. Slowly, I began to make a few more purchases for my home. I took my time, though. If I was looking for something and what I found didn't feel right or didn't really suit the ultimate me, I waited until I found what did.

Eventually I was able to do twenty push-ups at a time. I bought a bamboo table for next to my bed because I love bamboo. All I have to do is see some bamboo and I feel good. I also bought two chairs for my balcony that I'd seen in *Architectural Digest*. They were expensive, but I decided I was worth it and I could afford it.

I started telling myself I could do it — actually saying the words out loud to myself, which was probably having a much better effect on me than "there's just no way," which was what I was used to saying. My new things were saying something different too. I didn't think it would make much of a difference, but it did. I started walking into my home and feeling good. I don't have anything lying around or leaning against a wall because someone left it there or because I had space to fill. Everything is there to make me feel good in some way, and it does. Sometimes I catch myself thinking about my home while I'm at work, and that feels good too.

I had a few ups and downs, but I stuck to my new routine no matter what. After eleven months, I came out of the shower, looked in the mirror, and instead of grabbing two handfuls of blubber from around my waist, all I could pinch was a measly two inches, and it was mostly skin. The sixty extra pounds were gone, and I could do fifty push-ups at a time. Those first two months were a bit nuts. I felt like I was being pulled in so many different directions, but I stuck it out, and after a while I didn't want to stop. I didn't feel like quitting. I just felt like being myself.

What if the objects in your home were telling you that you're powerful, capable, intelligent, fun loving, and persistent, that you're forgiving and kind, that you're someone who is loved and who has a dynamite sense of personal style? What if every time you stepped through your front door this was the identity your possessions were reinforcing, instead of what your old things had you believing about yourself? What kinds of decisions would you make? What types of actions would you be inspired to take if this was the way you felt and how you saw yourself? What would your life be like then? It's your home, so why not create an environment that will have you feeling this way? Why not do everything possible to use your surroundings to your advantage?

You want your possessions and the environment you create in your living space to say to you that you care about yourself and that you are worth it. You want the things you bring into your home to give you confidence, to inspire you. It could be by their beauty, their uniqueness, their craftsmanship, or other positive associations. Whatever it is, if a possession makes you feel powerful, if it calls to mind your strengths and abilities, if it helps you to stay focused on moving forward with your life, then bring it on. It has earned the right to be in your home.

With each new possession, you have the opportunity to increase your good feelings and influence the changes you want to make. Hang a picture of your favorite athlete on your refrigerator. Have a giant wallpaper mural printed from a photo of Paris you love and put it up in your basement. Buy some new pieces of furniture or make a couple yourself. Leave the wall facing your bed uncluttered except for a small table holding a vase full of cherry blossoms. Hire a decorator whose vision you trust and start completely fresh. Always remember that what you bring into your home helps tell you who you are. Instead of having what the person you've outgrown and moved on from would have in his or her home, have what the person you envision yourself to be would have.

If some of the possessions you want to bring into your home aren't as agreeable to the people you live with as they are to you, remember that everyone has their own unique reaction to change. Be kind to those around you while still being true to yourself. Skip the anger, and use your cleverness and determination to resolve any conflicts that may come up.

If you do experience some friction over some of your new possessions, look up the classic movie, *A Christmas Story* (1983). In one scene, the father wins a lamp in the shape of a life-sized woman's leg in a trivia contest. He's so proud of the lamp that he displays it on a table by the main window in the front of the house, where it can clearly be seen from the street. Soon the neighbors gather outside to talk about and point at the lamp. For a short while the father feels powerful, but very quickly the lamp creates tension and conflict with his wife, and his powerful feelings turn negative.

If your actions are causing conflict with those around you, use your open mind to find out what works (A few of the techniques you will learn in Part 2 will help you.) If you have your own version of a lamp in the shape of a woman's leg that's driving everyone crazy, remember that this possession isn't the only thing that can help you feel powerful. On the other hand, if you are constantly backing down and giving in to those around you, ask yourself if that feels powerful. If you can't have a few things the way you want, you have to think about why you are putting yourself in such a powerless position.

Do what will help you in every aspect of your life. Do what the successful you — the ultimate you, the powerful you — would do. Use the techniques you will learn in Part 2, and you will leave your home each morning with the knowledge of your own awesomeness. Apply the principles of the Clearing to everything you bring into your home and make choices about your surroundings that will produce the best feelings in you. Fill your home with power, fill yourself up with those feelings, and then do what you came to do. Do your life. Do your happy, successful, awesome life.

PART II

CLEARING YOUR RESIDUAL THOUGHTS

19

TAKING CARE OF WHAT'S LEFT BEHIND

WHEN YOU WERE a kid and you thought about your future, you probably never imagined you'd be overweight. You probably never saw yourself working at a job you don't like or being married to someone you don't really love. You probably never considered that this or anything like it would be your life. But here's what happened: Certain events occurred that changed you, that made you believe that this person is you and this is the type of life you're supposed to have. Because you didn't know how to deal with them at the time, or how to feel different, the thoughts that came from these events stayed with you, and you started to believe that you were less than who you are. These thoughts are what I call "residual thoughts."

This is Part 2, and this is where you take care of what's left behind after you've Cleared your home. Any thoughts that don't belong, that are slowing you down, that don't suit your true identity—this is where you let them go and move on. Some thoughts are there because that's where you're used to them being, and they will dissipate as you become more involved with your new life. Others are there because there's still an action you need to take in order to leave them behind.

After she Cleared her home, things were better for my client Bianca, but something was continuing to block her when it came to her weight. During one of our follow-up sessions I discovered what that was, and what we did about it would eventually become the second half of the Clearing—Clearing residual thoughts.

"Maybe I just don't deserve to look good," Bianca said, sighing.

"When did you decide this about yourself?" I asked.

"I don't know. I'm a little surprised that came out of my mouth, actually."

"Well, what happened in your past that gives you these same feelings? What event made you feel so bad about yourself that you decided you don't deserve to look good?"

Bianca sat quietly and stared into her lap. For a while she didn't say anything, and then suddenly she looked up at me and, with tears in her eyes, blurted out, "I slept with my best friend's boyfriend!"

I'd never seen Bianca cry before. No matter what we spoke about in the past, she had always been very controlled, but with this confession came a flood of emotion. After wiping her eyes and taking a deep breath, she told me what had happened.

Bianca: I know you are going to think I'm a horrible person, and you'd be right to think that way because I am. I had too much to drink at a party one night during my senior year at college, and I ended up sleeping with a guy my friend was dating. I was drunk, and I know that doesn't matter because it was me that did it. No one made me drink that much, and no one made me act the way I did. Anyway, before I had a chance to talk to her about it, he went to her and confessed everything. She cut me out, and I couldn't blame her. Six months later we graduated, and I never saw her again. I think I'll always feel bad about that.

No matter how many good times Bianca had shared with her friend, she was stuck with how things were left in the end and felt powerless to do anything about it. What had happened created a dark cloud that covered her entire college career and gave her negative thoughts that stuck with her for years. She felt bad about school, her friendship, and herself, and nothing, including Clearing her home, had made her feel any different.

Bianca told me she would "always feel bad," and for the most part she did. Every time she looked in the mirror or got dressed, every time she saw a woman who was in shape or her husband saw her naked, every time she ate, was hungry, or shopped for food, she felt bad. To maintain this idea she had of herself as someone should feel this way, she was hurting herself like she had that night back at school, but this time, instead of alcohol, she was using food to do it.

Because of the emotion attached to this event, the thoughts Bianca took away from it became a big part of her life. Over time, she got used to what these thoughts told her. She started to believe what they said about her, and she ended up acting in ways that conformed to who they said she was. Bianca had made a mistake, but these thoughts didn't represent the truth about who she was or what she could do. She needed to replace them. She needed to create an ending that let her see who she really was. To do this she had to get back into the event, let her good parts come out, and continue the story.

"If you don't like the ending, why don't you come up with a new one?" I asked.

Bianca asked what I meant, and here's what I told her: "Well, look at what happened. Because of that one night, you have all these negative thoughts about yourself, and these thoughts have found their way into your life right now. You don't feel right because you're seeing yourself as someone you're not. You're telling yourself that what happened that night back at school is who you are, but it isn't you. It's only a tiny slice. It's a moment where there were infinite possibilities and you chose one that didn't work out.

"You have thoughts that have you feeling guilt, shame, regret, and frustration, and because you haven't resolved them and learned the truth about yourself, you are creating situations in your life today where you feel the same way. You're creating situations that mirror these ideas you have about yourself. If you go back, continue the story, and give this event a new ending, then you will see who you really are. These old thoughts won't fit, and they will go away."

I waited a moment, then asked Bianca, "If you could choose any ending you want for this event, what would it to be?"

"I don't really know," she said, "I guess I would want my friend to be happy and to forgive me."

"Sounds good," I said. "Let's make it happen."

We talked about the ending she wanted and mapped out the steps she would take to get there. Bianca looked up her friend from college, and when she was ready, she gave her a call.

Bianca: When she answered the phone and I told her who it was, I was surprised that she seemed glad to hear from me. After we talked for a minute or two, I went right to it like we had practiced. I told her why I was calling. I apologized for what had happened back at school and asked her to forgive me. I told her there was no excuse for what I did, and that I've regretted it ever since.

She was so great about it. She said that she had forgiven me a long time ago, that she wasn't "any saint" at school herself, and that she missed our friendship. I told her that I wasn't much of a friend to her because of what I did, and she said that it was college, and we were just making the kind of mistakes people make when they're young so they don't have to make them when they're adults.

I thought that was a very generous thing to say, and she was making an excuse for me, but it was true. I did learn about life from that experience. I learned that I never wanted to hurt someone like I had hurt her. Whenever I even hear that someone is sleeping with someone else's husband or boyfriend, or there's a scene in a movie where someone is cheating, I always cringe a little. That night gave me a healthy fear of drinking, too, which has probably saved me from a lot of other mistakes.

We talked more. She told me about her family and I told her about mine, and it was really nice. After I hung up the phone, I realized what a heavy load that had been for me. I'm married. I have a husband and kids now, but what happened back in college was still a big part of my life. After I made that call, I didn't feel the same about it anymore. The way my friend seemed to have let it go and her perspective on what happened made me think that it was time for me to let it go too. I had made a mistake, and I learned from it. I hurt people, that was true, but I had apologized, and I felt like it was OK now.

Now when I remember what happened, I don't really think about what went on at school. I think about what my friend said when we spoke on the phone. I think about how scared I was to call her but that I did it anyway, and I think about how good I felt after I had done it. I really just felt like I was floating.

When Bianca continued the story, she realized that she could take charge and make things right, and when she did, she could make herself and others happy. Her residual thoughts had been keeping the parts of herself that helped her do these things hidden. They had Bianca believing they didn't exist, that nothing could be done, and that she didn't have what it takes to feel different. These thoughts joined others like them and infiltrated her life. Instead of facing challenges and finishing the things she started, instead of doing what could consistently make her feel good, Bianca had been listening to what these thoughts were saying and stopping herself.

To Clear her residual thoughts, Bianca used the parts of herself she hadn't used the first time around, parts that, regardless of the truth, she was convinced that she didn't possess. She felt herself speaking up and being honest, strong, persistent, and compassionate. She felt herself taking a bunch of crappy emotions and turning them into good ones. She saw how powerful she was and what she was able to do, and she understood the truth. Her residual thoughts didn't fit. New thoughts came in. She felt different about herself, and she started losing weight.

The events in your life that ended badly are having an effect on everything you do. The thoughts you have from them stop you from getting the raise, finding love, and finishing what you start. They have you packing on the pounds, seeking out relationships with people who hurt you, and performing behaviors that slow you down in all areas of your life. They can keep you from doing what you need to do to be happy, and as long as they remain inside of you unchanged, they will continue to affect you just as they always have.

Maybe something happened when you were young. Maybe you mistreated someone or someone mistreated you. Maybe there's a friend you need to apologize to or someone you should forgive. Maybe you had an argument and you keep thinking about it, repeating what happened in your mind. You dismiss these thoughts. You blow them off, but your subconscious is like an internal Clearing device and it keeps bringing them back. It's trying to get you to take notice and make things right. It's giving you migraine headaches, lower back pain, and an expanded waistline. It wants you to do something besides pushing these thoughts away only to have them return later. It wants you to use what's inside of you to let them go permanently so they can never make you feel bad again.

You say things like:

"I'll never meet someone who's right for me."

"I'm not a people person."

"I'm terrible with money."

"My career is going nowhere."

"I'm not athletic."

"I'm an awful cook"

"I'm better off alone."

You think these thoughts are true, but they're not. Your residual thoughts have you seeing yourself in ways that hide the truth about who you are and what you can do. They are responsible for all the things you do that keep you stuck and that get you in trouble, and until you Clear them, they will continue to take form in the behaviors you find yourself repeating that are holding you back in your life today.

Sleeping with your ex-boyfriend when you could be out falling in love with someone who is actually right for you, talking yourself into being overweight and unhappy instead of sticking with your plan and feeling good about yourself, choosing to do what hurts you and continuing to do it even though you know the effect it's having on your life: These are all things you do because of what you're holding onto from your past. You do these things, or things like them, because of your residual thoughts.

With Bianca, her apology did the trick, and for many of my clients saying those two simple words, "I'm sorry," also worked like magic. When it came to Clearing residual thoughts, an apology was gold, but there was more. Some of my clients had events in their past where an apology didn't fit. Some were angry about things that had happened to them and needed to forgive. Others needed to confront and say what had been on their mind, sometimes for years.

Whatever residual thoughts my clients did have, I quickly discovered that Clearing them usually involved some form of confronting, apologizing, and forgiving.

This is what worked. This is what Cleared my clients' residual thoughts and created endings that inspired them, and I knew why. To confront, apologize, and forgive and do it right, my clients had to use the best parts of themselves. They had to use their calm, their courage, their cleverness, their experience, and their charm. They had to use the parts they didn't use the first time around, the parts that their residual thoughts had convinced them weren't there. When they did, it changed them. Now it wasn't just me telling them they were strong or that they could do it. They were *being* strong, and they were doing it. They were seeing it themselves and becoming aware of what they were capable of. They understood that their residual thoughts didn't belong, and they started acting in ways that made sense for who they actually were.

It was simple, really. My clients were coming to me with a bunch of negative thoughts from events in their past that had ended poorly. They were putting these thoughts into what they were doing to improve their lives, and it wasn't working. I wanted these thoughts gone. I wanted whatever kept my clients believing they were less than who they were out of their lives, and I focused on making that happen.

After they Cleared their homes, I asked my clients to make a list of five events from their past that had ended badly. Five was enough for them to make major changes in their lives without having to spend too much time in the past. After they had Cleared five events, my clients knew what steps to take and why they worked. This also gave them enough experience to take care of any other residual thoughts that might pop up as they continued on with their lives.

For each of their five events, I instructed my clients to write out whatever negative thoughts they took away about themselves. Once they did, I had them write the opposite of these thoughts, which I called the "the truth." Then I had them write down who they would confront, apologize, or forgive to create their new endings and what they would say when they did.

Initially, when it came to their new endings, many of my clients pictured failure and were stuck focusing on past experiences and the limitations they believed they had. Many were afraid of what would happen, so they imagined the worst. I knew these thoughts and feelings would cut them off from their abilities, and that the better they felt, and the more good feelings they created surrounding their new endings, the more access they would have to what they had inside themselves that could help them create the endings they wanted, so I moved quickly in the other direction. I took what I knew about my clients and created visualizations that would make them feel good and that showed them their success. I taught them to picture things going right again and again and to imagine themselves confronting, apologizing, and forgiving calmly, with style and grace. I had them say encouraging things to themselves throughout the day and to keep images nearby that inspired them, that made them feel good, and that focused them on their new endings so that when the time came to take action, they would be prepared. And they were.

Whether it was one thing we did in particular or a combination that led to the events that followed, I'm not sure. But in the end, the steps we took worked. Confrontations were made. Apologies and forgiveness were given and received. When my clients went to create their new endings, wonderful things took place. They started to understand who they really were and what they could really do. The new endings told them things about themselves that made more sense than what their residual thoughts had been saying. Their old thoughts lost their hold, and my clients were free.

Like Bianca and those who have Cleared their possessions before you, you've made important changes. You feel good. Maybe you feel better than you've felt in a long time: lighter, freer, energized, excited. But there could be something left over. There could be thoughts that are still hanging around, thoughts telling you that the things you are doing to make your life better aren't worth it, that you shouldn't bother, that you've done enough, and that you're not the kind of person who has what it takes to be successful or who sees things through to the end. You may think these thoughts are you, that what they say about you is true, but they aren't. They are only what, for the moment, you are choosing to believe.

Think about it. You didn't start out life believing a bunch of negative things about yourself. These thoughts are something you acquired along the way. Like Bianca, you have events in your past that ended badly. After these events ended, there was no resolution or change, so the thoughts you had from them stayed with you. You got used to them. You started to believe that what they said about you was true, that the difficulties you're having are just who you are, that the mistakes you've been making somehow make sense for you, and you cut yourself off from the talents and abilities you have inside of you that could be helping you to feel different and have a better life.

When I looked at these events with my clients, I saw that their residual thoughts weren't giving them the complete picture. Many had come to conclusions about themselves during moments when their negative emotions kept them from seeing things clearly. They were living their lives according to thoughts they had from events where they were being yelled at or someone was physically hurting them, events where they were caught off guard or were too young or inexperienced to know how to act or do anything about what was happening to them. Some made judgments about themselves when they were six, eight, or ten years old that were still playing a major role in shaping their lives twenty or thirty years later. Reactions they had to events they had no possible way to prepare for were influencing the actions they took every day, telling them who they were and what they were capable of doing.

My clients were living under identities that were keeping them from using their persistence, their humor, their compassion and patience. They were stuck using only a small part of their true potential, so they became frustrated. They held themselves back and repeated actions that got them in trouble because that's who their residual thoughts said they were. No matter what wonderful talents and abilities they had to choose from inside themselves, their residual thoughts made them believe these things weren't there.

This is what's happening to you right now. The trouble you've been having in your life is because you are stuck with thoughts from events in your past that are at odds with your true abilities. Instead of doing what you want, you end up being swayed by these thoughts. They create an identity that cuts you off from yourself, and this has you feeling frustrated and coming up short, instead of feeling good and succeeding.

It's important for you to realize that just because you aren't using all your potential, that doesn't mean it doesn't exist. Your potential is there (there's gobs of it). You are talented, you are persistent, and you have the ability to be charming, ingratiating, supportive, generous, and kind. All these things and more are there inside of you, and this is why the process of Clearing your residual thoughts is so important. When you give these events from your past that didn't end well new endings, you see that these parts of you exist. You're taking action. You're using your abilities, and you're using them on the event where they were absent. You're putting them back in, and when you're done, instead of your residual thoughts telling you who you are and what you can do, there will be a new ending where you made things right and new thoughts influencing your life.

If you're thinking that you don't have what it takes, that you can't do it, or that what you are doing to make your life better isn't worth it, this isn't actually you—it's your residual thoughts telling you these things. As you've been trying to live your life, they've been interfering. You do your best to change, and you do OK in the beginning. You lose weight, you put more effort into your career, you take a new class, you focus on making your marriage better, but then your residual thoughts return and you get in trouble. You gain the weight back. You quit the class. You have the same old fights with your spouse. You talk yourself out of the life you were meant to have and settle for what these thoughts are saying is right for you instead. You end up where you started or worse off, convinced that this is just who you are and all you're going to get out of life.

Bullshit. If this is what you are experiencing, this doesn't have to be your life. Follow the Seven Steps in the next chapter. Confront, apologize, forgive, and let go of the thoughts and feelings that are holding you back. Create new endings for the events in your life that ended badly and see who you really are. Maybe you will feel embarrassed when you do. Maybe you will be afraid of the reaction you might get, and that's OK. What isn't OK is to miss out on the life you could have because you didn't do anything, made excuses, and kept things the same.

Maybe you think that you don't have to deal with your residual thoughts and that to have the things you want you just have to try harder. But that has nothing to do with it. You have to change what you are putting behind the actions you take when you do try harder. If it's a bunch of residual thoughts, it's not going to work out. If it's thoughts from events where you took charge and used the best parts of yourself to confront, apologize, and forgive, the story will be different. The ending will tell you the truth about who you are, and you will create the kinds of thoughts and feelings that will help you to succeed.

Each time you sell yourself short ("I can't do it."), each time you think or make a negative comment about yourself ("Men always leave me."), each time you cut yourself down ("I'm fat. This is just who I am."), it comes from some place. You can find where that place is and continue the story. For the events in your past where things didn't quite turn out the way you wanted, you can take action and create new endings. Big, fantastic, fun endings. Sweet, warm, loving, exciting, hopeful, blissful endings. You can create thoughts that tell you something different about yourself and put them into the changes you're making in your life.

Maybe you're looking at some of the crummy things that have happened from your past and saying, "No way, it can't be done," but it can be done! You can take action. You can replace these old thoughts with new and better ones. You can take the events that have been causing you pain and messing up your life, turn them around, and use them to help you get what you want.

Don't hold yourself back or let your old identity talk you out of what you are about to do. Don't let fear steal away this opportunity to be happy. If you see yourself in what you are reading here, then commit to Clearing your residual thoughts. Why keep these thoughts anyway? Why read this chapter and say, "Screw this, I'm keeping my residual thoughts"? You have my book. You can do this, and when you do, you will feel the way you're supposed to feel. You will see yourself. You will know that you are awesome, and your actions will prove that it's true.

Your residual thoughts have been keeping you from what your life is meant to be and what you are here to do. You've Cleared your home; now complete the process. Use the Seven Steps in the next chapter and Clear your residual thoughts.

20

THE SEVEN STEPS TO CLEARING RESIDUAL THOUGHTS

I WATCHED MY clients realize that they were strong. I saw them change and become happier people. You will find this happening to you when you create just one new ending using the Seven Steps.

The steps are simple, but just as when you Cleared your home, you will need courage to take them. See for yourself that you are strong, that you can do the hard thing and experience the rewards when you do. Follow the Seven Steps below and get started Clearing your residual thoughts.

Step 1: Realize how brave you are.
Step 2: List events that ended badly.
Step 3: Prepare your new endings.
Step 4: Repeat your three communications.
Step 5: Write your commitment statement.
Step 6: Begin, and go until you're finished.
Step 7: Complete your closing ceremony.

STEP 1: REALIZE HOW BRAVE YOU ARE

Doing what you've done to get this far took courage. You could have run away from Clearing your home because it was different, because it took time, because it was hard, because you didn't want to think about what it made you think about, but you did it. Years, even decades, of the old identity being in charge didn't stop you. It's brave to Clear your home the way you did. It's brave to let go and venture forward the way you are doing now. You're stepping into a new world. Tell yourself you are brave because it's true. Go ahead and say it out loud, "I am brave!" (Don't wait. Do it right now. It feels good.) Your bravery is there inside of you. It's always been there, but because of certain events from your past, you have thoughts telling you that it isn't, thoughts that have you believing that you can't when you absolutely can.

You drive an enormous car with a huge engine at insane speeds, surrounded by people who may or may not be paying attention while doing the exact same thing. You get on airplanes and go up thousands of feet in the air. You face people you don't want to face every day. You make hard decisions. You have kids. You walk down the aisle and get married. You make sacrifices. You protect the people you love. You do brave things all the time. You've just gotten used to them, and that's why you don't see what you've done or yourself as brave anymore. But you are brave, and you are still brave even if you've made mistakes. Whatever you've done in the past doesn't take this away.

You used your bravery to take action and Clear your home. Now continue the story and continue to connect with this side of yourself. Any words I could say to describe how good it feels to let go of your residual thoughts won't compare to what it actually feels like when you do. Clear just one event, and you will understand. Then don't stop. Keep going. Be who you are, and use what's inside of you. Realize you're brave, *because you are brave*, and continue on to Step 2.

STEP 2: LIST EVENTS THAT ENDED BADLY

There are events in your past that ended badly, events you want to feel different about, but never believed you could. Maybe someone you trusted lied to you, or maybe you made a mess of a situation you could have handled differently. Maybe you got hurt by the one person in the world who was supposed to protect you, and you got stuck with thoughts that made you feel bad, thoughts that boxed you in and limited you. Because you believed these thoughts were true, they changed you and altered the course of your life. Now you realize what's been happening, and you want something different. You want success. You want to get rid of the gut, and take a few pounds off of your thighs. You want to have great relationships, and be consistently happy. To have these things, you need access to the person you are when you aren't being blocked by your residual thoughts.

For Step 2, grab a pen and a piece of paper, and go someplace where you can focus without distractions. Ask yourself what events in your past ended badly, and memories will start coming to you. When they do, write them down. A few events may have surfaced already while you've been reading. Include them in your list and keep going.

There could be an event from your high school prom, college spring break, or your best friend's wedding, one where you said what you shouldn't have said and did what you shouldn't have done, and you haven't felt right about since. Maybe there was an event when someone said something negative to you about yourself, and, even though it wasn't true, you believed it and allowed it to become part of who you are. Some events could be from decades ago; others could be from last week. Some could have to do with your kids, an old friend from summer camp, or your high school guidance counselor. Some events you may have forgotten about, and you will be surprised when they resurface. Others you may know very well because you've gone over them in your mind so many times before.

If you're having trouble figuring out what your events are or if you feel stuck at any point, you can ask yourself:

"What have I done in the past that embarrasses me?"
"What moment from my life do I wish I could take back?"
"What happened in my past that makes me feel the worst?"
"What events from my life would I change if I could?"
"What events from my past made me feel powerless?"

Since you will be confronting, apologizing, and forgiving to create your new endings, you could look at your past and ask yourself:

"Who do I need to confront?"

"Who do I need to apologize to?"

"Who do I need to forgive?"

You could also think of some of the specific ways you act today that aren't working out for you, focus on each one individually, and ask yourself:

"What event in my life did this behavior come from?"

"What event started me thinking that I was someone who does something like this?"

"When was the first time I remember feeling the way this behavior makes me feel?"

You can do the same for any negative beliefs you have about yourself. Look into your past and ask yourself:

"What event made me start thinking I'd always be fat?"

"What event told me I wasn't good looking?"

"What event told me that I'm someone who always picks the wrong guy?"

Modify the questions according to what is going on with you and your life. As long as you're in some way asking yourself which events in your past ended badly, you can use any variation you want.

Most of your events will come to you when you ask yourself these questions. Others may pop into your head as you go about your day. You could be loading groceries into the back of your car and suddenly recall being bitten by a donkey at the petting zoo when you were six and understand why you haven't asked for the raise you deserve at work. You could be putting the dishes away in your kitchen and suddenly remember playing Spin the Bottle at your fourteenth birthday party, kissing a boy you didn't really like, and how you did the same thing twelve hours earlier when you said goodnight to your husband.

Understand that your subconscious is ready for this. It's ready for you to take out the garbage, and it's standing at the front door with two full bags. Wedge it open just a little with your questions, and it will start pushing events through. When it does, don't waste time trying to deny what's coming to you. These memories are finding their way into your focus because you are asking for them. You may think some of what comes to you isn't important, but resist the urge to brush away certain events by telling yourself they don't matter. Write them down regardless of how you initially feel, and give yourself a chance to discover why your subconscious is bringing them to your attention.

Nicole: I was talking to John about residual thoughts and what I had been doing to Clear them. While we were talking, I mentioned a work meeting I'd been in recently during which there were several times that I didn't feel like my suggestions had been listened to or considered. He asked me, "When was the first time you remember feeling like your efforts weren't appreciated or like you weren't getting the credit you deserved?" Immediately, something that happened twenty years ago popped in my head, and I thought to myself, "Well, that doesn't make sense." However, by now I had worked with John long enough to know that I should trust what messages my brain gives me. So I said, "Well, I don't think this is it, but when I was fourteen my friend and I were partners on a history fair project about the Battle of Vicksburg. We won first place, but the school had only bought one trophy. The teacher who was presenting the award to us didn't know what to do. She looked at my friend and said, "Here, you have boobs, so I'll give this to you." What was crazy was that I was the one who had done all the work on the project, and now my friend was getting the trophy, and she was getting it because she had boobs.

As soon as I'd told John the whole story, the connection to my current issue was obvious. John told me that was an important residual thought because we had been talking about how a big issue for me is that I crave appreciation and resent people when they don't give it to me. Initially, I second-guessed my brain bringing up that memory, but I'm so glad I talked it through.

Whether it took place when you were eight years old, fourteen, or forty, whether it was last week or last year, if it's popping into your mind, go ahead and write it down. When you're done, there could be ten, twenty events, or more. There could be several events that all involve the same people or where the same thing keeps happening again and again. There could be events popping into your mind that you believe have nothing to do with the way you're feeling or what's been going on in your life. For now, take down everything that comes to you.

After you have your events compiled, circle the five that you have the strongest feelings about. Remember, you're getting rid of the negative thoughts you have about yourself from these endings, so pick what you don't want influencing you and what you could definitely do without having to think about for the rest of your life.

If you're looking at one of the events you wrote down and thinking, "I really don't want to deal with that one," then that's definitely one for your final list. Put simply, the more you don't want to Clear an event, the more it needs to be Cleared. The good part about this is that the potential reward from creating new endings for events like these is tremendous. Sometimes to get the most benefit you have to choose what you may believe is the hardest thing to do. Don't allow your old identity to influence you to avoid choosing certain events for your list in favor of others you may believe are easier to deal with. Don't allow your old identity to talk you out of connecting with the truth about yourself or hold you back with these events any longer. This is your moment. Let go of your fear, and free yourself.

Once you have your list, you may feel there are some events that didn't make it into your final five that need new endings, and that may be true, but Clearing residual thoughts isn't about correcting every single incident that may have gone wrong in your life. Too much focus on your past can work against you. For your Clearing, you want to spend as little time there as possible while doing the most good. If there are still events that you feel need to be addressed once you've completed your Clearing, I say go ahead and Clear them. For now, focus on the five you've chosen and continue on to Step 3.

Step 3: Prepare Your New Endings

Next, I want you to prepare what I call an "event chart" for each of your five events. Take two pieces of plain paper and go to where you won't be distracted. At the top of your first piece of paper, write "Event," and give yourself some room to describe the event you will be working on, then divide the space beneath into four columns. Title your first column *Residual Thoughts*, the second *The Truth*, the third *What I Will Do,* and the fourth *What I Will Say*, as in the illustration below. At the top of your second piece of paper, write *What I Will Say (cont.)*, and leave the space beneath it blank. When you are through, make four copies so you have one set for each event on your list.

Event #1: _____

Residual Thoughts	The Truth	What I Will Do	What I Will Say
			(continued on next page)

Once you have your five sets of event charts, fill out a chart for each event on your list. Start at the top with a brief description of what happened. Then under your first heading, *Residual Thoughts*, ask yourself what negative thoughts your event gave you about yourself, and write down what comes to you when you do. Forget about everyone else who was there for now and how bad you may think they suck. You could be angry at other people, but your residual thoughts are about you. Look at the event you are creating a new ending for, look at the part you played in what happened, and ask yourself what you did or didn't do that could have you thinking something negative about yourself. What does this event say about you as a person that isn't so great, that you might not want to think is true about yourself? Own up to it now so you can let it go and not have to deal with the effect this event is having on your life any longer. Decide to be completely honest. (Why not? What you write is between you and a piece of paper. You don't have to be concerned with what anyone else thinks.) Start your chart off right. Focus on what this event says about you, and get started filling in the first column.

Under your second heading, *The Truth*, look at what you wrote in your residual thoughts column, go sentence by sentence, and simply write the opposite. If, for instance, one of your residual thoughts is, "I'm a loser," write, "I'm a winner," in your Truth column. If you wrote, "I give in even when I know it's wrong," and, "I lie down in the face of adversity," for *The Truth* you can write, "I keep going when I know it's right to," and, "I stand tall in the face of adversity." If your residual thoughts are, "I have no self-control," and, "I say anything that pops in my head without thinking and hurt people's feelings," for *The Truth* you could write, "I control everything I do," and, "I think about the things I say before I say them. I respect other people's feelings and take care to protect them." Even if you don't believe what you are writing yet, go sentence by sentence and write the opposite of each of your residual thoughts anyway.

Under your third heading, *What I Will Do*, look at your event and decide who you need to confront, who you need to apologize to, and who you need to forgive. It may be one person, or it may be a whole group of people. Many times, in order to release your residual thoughts, you will need to confront, apologize to, and forgive yourself. Think about what you will do and who you will need to speak to create your new endings. Write down the person's name (even if it's you) and which actions you will perform, whether it is one action or all three.

Under your fourth heading, *What I Will Say*, write out what you will say when you go to confront, apologize, and forgive. To help you come up with the best possible words to use, I want you to employ a simple technique that I teach all my clients and that I use myself to help create the kind of endings I'm looking for in my own life, a technique I call "seeing the destination."

Seeing the destination is exactly what it sounds like. To do it you simply imagine the destination you want your event to have. You paint a picture in your mind of everything turning out the way you want. To help you determine what you will say for a new ending, see the destination you want for your event before you begin writing. Take your event chart and go somewhere you can be alone. Breathe deeply a few times and let your body relax. Then close your eyes and focus on what you want to happen during the final ten seconds or so of your interaction. Concentrate on picturing the moment when things are working out, when you're saying the words that are changing everything.

In the past when you had to figure out what you were going to say to help resolve a difficult situation, you may have envisioned all the things you didn't want to happen or that could go wrong. You may have pictured failure and experienced fear, and with these images in your mind and these feelings in your body, you made decisions that weren't the best, and things didn't work out. This time, instead of creating images depicting revenge, more conflict, and frustration, and putting these things into your decision about what you should say, go in the opposite direction and imagine the ending you actually want in all its glory. Envision it just how you want it to be. Experience all the good emotions this brings, and when you're smiling and enjoying what you see in your visualization, when you are truly connecting with what you're picturing, open your eyes and begin writing.

To create different endings from the ones you did before, you have to access different parts of yourself. You have to connect with the talents and abilities that you didn't use the first time around, and seeing the destination you want will help you to do it.

You're in charge of this, and you have total control, so when you see the destination for your event, make the image you see as sweet, as triumphant, and as magical as it can possibly be. See the hugs, the kisses, or the enthusiastic handshake. Witness yourself at your best. Focus on the good feelings that are there during this moment, and the words will come.

The more good feelings you create when you do this, the more you increase access to everything you have inside of you that will help, so as long as you're seeing the basic ending you want, you can add to your imagery to increase those good feelings. Maybe see your successful confrontation and then, to get your good emotions going even more, see a crowd of people lining up, all clamoring to meet you and get your autograph. Maybe see yourself holding two puppies as you go to apologize; your co-worker notices them, and it's impossible for you both not to smile. Maybe you're forgiving someone, and as you finish, you see the Dalai Lama walking toward you, surrounded with pink and yellow butterflies. He's there to give you this year's "Most Benevolent Person on Earth" award.

See what you like. See what will make you smile and laugh. Get your good emotions up, then ask yourself what you should say to create the ending that will give you these same good feelings, and write what comes to you. Create the vision, make it enticing, make it something that you want, and feel the emotions of your success. Once you've done this, create what you will say to make it happen. Go ahead and repeat your visualization as much as you need to while you are writing. If you start feeling frustrated or like the words just aren't coming, indulge in your destination and give the good stuff a chance to get through.

This technique works. It changes the way you feel, and that allows you to have different thoughts. Instead of being blocked from your potential because you are angry about what happened or anxious about confronting someone, when you see the destination, you can step around these emotions and connect with what you have inside yourself: your courage, compassion, your charm, your humor and tenacity, all the things you have that can help you. That's why no matter how much your old identity may tell you that doing a visualization like this is a waste of time or some cheesy new-age fluff, you must bust through this wall, take the few moments required to do this, and see the destination before you come up with the words you will use to create your new endings for each of your events.

Think of what you've been getting with your old techniques, with the yelling and screaming or with the ignoring and denial. It doesn't have to be like that anymore. Seeing the destination takes you out of the negative cycles you're stuck in with some of the people in your life and helps reveal options that are more positive and effective. By seeing the destination and then deciding what to say, you can step past anger and resentment, past the temptation and pitfalls of finger pointing, and past the disappointment of realizing that you've done the same wrong thing all over again with much the same results. It gives you a chance to make this about you, your growth, your feelings, and your becoming who you are instead of about what the other person did wrong.

Whether you use a few sentences to say what you need to say or you end up with several pages of material, it's OK either way. Follow the instructions here in Step 3, and, no matter how many words you use, you will find the right ones. Practice reading what you've written out loud a few times; then look at your event chart under *The Truth*, and ask yourself whether what you have fits what the person described there would say. If it does, then what you've prepared is ready. If it doesn't, focus on using the words this person would use and modify what you've written accordingly. When the time comes to act, what you say doesn't have to be exactly like what's on your chart. If you follow the steps and let your visualization influence you, if you keep going even if you make some mistakes, you will end up saying the right words no matter what you've prepared.

If you need to confront, apologize, and forgive yourself, or if you need to forgive someone who hasn't apologized to you, or if your new ending involves someone who is deceased or who you are unable to locate, if there is no one else to talk to or to hear you say the words you need to say, go through the process just as you would for any other event for which you are creating a new ending. Complete your event chart, and follow the instructions for creating a Second Action coming up after the Seven Steps.

Before you take action to create your new endings, you have several more steps to take. Right now you could feel ready to get started confronting, apologizing, and forgiving, or you could be thinking, "I've done these things wrong so many times in the past; how do I actually do this?" At the end of the steps I've included more instructions on confronting, apologizing, and forgiving, as well as a few client experiences, to help you. For now, have a look at the three client examples I've included below to see how others have completed their event charts. Once you have, finish step 3 by filling in your charts for all five events, and then move on to step 4.

EVENT CHART EXAMPLES

For creating new endings, your event charts just work. If you fill them in with a strong desire for the future you want and follow the instructions in step 3, they will help you move past your residual thoughts and connect with the talents and abilities you have that can make your new endings go your way. The three examples that follow will give you ideas on how to complete your own event charts. What you write and what you end up saying can be as short or as long as you want it to be, so don't be put off by the length of some of the stories or how much the people in the examples said to create their new endings.

Event Chart Example #1:
Dodgeball: One Game with Long-Term Effects

Gretchen: I was in the third grade, and we were playing dodgeball during gym class. There was one boy who wouldn't throw the ball. It was down to only three people, and he was just standing there, so I yelled out, "Chicken!" The gym teacher immediately stopped the game and wanted to know who had said it. I didn't say anything. I'd never gotten in trouble at school before, so I was petrified about being caught. Because I didn't admit it was me, we all had to leave gym early and have quiet time in our classroom until the person who said it came forward. Our third-grade teacher told us how disappointed she was in whoever said that and then didn't admit to it. She turned off the lights and told us no one could move or talk until the person came forward. Then she walked up and down the aisles, giving us a pretty hefty guilt trip. I was mortified and ashamed. I'd done something wrong, and I was embarrassed that I'd been bad and afraid I'd get caught. I wanted people to like me. I didn't want my classmates to know I had gotten them in trouble.

Event:
Yelled out, "Chicken!" during dodgeball and got my class in trouble.

Residual Thoughts:
I disappoint myself and other people. I don't have honor, and I'm a coward. I hurt people with the things I say. I'm a scared person. I don't admit when I've done something wrong.

The Truth:
I impress myself and other people. I'm honorable and brave. I make people feel good with the things I say. I'm a brave person. I do admit when I've done something wrong.

What I Will Do:
Confront, apologize to, and forgive myself.
Apologize to the boy.

What I Will Say:

To myself: You were scared to say what you had done in front of your classmates and your teachers. You were very young, and it's OK that you didn't speak up because you didn't know how to handle your fear at that time. What happened back then doesn't determine what you can do now. You've spoken up in difficult situations since then and proven you can do this. Remember when Celeste had to go to the hospital? Remember David's party in the woods? Remember the night of the car accident? I forgive you for not speaking up when you were eight years old, and I want you to know and realize that isn't who you are. You know how to apologize. You did it with your third event when you spoke to Susan about that night at the dance, and it turned out great. You did it when you told mom and dad about losing your scholarship. You did it when you spoke to Brandon about what happened at the bachelorette party.

I remember other times when you didn't apologize, when you didn't speak up, and things didn't turn out well. Remember when the statue broke by Grandma's pond? Remember when you yelled at Steve that day in front of his friends? You knew you hurt him, but you never said anything. This makes you feel bad, and not saying anything causes you to hold onto your bad feelings, and you just end up thinking about what happened for way too long. I'm sorry that I chose to let this event define you, instead of all the other events where you did speak up and do the right thing. You have confidence now, and you do speak up, and if someone is acting like a chicken, including you, you have a lot of choices for what to do about it. You can do the right thing all the time, and if you don't, then you can do what is necessary to make it right.

To the boy: In the third grade, we were playing dodgeball, I called you a chicken, and the teacher stopped the game. I recently remembered what had happened, and I wanted you to know that even though it was a long time ago, I'm sorry I did that. I'm sorry I called you a name instead of cheering you on. You were on my team, after all. You were a cool kid with a Rolling Stones T-shirt who was having a normal reaction to having to play a pretty terrible game that you probably didn't really want to play. You weren't chicken, you were brave, and you were the only one left from our team, so you were better at playing the game than the rest of us. I wanted you to know this, and I hope you accept my apology.

Gretchen: I didn't really feel the need to deal with my teachers. My residual thoughts weren't about them anyway. What would I confront them about, the fact they acted like idiots twenty years ago? What could I apologize for, acting like a normal kid to the threat of being called out in front of the entire class and being held responsible for what happened when none of us should have been placed in that position in the first place? This was about me and the way I behaved and not how they reacted. That didn't matter to me as much as Clearing my residual thoughts, and mine were coming from what I said to the boy and then what I did afterward. Could the teachers have handled things differently? They sure could have, but I wasn't going to waste time holding it against them.

Looking my old classmate up just seemed ridiculous, but I couldn't think of anything else to do, so I did it anyway. I found him online and sent my letter. He didn't know what I was talking about, but I did and it was over. I thought I would be embarrassed about this, and I was a little at first, but mostly I'm proud of myself for speaking up. I feel different about what happened now, and that's what really mattered to me.

Example #2: Rock-Hard Brownies: Clearing the Way to Culinary Excellence

Jessica: When I was fourteen, I decided it would be a nice treat to make brownies for my family. I made the brownies from scratch, and when we tried to eat them, they were rock hard. My family teased me about it for weeks. On occasions since then, whenever the subject comes up or someone says "brownie," I have to suffer being good-natured while hearing the comments. This is what I became known for. I completely gave up on cooking, and it kind of became part of who I am. I would walk around saying things like:

"I can't cook."

"Cooking? I wouldn't know the first thing about it."

"I don't make dinner, I make reservations."

"Slapping two pieces of bread together with some jelly is about as gourmet as I get."

Event:

When I was fourteen, I made rock-hard brownies for my family, and they teased me about it.

Residual Thoughts:

I am a terrible cook. I hate cooking. Some things I just can't learn. I try things once, and if it doesn't work out, I quit. I let other people tell me who I am and what I can do.

The Truth:

I'm a terrific cook. I enjoy cooking. I can learn anything I want. I try things once, and, if it doesn't work out, I keep going. I tell myself who I am and what I can do.

What I Will Do:

Confront, apologize to, and forgive myself. Confront and forgive my family.

What I Will Say:

To myself: When you were fourteen, you made brownies that didn't turn out well, and everyone teased you about it. You decided this meant that you're a terrible cook, but that isn't true. You can follow a recipe, and you can create delicious food. It's OK that you didn't make good brownies the first time, and it's OK if you don't do things perfectly the first time you try something in your life today. I'm sorry I've been so hard on you. I'm sorry I've let what happened with the brownies repeat again and again and hold you back from not only learning how to cook, but also from standing up for yourself with other things, like your relationship with Jack or that project at work that you let Courtney finish for you. (You know that's why they made her manager and not you.) I'm sorry I sold you short and stopped you from being who you truly are just so you could get along with people who don't see your true potential. I'm sorry I let fear of failure cause you to accept much less than you deserve.

I forgive you for these things. I forgive you for determining from that one event and from your family's reaction that you are not a good cook and letting that stop you from even trying to cook anything. Now it's time to change and live the truth, starting with where this all began. Get some eggs, sugar, cocoa, salt, and milk and make this right. Keep going. Never let anyone tell you who you are again. Tell yourself who you are with your actions. You are a good cook. Now get cracking!

To family: I'm sure you all remember when I made brownies for you that one time when I was fourteen. It hurt my feelings when you teased me for so long about being a bad cook. Because of the way you reacted, I've always thought that I was a terrible cook. I shouldn't have let what happened and all your teasing over the years sway me into thinking that about myself. I decided to do something about it, and here it is.

Jessica: I waited for the holidays when we were all together. I said just what I wrote, and then passed around my plate of brownies. I had spent the previous four weekends making batch after batch until I got it just right, and I must admit they were awesome. Everyone loved them. I even received apologies and congratulations. I am the brownie expert now and about to expand my repertoire. Now whenever anyone mentions brownies or cooking, I smile a little and think about what I'm going to make next.

Example #3: Persona non Grata: Seeing the Truth About a First Love

Scott: When I was in the eighth grade, I had a girlfriend who broke up with me to go out with my friend Jeff. She just came up to me and told me the way it was, just like that. One day we were holding hands and walking down the halls of our school together, and the next she was doing the same thing with Jeff and I was out of the picture—*persona non grata*. At first I laughed when this event came up. It was so long ago, how serious could it have been? But I was rejected, and the truth was that even though I was young, it hurt like hell. I remember walking around for a while after that, deflated like a half-empty balloon sort of flopping over on itself.

Event:
Rejected by a girl in the eighth grade.

Residual Thoughts:
I'm disposable. I'm someone who gets dumped. I'm not good enough. I'm no good at relationships. I get hurt when I'm in a relationship. I'm better off being miserable and "safe" than actually being happy and really living my life. I'm not good at having a girlfriend. When I get close to women, I get hurt.

The Truth:
I am valuable. I'm someone who is cherished. I'm more than good enough. I'm good at relationships. I feel great when I'm in a relationship. It's better to be happy taking "chances" than being unhappy

and not really living my life. I'm good at having a girlfriend. When I get close to a woman, I feel better.

What I Will Do:

Confront, apologize to, and forgive myself. Forgive first girlfriend.

What I Will Say:

To myself: Scott, you were in eighth grade; what was she supposed to do back then? Profess her undying love to you and start making wedding plans? Everyone gets rejected. She did the best she could. It's time for this event to make you a better person, not a scared one.

You've learned and experienced a lot since you were thirteen, and you can make good judgments about who you should be with. Just because you got dumped in the eighth grade by a girl you barely knew, that doesn't make all women untrustworthy, and you don't have to break it off with every woman you start to get close to now just so you can avoid it happening to you again. I know you don't want to admit that this is what is going on, but it's OK. You need to know that you can handle being in love and that being hurt isn't the end of the world. It's part having a real life. Do you want to die having never really loved someone? Remember Crystal and how good you felt? Remember how you screwed things up with Natalie? You are stronger than this, and you have to stop hurting people just because you're scared.

Listen to John and do something different. You know relationships can feel great. It's time to let what happened go. You are strong enough to handle trusting people, and not all women are the same or just out to hurt you. Remember when Molly asked you to the prom and then became one of your best friends? Remember how Mom wrote you letters when you were at camp to tell you about the family so you wouldn't be homesick? Remember when Miss Wilson tutored you in algebra after school for a month to get you ready for finals? Remember when Aunt Vickie loaned you money for your first car? You didn't even know yourself back then. Now that you do and you have some experience, you know the truth and you can let this go. Not every girl has to be in love with you. If you let it happen naturally, you will find the right one.

I'm sorry I've let these feeling exist inside you for so long. I'm sorry I've let what happened have such a strong influence, when the truth is, now that you look at it, what happened isn't a big deal. It's time to stop basing such a large portion of your life on something that happened when you were thirteen. It isn't stupid that you were hurt back then, but it would be stupid to let this event stop you from being happy now.

You treat others great, and people like you. Remember when you let Bill live with you rent-free for that year after his divorce? Remember your birthday party when everyone showed up and surprised you by taking you to that Eagles game? These old residual thoughts you are carrying around from what happened in eighth grade aren't you. They aren't who you are. They aren't true, and it's time to let them go. You are an amazing person who enjoys making people feel good. You are someone who loves relationships, someone who is happy to be in other people's company, and someone who will find the right person to love.

I apologize for the mistakes I've made. I forgive you. And now that I've really thought about it, my eighth-grade girlfriend doesn't need to be forgiven because she didn't do anything wrong. No one did anything wrong. In fact, she was brave to come up and tell me that it was over. Just like you were brave to admit how this event made you feel and to do something about it.

When you get past the fear and apprehension, when you push everything else aside, you'll see that the truth is that confronting, apologizing, and forgiving are actually simple things that usually require very few words and take no more than a minute or two to actually do. Have faith in your abilities and the process. If you commit yourself to what you are doing and to following what is written here, you will find that you can confront, apologize, and forgive, and that you are actually good at all three.

There's something really nice waiting for you, something better than nice, but you have to do something first to have it. There's a trade that has to take place. The good news is that this is going to be the best deal you ever make. I wish you could see here, from the start, the life you could be living without your residual thoughts so you could know what's coming. I wish you could realize in the way that I do, having seen what I've seen, what your life could be like. All I can tell you is to keep going no matter what happens. Clear your events and experience it yourself. Instead of struggling and lugging around the negative thoughts from your past, give yourself this chance to let them go, to regain your power, and to see what you can do when you connect with it and use it to pursue the things you want.

STEP 4: REPEAT YOUR THREE COMMUNICATIONS

How are you going to create your new endings and make sure they turn out the way you want? How are you going to make this different from all the other times you attempted to confront, apologize, or forgive? Maybe you're thinking you're no good at this. Maybe you're thinking this isn't going to happen the way you would like because it's never worked out before, so how could this be any different? Maybe you've written down what you wanted to say in situations like these in the past and even practiced so you would be ready. Maybe you went into it with the best of intentions, and it still went horribly wrong. Now you're wondering how you can possibly do this. The answer is that you can do it by using your three communications.

Your three communications are what you see with your eyes, what you see in your mind, and what you say to yourself. They are how you send messages to yourself, and, whether you are succeeding or failing, these communications play a role in the outcomes you create. Harnessing their power will help create success not only with your five events, but also with the endings you want to create throughout the rest of your life.

Not convinced? Maybe you're thinking the three communications aren't a factor with what is happening in your life and this doesn't apply to you? Well, think of the last time you tried to lose weight, and then think of what you had in your home before you Cleared it. Think of the identity you were reinforcing with what you saw there every day. Maybe when you went to modify your diet you pictured strawberry cheesecake, burgers and fries, extra-large icy sodas, and all the other foods you were attempting to avoid.

Maybe you envisioned yourself wearing your fat clothes to your friend's wedding. Maybe you said things to yourself like:

"I'll never lose this weight."

"It doesn't matter what I try, nothing works."

"I'm just a blob."

You thought you were expressing yourself or "just venting." You didn't think you were actually asking for these things, but you were.

I know it may sound crazy, but when you failed in the past it was because you were telling yourself to. With the things you saw, the images you placed in your mind, and the words you said, you told yourself not to work so hard, not to do your best, to stay down when you fell, to retreat when things got tough, and to quit after you made mistakes. As difficult as it may be to imagine, it isn't other people or what's happening around you that's the reason things aren't working out the way you want them to. Look at those instances you came up short in the past and you will realize that *each time you didn't create the outcome you wanted you did so because you were requesting one you didn't want all along.*

If you're continually having difficulties with your coworkers or you keep picking the wrong guy, think of what you see around you that doesn't make you feel powerful and keeps you focused on the past. If you aren't as successful in your career as you would like, take a look at the images you have in your mind before you go to negotiate a new deal or attempt to resolve a conflict. If the weight isn't coming off, think of the words you say to yourself when things get tough. When you do, you will see how these communications correspond to what's happening in your life.

If you're constantly looking in the refrigerator at your roommate's chocolate cake, if you keep bringing images into your mind of a recent fight with your significant other, if you're saying things like, "I'll never meet someone who is right for me," you are telling yourself that you want these things or things like them. You're commanding yourself to move toward them and create more of the same. You're saying, "Look, self, I want you to put all of my powers behind finding people to have terrible relationships with, and no matter how much talent I have or what I can actually do, I want you to make sure that I never win. Now walk me over to the refrigerator because I want some chocolate cake before I fight with my boyfriend."

Your three communications can be used to turn your life into a disaster, or they can be used to create success. Whether it's a business deal, a conflict in a relationship, or something going on with the new guy in the cubicle next to you who talks too loud on the phone and likes to heat up his two-day-old fish in a microwave ten feet from your desk, whether the end result of your interaction is failure or success, these three communications are what you are using to create the outcomes you're experiencing.

Maybe right now you're thinking, "That all sounds nice, John, but it's not like I can look at some knickknacks, photos, and things that inspire me and find myself changing. It's not like I can picture myself being thin in my mind, and, *voila*, I'm a size 4, or tell myself to be skinny, that I can do it, and it just happens." But that's exactly how it happens. That's how you became overweight in the first place. That's how you started holding yourself back. You saw, imagined, and said certain things, and then you took actions that corresponded to these communications and the way they made you feel.

For step 4, I want you to keep using your three communications, but instead of requesting what you don't want and sabotaging yourself, I want you to use them to tell yourself what you do want and to move in the direction of the endings you truly want to create. Here's how:

Your First Communication: What You See with Your Eyes

For your first communication, page through a few magazines or go online and find a photo that makes you feel good. Look for images of people having fun. Look for expressions that bring a smile to your face and can quickly inspire positive feelings in you, ones that make you say to yourself, "this is the way I want to feel after I create my new ending." Your picture could be something like an athlete crossing a finish line, looking victorious with arms raised in the air, or a woman appearing happy and confident as she gives a presentation, or a man smiling while throwing a Frisbee to his dog. If what you find makes you laugh, that's great too. Maybe you come across a photo of a horse wearing sunglasses, and it has you in hysterics. That works. Use it.

I suggest using a different photo for each event, unless you feel strongly that what you are using is continuing to give you the good feelings you need. Just make sure that the pictures you choose aren't of people you know personally so that there are no associations or memories to distract you. I know you love your children and your family pet, and all those photos you have of them are great, but go with something that you don't have a connection to already or that you've used for anything else.

A few of my clients have used objects for their first communication, and if you find one that gives you the feelings you're looking for, something that inspires you and doesn't cloud your mind with thoughts and memories of the past, then go ahead and use it.

Choose what helps you experience the good feelings you want surrounding your new endings, and choose what you can either carry with you or see for most of the day. If what you find makes you smile, if you're feeling the emotions of the person's expression in your photo, then it's a pretty good indication that you've found what you are looking for.

Ryan: For one of my events, I used a picture of a popular singer and TV show host for my first communication. I'd never seen his show and couldn't name a single one of his songs, so there were no conflicts or distractions. The expression just caught me. He had such a carefree smile. It matched the way I wanted to feel perfectly. I cut out the tiny square of his face from the back page of a magazine, kept it on my nightstand, and took a photo of it for my home screen on my phone. My girlfriend was curious as to why I had a picture of this guy smiling on my nightstand and my phone, and I never considered it the way she did, and that was pretty funny. I told her it was part of what I was doing with my Clearing and explained what I was using it for. Now she's decided to do the Clearing too, which is a good thing. The only downside is that now I can't blame every weird thing I do on this.

KC: I chose a picture of Kate Middleton for one of my events. She has a lot of characteristics that I admire and that I would like to have. She is graceful, athletic, joyful, stylish, patient, and kind. I cut some pictures of her smiling out of magazines and put them on the door of my closet, where I see them several times a day. I put my favorite picture on my phone, and when I'm at work, I look at it when I go through my communications. When I'm getting ready in the morning, and when I put up my work clothes at the end of the day, I see her in my closet, smile back at her, and think to myself, "I can be like that." I see the destination for my event, I tell myself I can do it, that I can create my new ending, and it feels good.

Brandon: For my first communication, I was looking for a picture that would capture the way I wanted to feel, and what ended up catching my eye was a sculpture of a hand I saw in a local gallery. It looked like it was reaching out for a handshake, and it instantly made me think about the new ending I wanted to create. I smiled when I saw it because I knew it was perfect. It made me feel great, and it also made me focus on my goal, so I bought it, put the sculpture on my desk, and used it for my first communication.

Your Second Communication: What You See in Your Mind

For your second communication, see the destination you want your event to have. Show yourself where you want to go, and create the emotions that will give you access to the abilities that exist inside of you and that can get you there. (This is what you did in step 3 to help you decide the words to say to create your new endings.) Remember, you don't have to be concerned about visualizing everything that's going to happen during your interaction. Instead, focus on the final moments, on seeing yourself saying the last few words that are making everything right:

"Thank you."

"I appreciate what you've said, and it means a lot to me."

"That's exactly what I wanted."

"I'm so glad we spoke. I missed you."

"I'm so happy we're friends again. This is truly a splendid day."

"You're a great listener, you have an exceptional body, and I love you." (Who says your new ending can't be fun?)

Things may change as you continue the story, and often the actions you take and the words you end up using will vary from your original plans. This is why, if you prepare by focusing simply on images of your destination, instead of on images of all the actions you plan to take to get there, you'll show yourself where you want to go without limiting yourself to any one way of getting there.

For your second communication, see the destination for the event you are working on in your mind. Focus on the agreement and resolution. Make what's happening fantastic, make it exceptional, make it just the way you want it to be. Soak up all the goodness that is there, and feel every wonderful emotion you can. Once you do, you are ready to move on to your third communication.

Your Third Communication: What You Say to Yourself

For your third communication, tell yourself that you can do this (just like you did in step 1 when you Cleared your home). Go ahead and get specific about what it is you can do: "I can do this! I can apologize to Karen and let my guilty feelings go." Then add something from *The Truth* column on your event chart: "I'm great at apologizing, and I'm a genius!" or, "I'm someone my friends can always count on!" or, "I confront with grace and style!" Choose a sentence or two. Pick out something you feel is important to hear. It doesn't matter if you believe what you've written; the real you knows that it's true. Then, when it's time to do your third communication, start by saying "I can do this." Describe what it is you are going to do, and then add what you've chosen from your chart.

Putting Your Three Communications Together

Print five copies of the three communications sheet I've given below, one for each of your events. For your first communication, "What I see with my eyes," attach a copy of the photo you are using to your sheet. For your second communication, "What I see in my mind," write a brief sentence that will help you to quickly summon images of your destination for your event. For your third communication, "What I say to myself," start with "I can do this!" then add a short description of what you will do and anything else you've chosen to include from *The Truth* column on your event chart, and you're ready.

As soon as you begin working on a new ending, find a picture, and fill out your three communications sheet for your event.

Three Communications:

1. **Photo** (what I see with my eyes): Look at your photo. Connect with the emotions.

2. **Visualization** (what I see in my mind): See the destination you want your event to have and increase your good feelings.

   _____

   _____

3. **Sentences** (what I say to myself): Bring the good feelings from your first two communications into your third and say your sentences out loud (and really mean them). Start with "I can do this!"

   _____

   _____

When the time comes to do your communications, go somewhere you won't be disturbed: the bathroom, the closet, your backyard.

Set up a chair in your garage if it's the best place you have to be by yourself. Stand or sit, whichever you prefer. Take out the communications sheet you prepared for your event, start focusing on your picture or object, and allow yourself to connect with it.

Once you're smiling and feeling good, move right into your second communication. Close your eyes, take a deep breath, and for the event you are working on, see the ending you want. Make it fantastic; make it exceptional; make it just the way you want it to be. See the last few moments of your interaction. See the final words being spoken and your ultimate success. See the expression of joy and accomplishment on your face. Maybe you're crying with relief in your vision. Maybe you're walking away with a confident smile knowing you did your part, you were kind, you were excellent, and you displayed the truth of who you are. Feel the triumph. Get all the good feelings you possibly can out of your vision, like you're squeezing the last bit of juice from the most perfect-tasting orange.

Next, move right into your third communication and say your sentences. Say them with meaning. Shout them out if it helps get your emotions and your determination going. Jump joyfully into the air. Pound on the walls or quietly focus your attention. Do whatever it takes to ignite your enthusiasm because the emotion that you build up helps push the messages you're sending yourself past your residual thoughts and your old identity. Once you're done, simply move on with your day.

Create a schedule. Program a reminder on your computer or set a timer on your phone to go off three times a day. When you hear it, go through your three communications like they're the most important thing in the world. Take every emotion and desire you have for an awesome future and put them into what you're doing. If at any point you find your mind drifting—if, in the midst of your visualization, you're suddenly thinking about your grocery list or what your friend said the other day—you're probably taking a little too long to do your communications, or it may simply be time to take action and create your new ending. If this is the case, let go of your apprehension and finish your new endings at a brisk and inspired pace.

The more you see with your eyes what creates good feelings and keeps you focused on your destination, the more you use the images in your mind to put yourself into the moment of your success, the more you tell yourself with your words who you truly are and what you want to have happen, the more all the parts inside of you get exposed to the idea that this is you, that you are this successful person, that you are someone who feels these feelings and creates these endings, the more likely you will be successful at what you're doing.

Maybe you're thinking, "Why should I tell myself I can do something I'm not really sure I can do? I don't want to lie to myself." But when you tell yourself that you can do this, it isn't a lie. Within you is the potential to continue your five events successfully. It's only your residual thoughts that have you believing otherwise. They're what's telling you that this isn't the right time, that the other person is such an asshole that it will never work, that these events from your past that ended badly aren't having an effect on you. It's your residual thoughts that are telling you that you don't have to create new endings because eventually these bad thoughts and feelings will go away on their own.

But that's not how it works. Time doesn't heal all wounds. Your residual thoughts don't go away on their own. They hang around and become a part of you instead. They become that new wrinkle between your brows, another failed relationship, and the five pounds you're packing onto your thighs with every passing year. They become the repetitive fights, the financial wrong turns, and the friendships that for some reason just seem to bite the dust. The truth is, your residual thoughts live on, doing their damage, until you step up and do something about them.

Think about it. No matter what, your eyes are going to take in what you have around you and you are going to be influenced, so why have anything other than what makes you feel good and keeps you focused on your goals? You are going to imagine yourself in different situations, getting different reactions and creating different outcomes and it will affect the actions you take, so why envision any of these things going wrong? You are going to be talking to yourself throughout the day and the things you say will affect the way you feel and the actions you take, so why say anything other than, "I can do this. I can make this happen"?

There is no prize for predicting your failure. There's no upside to focusing on things turning out badly. Why work against yourself? If you want to be happy, why picture anything other than yourself, in all your awesomeness, looking good, succeeding, and enjoying life? Why be anything other than on your side?

And what if you do fail or fall flat on your face? So what? I do those things too. We all do, but from what I know about myself and what I've seen with my clients, the frequency of failing and face-fallings decreases dramatically when, instead of using your three communications to tell yourself what you don't want, you use them to tell yourself what you do.

Now this isn't something you can just read about here and say, "That's interesting," never practice, and expect things to suddenly start working out for you. The more you run through your three communications, the more of yourself you put into them each day, the more you focus your passion and repeat them, the more your fear will diminish and your confidence will grow, and the easier it will be for you to see the truth and to make your new endings happen the way you want them to.

Before you begin work on your first event, fill out your communications sheet. Then, prepare for your new ending by using your three communications three times a day and as often as you can in-between. Once you've Cleared your first event, immediately begin filling out your communications sheet for the next, and follow this process until you've Cleared all five. If you will be Clearing several of your events at once, fill out your communication sheets for each event, take the sheets for all the events you're working on, start with the first you will be Clearing, and one at a time, go through the communications for each.

The more you do your communications, the more these new endings will feel like they fit, and the greater tendency you will have to take the actions and say the words that will make them happen. Prepare your communications for your first event now, begin repeating them, and then move to step 5.

STEP 5: WRITE YOUR COMMITMENT STATEMENT

What if you decide right now that you are going to follow the steps, that your residual thoughts don't stand a chance, that your five events are getting new endings, and that, no matter what happens, you aren't going to stop until you're done? The dramas, the problems, the bad feelings that keep repeating in your life—without your residual thoughts, they won't fit. Your energy will go elsewhere, and they will fade. In the space they once occupied, you get to put the things you want: the body you want, the job you want, the relationships you want, the projects and interests you want to pursue, and whatever feelings you choose to create.

Imagine having conversations with your family and friends, enjoying relationships at work and at home, playing or relaxing without your residual thoughts telling you who you are, limiting you, making a mess, and then keeping you distracted with the cleanup. Think of the things you could accomplish without the bad feelings these thoughts create and the doubts and fears they introduce into the things you do each day. Think about what it would be like if they weren't influencing you to fly off the handle over little things, to be short with those around you, or to be quiet and resentful instead of speaking your mind. What if it was just you being calm and relaxed, patient and understanding, and enjoying your life because you're doing what you want and feeling good about yourself?

There's something that happens inside of you when you commit, when you tell yourself, "I'm doing this, and nothing is going to stop me." This is what needs to happen now in step 5. It's time to commit. It's time to say to your residual thoughts, "Look, there's no discussion. These new endings are happening. You are no longer running the show. Step aside. STEP ASIDE."

You've read up to this point. You understand what you will be doing and why. If the Clearing is what you are going to do, then give yourself over to it. Cut the ropes on the bridge to the world where the residual thoughts from these five events told you who you are and what kind of life you are capable of having, and commit to moving forward.

Remember what these thoughts have stolen from you, the good feelings they've squashed, and the repetitive problems they helped create and reinforce in your life. Remember the relationships they've ruined, the opportunities they stopped you from taking, and the mistakes they've pushed you into headfirst. And then commit to ending their rule. Commit with every part of you, and refuse to stop your Clearing until you are done.

For Step 5, create your commitment statement by writing down what you are going to do, when you are going to do it, and how long you plan to take. Then finish with a promise that you will not stop until what you've started is complete. Once you have your statement written, sign it, and you're ready to go. It isn't necessary to read it each day. What is most important for Clearing your residual thoughts is to commit to what you are doing, and then put everything you have into your three communications and the actions you take.

You can copy the example below for your commitment statement or use it as a guide for writing your own.

> I, _____, promise to Clear all five events on my list by following all of the Seven Steps. I promise to use my kindness, my cleverness, my intelligence, my good feelings, and all the best parts of myself to continue each story and create new endings that make me feel good and reveal who I truly am. I will begin on _____ and finish on _____.
>
> _____
> Signature & Date

Writing out your commitment statement as I'm suggesting here could be one of those situations where your residual thoughts will come rushing in to tell you, "You don't have to do this. You've read it, and that's good enough." That old stinker of a voice could suddenly appear, saying, "You've got the gist of this. It isn't going to make any difference if you write it out or not." But it will make a difference. There isn't one part of the steps that isn't necessary, that isn't going to play an important role in creating your success, so tell that voice to take a hike, and take a few minutes to honor your commitment and do this right.

Lauren: Literally writing out the commitment statement was an important step for me. It pushed me to make a promise to myself, and I take promises much more seriously now since I Cleared my possessions and realized that many of my residual thoughts and the problems I'd been having revolved around lying to myself. I really don't think I would have written it out if I hadn't told John I would follow all the steps exactly as he had laid them out. I think normally I would skip something like this, but he was so big on commitment, I think I felt I would be letting him down if I didn't do it. I knew it was really me who I would have been letting down by doing things like I used to and not following instructions. It definitely made me think to myself, "Look, do this correctly, and then there will be no one to blame and no excuses." It only took two minutes to do, and I think it helped strengthen my resolve in the process.

Before you sign your statement, consider that, as with Clearing your home, if you don't complete what you've committed to and create new endings for all five of your events, the events on your list that are left will always be there to tell you that you are someone who doesn't finish what you start, and you will be stuck living with these thoughts influencing your life until you take steps to do something about them.

Avoid this destructive scenario. Once you sign your statement, take your commitment seriously. No matter how happy you feel after Clearing your first event, don't stop. No matter how excited you feel about your life after Clearing your second event, don't stop. No matter what kind of success you're experiencing at work after

Clearing your third event or how enthusiastic you start feeling about your personal relationships after Clearing your fourth, *don't stop*. No matter how much you start loving yourself and your life, don't stop until you've created your new endings for all five events.

I'm not going to sell you short. I have no residual thoughts regarding you and your abilities. I only have the truth, and the truth is you can do this and you can feel good consistently. Sure, your old identity could try to get you to skip steps like this one or tell you that you only have to do certain parts, but you are worth more than skipping steps and only doing things halfway. You've done those things before. We all have, and it hasn't worked out for any of us.

Write your commitment statement, sign it, then move on to step 6. If you have to adjust the end date after you begin, then go ahead, but no matter what happens or comes up, keep going. Don't let anything stop you from revealing your true self and completing your Clearing.

STEP 6: BEGIN, AND GO UNTIL YOU'RE FINISHED

You want your residual thoughts to stop having an influence on your life as soon as possible, so prepare and then get right to it. Don't put this off. Don't find reasons to delay or pause to allow the old identity back in to slow you down. You're doing things differently now, so stick to what is different. Make Clearing residual thoughts your priority. Be passionate about the life you want to create, and, no matter what is going on around you, once you begin, go until you are finished.

When you speak to the people on your list, be direct. Avoid dancing around the subject or alluding to what you want to talk about. You've prepared something to say, so say it. Stick to what you've practiced while allowing for changes along the way. If things veer off in a direction you didn't foresee, use your charm and your patience to bridge the gaps and keep things moving forward. If the people you speak to have something to add, allow them to have their turn, and listen to what they have to say. (After all, how can you expect them to listen to you if you won't listen to them?) If you hear something upsetting and you lose your cool, recover. The steps you've taken to prepare will steer you in the right direction by influencing you to make good choices. Focus on your destination, honor your commitment, and you will create new endings that will give you the feelings you're looking for.

After you finish your first event, start the next one on your list. You could do all five in one day, or you could spread them out over several weeks. How long it takes is up to you, but Clear your events with a sense of purpose and urgency. The potential effect of what you are doing is beyond my abilities to estimate. What I do know is that it will be big, enduring, and worth every effort you make.

You could be moving through life with a lot less baggage and interference from your past. You could be happier without the parts of your identity your residual thoughts stuck you with. Don't allow them to block another glorious moment, not one more fabulous success, not one more amazing kiss. Don't allow them to keep you from realizing who you truly are. Even if things get intense and an interaction gets heated, don't let what's happening push you away or have you thinking that you should quit. You're not a quitter, so why pretend you are and suffer the consequences? You've come this far. You're doing it. You're continuing the story. You're creating new endings. You're taking control of your life, and that's an amazing thing.

If one of your new endings isn't giving you the feelings you want, put it through the process again. Use your experience and good feelings to make it right by creating another ending, or ask yourself if there is a Second Action that will give you what you are looking for, and if there is, plan it out and get started (see the section below, "Taking a Second Action").

What's the downside of completing Part 2 of your Clearing? There isn't one. From experience, I can say with confidence that if you follow the steps, you will love the feelings you get from creating your new endings and releasing your residual thoughts. So far, no one has come to me and said, "John, you know those thoughts from my past that were bumming me out, that had me eating fistfuls of pie and bacon? Yeah, well, I really miss them." It just doesn't happen.

You can do this. You are powerful. You can do things that are a hundred times harder. I don't care what you did in the past, and it doesn't matter anyway. Starting right now, make this who you are and live your true life. You are someone who finishes things. Why lie to yourself and say that you're not? Why live with that pain or bother wasting time and energy carrying around what these five events have left you? Begin. Continue the story. Confront, apologize, and forgive. Create your new endings and the thoughts and feelings you want. Go until you are finished with all five, then continue on to step 7.

STEP 7: COMPLETE YOUR CLOSING CEREMONY

Once you've created your new endings for all five of your events, it's time to perform an action that signifies something important has happened, one where you let go of your list and any notes that you used in a symbolic way. What you've done and what you will do during the next few months will play a significant role in determining how the rest of your life plays out. Your closing ceremony is your chance to honor this moment, let go of what you no longer need, and complete actions that mark the start of your new future.

First, take a pen, some paper, and your event charts, go someplace where you can focus undisturbed, and put what you've written for each of your five events under *The Truth* onto one piece of paper. After you've done this, write down anything else you learned from your experience that you feel is important to remember. Maybe there are a few things you did that worked so well that you want to make sure you do them again, or maybe you have some advice for yourself that will help you with your future. Thinking over what happened and taking note of what you learned will help you retain your good memories and make them more a part of your life, so go ahead and take a few moments to review all the things you've done and start writing.

Forget any knee-jerk negativity your old identity may have had you using whenever you evaluated yourself in the past, and stick to the good stuff. Half-hearted compliments, or subtly cutting yourself down by writing things like, "I'm sort of good at apologizing, and some of the time I can confront people," isn't what you are looking for. If you learned that you are better at apologizing than you thought or that you can make bad feelings go away a heck of a lot faster when you say you're sorry than when you don't, write it down. If you surprised yourself with your confrontation techniques or how good it feels to forgive and let go, if you've realized that you're persistent and pretty darn clever, that you can get much different results depending on what you do to prepare, then go ahead and write these things down as well.

Write as little or as much as you want, and have fun with this. You get to tell yourself the truth and whatever else you feel will help you as you move forward. You get to really be on your side. It's a great position to be in. Make sure you take away what is important for you to know and what will give you an advantage in similar situations in the future. Have a look at your event charts and get started. You can make a bullet point list, you can give the details of what you learned in a paragraph or a page, or you can write the truth about yourself and what you want to remember in a more conversational way in a letter to yourself, as in the example below.

Letter to Myself: What I Learned from Clearing My Five Events

Dear Meredith,

I look back at what you've done, and I'm blown away. You actually did it. Remember how good this is. Whenever you read this letter I want you to be able to remember the way you feel right now.

Remember how impossible you thought Clearing five events was. Remember the reactions you got that were so different from what you thought they would be. Now look at the way you feel, and never forget you can do this in any tough situation. Never let the bad things that happen repeat in your mind for too long. Always do something about them Remember how when you saw the destination, it made you feel good. Remember how it made you see things in a different way and how the answers started to come to you when you did. Remember when you were angry and that was all you could be. Now you don't feel the same way anymore. Remember how quickly you made that happen.

You are smart and resourceful. Look at the way you turned things around with Pat after you hadn't spoken to her in years. Look at how much better your relationship is with Mom and Dad now. Never forget how good it felt after you apologized to Coleen and saw the look on her face right before she started to cry. Look at what you did for her and yourself. Remember how Daniel didn't want to listen to you the first time you tried to talk to him about what happened at the pool party, but then, when you went back a second time, he did. You used to give up after trying once. You didn't do that this time, and it paid off. You prepared with your Clearing, you kept going, and that's what made things turn out the way they did. So keep doing it. Always prepare, and, if it doesn't work out, keep going. Remember how you didn't want to do the three communications, then, after watching yourself for a few weeks, you realized you were using them just like John said were, only you were telling yourself to mess everything up. Stop doing that. You are always using these three communications, so use them to help you. This worked Meredith, so keep doing it!

You learned a lot about yourself from this. You learned that you are strong, that you control the way you feel, and that it's better to prepare and take action than to think about the mistakes you made over and over again and do nothing. When you feel bad, it's always because you need to confront, apologize, or forgive, so get off your butt and do it. If you are reading this now, it's because you need to.

It's because something is going on. I want you to stop. Take a deep breath, and put what is happening through the Clearing. Use your communications and make this right. You can do it. I love you, and I'm looking out for you. That's why I'm writing you this letter. You can do this. I'm telling you the truth, and you know it.

Love,
Meredith

When you're finished, put what you've written aside; then take your list of five events from your Clearing and begin making it unreadable. Rip it into tiny pieces or run it through a shredder. You can include any notes you no longer need and your five event charts as well. Taking away *The Truth* from your events and the memories of the actions you took are all you need from completing the steps. If you feel your event charts have added value and that it's powerful to keep them, then do it. Otherwise, let them go. Throw the majority of your paper into your recycling bin, and take half a handful or less and save it for your ceremony. If you have a fireplace, you have the option of burning your papers, and after the ashes have cooled, gathering a small portion into a glass or metal container.

Next, put what you've written aside, find a garden shovel, or even an old spoon or fork (anything you can make a small hole in the ground with), gather up the remains of what you put aside, the paper where you wrote what you learned from Clearing your five events, and this book, and go to a place you don't usually go. Take a hike in the mountains or a walk on the beach. Go to where there is nature and where you won't be disturbed. Take a drive if you have to. Get on a bus and go two towns over. Once you are there, turn off your phone, take out your letter or paper where you wrote what you learned from your new endings, and read it. Think about what you wrote. Think about all the things you've done to Clear your home and your residual thoughts. Consider what you've accomplished. Dwell on what you've done right with your Clearing and all the good things you experienced. Recall what you did to create your new endings and the moments that gave you the best feelings, and have a good time thinking about them.

Maybe some of what happened during your new endings seems funny to you now. If it does, then laugh and feel good. Maybe the actions you took make you feel so relieved you want to cry, so go ahead and cry. If some of the things you did impressed you, go ahead and be impressed with yourself. It's OK. Think of the bold actions you took and the brave things you did, and let them sink in. You've done something fantastic. Take some time to feel good about it.

Next, think about who you really are, and get into being you again. Get into your life because this is what you've got. You've got the greatest thing that ever existed, and it's time you realize this and make a promise to keep going in your new direction. Promise yourself that you will continue to use your three communications and pay attention to what you see with your eyes, see in your mind, and say to yourself. Promise to make sure you're focusing on the things you want instead of what you don't, and when things don't go well and you get upset, promise that you will create a new ending and never let residual thoughts control your life again.

Then, get out the remains of your papers and what you brought to dig with, pull back an inch or two of grass or dirt or sand, and put the remains of your list and notes into the ground. If you have ashes, let them go in the breeze. Don't get into trouble or start trying to bury big piles of paper in some guy's yard three blocks down the road who you heard might be on vacation. You can rip a small piece of paper off your list and push it into the dirt with your finger and it would work well for your ceremony. No matter where you are or how you do it, be safe and respectful of other people's property.

Save your letter or paper where you wrote about what you learned from creating your new endings and review it whenever you feel you need to. There may be moments where things get tough or where you may want something extra to boost your confidence; in these cases, read your letter and reconnect with the truth.

Once you are finished, put your tools away, grab a seat, and think about what you want to accomplish moving forward and all the good things you want in your life. Talk to yourself about your new destinations, and begin seeing them in your mind. Enjoy imagining a future where things work out. It doesn't matter if you only have a few ideas and haven't completely thought things through yet. Allow yourself to enjoy exploring and dreaming about the possibilities. Smile and feel good.

Once you've indulged in these visions of the future, it's time to use what you've learned and continue creating the next part of your life. Decide it's going to be awesome. Combine what you have here with what you have inside you, and make it so.

21

DOING THE SEVEN STEPS: TAKING ACTION

SURE, I'VE TOLD you what you need to do to create your new endings, but how do you do it? The next section of the book deals with how to confront, apologize, and forgive in the way that will create the best endings possible. Read "Doing The Seven Steps: Taking Action," the "Do's," the "Don'ts," and the Q&A before you begin to Clear your events and as often as you need as you move through the process.

CONFRONTING

Many people have negative connotations when it comes to confronting, but it doesn't have to be this way. Instead of being a prelude to an argument or increased tensions, when done correctly, confrontation can be a source of good feelings, and it can free you from the weight of misunderstandings and hurt. When you confront, you're simply telling someone what you like or what you don't like. Most of the time, a few simple sentences are all it takes. That being said, what those sentences end up being, the manner in which they are conveyed, and the effect they end up having can vary greatly depending upon what you do before you create them.

Nancy: When John and I were discussing Clearing residual thoughts, an event popped into my mind. Three years earlier I had lied to my sister, and I knew I had to apologize to her and to confront my brother-in-law. One Christmas, the three of us decided that to make the family gathering a little more fun, we would drink a little during the day. My sister and I almost never drank, and my brother-in-law was an alcoholic, so deciding to drink was probably not the wisest decision. My sister and I were able to get one drink down and enjoyed the effects, but my brother-in-law kept drinking throughout the day. At one point he got a little too close to me and looked like he was about to kiss me. Hours later, as I was getting ready to leave my parents' house, he grabbed a basket to take to my car, as if he was helping me. He loaded it in the trunk and then asked me if that had earned him a kiss. My body kind of seized up for a second. I ignored what he said and quickly went back into the house.

A few days later my mom and I went to my sister's house for a visit. My brother-in-law came out and met us on the front porch and said that my sister didn't want to see anyone because she was upset about Christmas and had accused him of hitting on me. This is where I really screwed up and instead of telling the truth, I lied. In front of my mother, and with my sister probably listening inside, I said, "Well, that didn't happen." I shrank away from the confrontation and the truth, and my mother and I left. I was so uncomfortable about the whole thing that I didn't know how to handle it, or at least that's what I thought at the time. Of course I could handle it. I know that now. All I had to do was tell the truth. This wasn't my problem; it was my brother-in-law's, but my lies and excuses made it mine, and I was holding on to it.

Two years later, my mother had a birthday lunch for me. My father, my sister, and my sister's husband were there. I was in a really great mood because I had just spent most of the previous day reading a Harry Potter book. I was telling my mother about the book when my brother-in-law made a joke about the whole Harry Potter series being Satanic. I felt anger fill my entire body in a flash. I simmered silently for a few minutes, and then I let it loose. I loudly told him that I didn't appreciate his joke or him ruining my birthday that I hadn't even invited him to anyway. Everyone at the table was silent. My brother-in-law got up and left. No one knew how to respond because what I did was so out of proportion to what my brother-in-law had said.

The fallout from that outburst was that my sister said that she felt like she couldn't be around me anymore, and my brother-in-law informed us that he wasn't going to come to any family events. I called my sister, and she said she felt like she was having to choose between us. I completely ignored what I was really upset about and apologized for blowing up at him, and she decided we could still hang out.

As John and I talked about all these events, I told him I didn't want to Clear this one because I didn't want to have to tell my sister that her husband kept trying to kiss me at Christmas, even though she obviously knew something had happened. I also told him that whenever I had confronted my family in the past it hadn't gone well. He asked for an example and I told him the "Harry Potter incident" was a pretty good example. John pointed out that my passive-aggressive response must have only confused my family, who had no idea what I was really angry about.

When I wrote out the event and the details of what happened, I uncovered residual thoughts that I didn't realize were there. I knew what they were. It was obvious. I don't stand up for myself. I lie rather than confront, and I don't protect the people I love. I didn't speak up during this event or after. I didn't speak up in many events before. I was being passive-aggressive, and the things I wanted to say were coming out of me in ways I didn't like. I hated how I felt. I was putting off doing anything about it because it was uncomfortable and I didn't want to think about it, so instead I let my relationships with my family and the way I felt about myself suffer.

I started creating visualizations of myself confronting successfully; then I focused on the future and some of the things I'd be doing. I felt wonderful as I watched myself giving speeches, standing up to people, being confident, going to the places I wanted to go, and doing the things I wanted to do. I saw people smiling at me and going out of their way to help me out and be nice.

When I began feeling good, I opened my eyes and started writing what I wanted to say to my family. Sometimes, when I was feeling tired during the process, I would visualize sitting on a beach and feeling the warm sand on my feet. I did these visualization before each new "script" I wrote.

When John and I first talked about this event, I wanted to write letters and mail them, but one morning I woke up and I knew I was going to have to go to my sister's home and do this in person. I didn't really consider calling ahead. I didn't want to get everyone riled up or anxious. I think with my family, if I had called ahead and said I needed to talk about some things, it would have been nerve-wracking for them to wait and wonder what I needed to talk about. For my situation, I decided that just going over there was the best way.

When I first got into my car, I practiced reading each letter out loud and made a few edits. I was going to Clear several events with several different people that day, and I was starting with the hardest one first and that was definitely the event with my sister and her husband. I did my visualizations. I said to myself, "I am brave," out loud, and I meant it even though I was nervous and a little scared. Then I started driving. As I got close to my sister's home, I started to feel anxious, so I did my visualizations with more frequency. Oh, and I didn't listen to the radio on the way there. I wanted to be completely focused.

When I got to my sister's home, I told her that I needed to talk to her. We chatted a little, about her two dogs and a few other things, and then I told her I was going to read to her because I didn't want to forget anything I wanted to say. She was kind and patient. My sister and I both teared up when I was reading. When we were done, I went to my brother-in-law's workshop and spoke to him. I did things the same way as I did with my sister, and he actually apologized to me when I was done.

When visualizing my destination for these new endings, I started out with my boyfriend smiling at me and hugging me when I got home, but I changed from that visualization when I realized I needed something more immediate to the situation. I pictured hugs and smiles with my sister. I didn't visualize that with my brother-in-law, though. I visualized speaking with him and then smiling in my car as I drove away from their home. I guess that's more fitting given the circumstances. I visualized this again right before I walked into his workshop to confront him. All of these visualizations are pretty much what ended up happening.

With confrontation, there could be some anger or other negative emotions that are left over from the original event on either side, and this is where seeing the destination is a tremendous asset. By seeing the destination before you decide what to say, you're changing your emotions. By changing your emotions, you're allowing different parts of yourself into your words and actions, and that changes everything that happens as a result. But what if you are so angry about the original event that you can't see a destination that doesn't somehow involve clobbering the other person you are confronting? What if there is no scenario that you can imagine where this ends up working out?

If anger or old hurt feelings are getting in the way when you do your visualization for your confrontation or any of your new endings, add something to your images that makes you laugh and smile. Start by seeing the destination you want. Imagine those last few seconds. If there are hard feelings you're finding it difficult to get past, don't worry about it. Just make it as congenial as possible. Then see yourself walking away smiling because you did it. Suddenly, you look up and you're surrounded by a stadium full of people all cheering you and calling out your name: "Susan, we love you! We knew you could do it! You are so frickin' hot!" You're rising up on a platform center stage with lights flashing all around you as people shout, "Rick! Rick! Rick! Nothing can stop Rick! It's hard to keep our clothes on when Rick comes in the room!" Or maybe you're skipping across a clear blue sky on top of fluffy white clouds or water-skiing off a yacht in the Mediterranean. Your pet dog or cat streams by a few yards away, parasailing and eating a Twinkie.

I'm serious about this. It's funny, sure, but it really works. As long as the basic ending is there, as long as you visualize those last few seconds of your interaction, of you turning things around and being amazing, you can get creative and tag on whatever you like to your visualizations to amp them up a little or a lot. These embellishments get your good emotions going, and this opens the door wider, creating more access to your abilities and a stronger connection with your true identity. Because they make you feel joy, these visualizations free you from the grip of your residual thoughts and allow the best parts of you into what you are doing. If you try to access these parts and work on what you want to say when you're picturing disaster and focusing on your fears or when you're angry and consumed with thoughts of revenge, they will be hidden from you. The store will be closed, and you will be stuck with what you've already tried in the past.

Julie: I started my Clearing about a year after my husband had an affair. After going through my home and getting rid of practically everything, I still wanted to go over to his place, tell him what a scumbag he is, and beat him with his golf clubs. John convinced me that wasn't a good idea, and I started doing the steps for Clearing my residual thoughts instead.

The visualizations are really what changed everything. I would end up laughing at the ridiculous positions I would imagine my ex-husband in. Sometimes I would visualize dropping him off at work and pushing him out of the car without his clothes on and then going straight to the airport, flying to the Florida Keys, and starting a new job. I did visualizations like that for a few days as I worked on what I would say, and I realized that this didn't really have to be a visualization. This could really happen—not the naked-ex-husband-getting-tossed-out-of-the-car part, but the new job in the Keys. I had always wanted to live there. I was qualified. I had been working in the hospitality field since college and had moved up the ranks of several well-respected companies in the industry.

So I started sending out my résumé. As I got more involved in pursuing this new career path, I began to see things with my husband differently, and when I wrote down what I wanted to say, it ended up being very different from my you're-a-scumbag-golf-club-to-the-head idea. This is what I wrote and pretty much what I ended up saying to him:

"I was mad at you for cheating on me, but now that I've looked at it without being angry I'm glad you did it. We would have kept going, kept trying to work it out, but now I'm free and you can be free. I thought that was me — my life with you and the way I felt — but it wasn't. I just didn't want to admit it. I didn't want to think that I was wrong and that we wasted so much of our lives together. I was too afraid of what that meant, but all it really means is that it's over and we can have different lives now. We weren't happy, and we just got used to it. I was afraid of being on my own, and that's a terrible excuse to stay together. I think in a way I was just using you, and I'm sorry about that. Now I don't feel the same way about what you did. I forgive you, and, as strange as this sounds, I thank you."

Julie could have held on to her hate and allowed what her husband did to continue to live on in her this way. She could have continued to carry these thoughts around with her, letting them make every aspect of her life a little less better, a little less good, but the steps she took allowed her emotions to change. She saw things differently after that, and with this change she was able to create the words that gave her the ending she wanted and what she needed to start her new life.

By going through the visualization of your successful ending, you create feelings that give you access to your clever parts, your wit, your ingenuity, your calm, and your strength and kindness. When you use these parts to prepare, you come up with different answers. Instead of pointing the finger and saying something like, "You did this, you bastard, and you are going to listen to what I have to say whether you like it or not!" and creating an ending you don't want, you will find yourself asking, "Can you help me with something? I'm doing this process where I'm changing events that are making me feel bad. All you have to do is listen," and creating the ending you do.

You are in charge of this new ending, and you have advantages you didn't have when the original event occurred. You have this book. You have the experiences of my clients, and you have the greatest advantage anyone could possibly have—you have you. If you prepare and follow the steps described here, your old ending and the old thoughts will fade. What you say doesn't have to be perfect. There are many ways for this to happen and for you to be successful, so insisting that things must go according to a rigid plan or exactly as you rehearsed doesn't make sense. Your familiarity with what you've written and practiced will find its way into what you do and say, and that's all that is necessary.

No matter what happens, keep moving toward your destination. Avoid overcomplicating what you are doing or allowing anything to delay you. You want to get these residual thoughts out. You want to change these stories as soon as you can. Be suspicious of any thought that pops in your head that slows you down, and fight back against interruptions by focusing on the steps and taking action. The sooner you get started creating your new endings, the sooner your residual thoughts lose their hold and you can begin living your life without them.

OPTIONS FOR CONFRONTING

There are many ways to confront. To get a better idea of your choices and how to go about making what you choose work for you, take a look at the three options discussed next—confronting in person, confronting using a letter, or confronting over the phone. If you need to confront someone who is deceased or if you'll be confronting yourself, complete your event chart and the steps just as you would for any other confrontation. Read aloud what you've written under *What I Will Say*, and follow the instructions under "Taking a Second Action" at the end of this section.

Option #1: Confronting in Person

There can be a certain amount of fear when it comes to confronting someone in person. When you face that fear using the Seven Steps, something happens that makes it all worthwhile. Sure, you get the relief of saying what's on your mind and not having to think about the old endings anymore. You get the good feelings and the resolution, but you get something else too. You get to see aspects of yourself that your residual thoughts have kept hidden. You get to use the talents and abilities that you didn't use during the original ending and that may have been missing from your life ever since. You get to see that these parts of you actually exist and realize that the truth is you can use them whenever you want.

If you're thinking, "This isn't me. I can't confront. I don't do things like this," it's just your residual thoughts talking and limiting you. Of course you are someone who does things like this, but instead of confronting and receiving the benefit, you've been putting your effort into stopping yourself, carrying the weight of these bad feelings, and suffering the pain of slowing yourself down. You've been letting your fear win out and it's affected every part of your life, whether you are aware of it or not.

You need to discover certain things about yourself and what you are capable of, and your confrontation will help you do this. You may be thinking, "Yeah, but I could do without all that messiness of doing this in person." The truth is that, when you follow the steps, confronting may be a lot different from what you might think.

Celine: I was surprised by the amount of laughter there was, and not nervous laughter but sincere laughs. The stuff I was saying to my parents wasn't the most pleasant to hear. I really didn't give that much thought to what would actually happen during these interactions, but I suppose I did expect my confrontation to be more somber. Then I remembered that I had repeatedly pictured us hugging at the end of the confrontation, and I know that we probably wouldn't have gotten to an ending like that if it wasn't in my mind already. Normally I never would have imagined a successful ending. For a confrontation, and with my parents to boot—no way.

Was I subconsciously doing what would create the laughter so I could get to that ending? Maybe I was, and maybe this allowed me to say things in a way that we could get to the hugs that I had imagined. I was never too good at these situations before. I mean, I would never go into a confrontation thinking, "I'll have them rolling in the aisles and slapping their knees in no time," so I can't help but think repeating this image in my mind played a role in how things turned out. At first the connection didn't really click for me, but when I thought about it afterward, I realized that what I was seeing in my mind actually did happen.

Nancy: People will surprise you during the process. I remember being concerned about confronting my brother-in-law and thinking that I needed to make sure I have my coat on so my mace would be nearby. I thought about having to start parking my car somewhere else because he knew where I live and could vandalize it. I don't know if my mind was trying to scare me away from what I was going to do or if it was trying to give me excuses to get out of it. Regardless, he was very polite, listened to me, and then he apologized. He was never a violent person, so it was pretty irrational for me to have those fears in the first place. I just had never approached anyone and spoken to them like that before. For some reason a part of me believed that when I did, all hell would break loose. Instead, things worked out.

It was a struggle at first to get myself to see the ending I wanted. If I hadn't, though, getting a good reaction from my brother-in-law would never have entered my mind. I would only have been thinking of things going wrong and been filled with fear. I was still afraid when I did it, but I was something else too. I was excited and relieved to actually be doing it. In the end, I liked the feeling of what I did a lot.

Confronting face-to-face yields tremendous benefits. Don't let the sound of it scare you. You are with people all day, and in some way you are communicating to them what you like and what you don't like. You've actually confronted others hundreds of times in the past. You just may not have been aware that you were doing it or that you were capable of doing it with greater success.

Things are different now. You don't have to be afraid. You have the steps and you know what to do to get past your residual thoughts. If there is some trepidation, keep doing the three communications from step 4 to help get you through. Trust the steps and, whenever possible, confront in person. If you have to deal with someone who is prone to violence, obviously this isn't a good idea, and you should consider using one of the other options that follow instead.

Option #2: Confronting Using a Letter

You can read your letter in person, you can mail it, or you can place it where you know the intended party will find it. I recommend reading your letter in person. In person is always the best for a confrontation because it offers the greatest potential reward for you. Facing your fears, standing up for yourself, and saying what you have to say will reveal your strengths to you in a way that is difficult to recreate without a face-to-face interaction.

In some situations, especially when the person you are confronting isn't the best listener, reading what you want to say offers some advantages. Like an unopened present, when you get out your letter, the people you are confronting will want to know what's written in it. Their curiosity will be piqued, and, once you start reading, it will be as though you're reading a story. They will want to hear what happens next. After all, they play a starring role.

To confront using a letter, simply follow steps 1–5 like you would for any other confrontation, only this time fill out your *What I Will Say* section on your second page so you won't have to take your entire event chart with you when you go to confront. When the time comes, meet up with the person or people you want to speak to, ask if they'll listen to something you've written, then take out your letter and begin.

If you're interrupted while you are reading, that's fine. Be patient. It's all part of the process. The people you speak to can add to your understanding of yourself and the event. Let them talk and ask questions if they want. (This goes for all your new endings and whatever action you take.) Listen, answer, and then continue. Focus on your destination, on getting these words and thoughts out of your body as calmly as you can. Keep going no matter what happens, and you will have your new ending.

If the person you need to confront, apologize to, or forgive is deceased, or you are unable to locate them, you still have to take an action to release your residual thoughts and create a new ending. In these instances, a letter may be the best way to continue the story.

My client Steven found himself in this position and was stuck carrying the negative feelings from a string of events where things had ended badly with his deceased father. The first one he recalled was a high school basketball game he attended with his family when he was twelve. Steven's father got drunk, fell off the bleachers, and ended up hitting his head and having to go to the hospital. Steven's friends and the other kids from school saw what was going on, and he remembered being embarrassed by what had taken place and feeling like the entire gymnasium was looking at him.

Steven: When I started thinking about residual thoughts and what events I wanted to put on my list, my high school graduation was one of the things that came to mind. My father showed up late, smelling like he had taken a bourbon bath, and started screaming during the commencement address. Another time, I brought a girlfriend home on winter break during college and he drunkenly made a pass at her, and then blamed it on my mother. This somehow made sense to him. There turned out to be a lot more memories like this, many I had forgotten about or hadn't thought about in years.

Back then I felt like everyone I met knew something embarrassing about me, so I started shying away from social situations. I became guarded with people in town and avoided many of the kids from school except for my closest friends. I just didn't want to deal with it. I didn't want to talk to people because I didn't want my father to come up. I felt like everyone was judging me and categorizing me in some way. Like, there goes the son of the drunk guy, and they were right, or so I thought.

When I met new people, I wouldn't be interested in them or pay attention to what we were talking about. I just went through the motions. The whole time I'd be worrying about whether or not they knew about my dad. I would shy away from people in college, too. Even though I went to school far away from home and no one knew about my family, I still kept these behaviors and thought that's just the way I was.

When I started writing down these experiences, I realized I was doing the same thing at my job. My dad had passed away a while back, and I didn't think about him anymore when I talked to people today, but I was still pretty guarded. It didn't matter if no one knew my family or my history. It just became the way I acted.

You told me that the negative things I think about myself aren't true, that they were just things I believed because of these events that didn't end well. And at first I couldn't see it. I thought this was me. I'm Steven, and I'm not good with people. I'm not good in social situations. I'd insult people or say something weird to someone when I went out. Then I would drive home in my car and be mystified as to why I had said and done the things I did. I didn't want this to happen. I didn't want to make people feel bad or push them away. It didn't feel right to me.

It seemed crazy to me when you told me that I felt this way because what I was doing wasn't natural to me, that it wasn't really me, and that's why it felt bad to think the things I did or to act in ways that made my life difficult. You said I was carrying around something that didn't belong and those bad feelings and thoughts I experienced again and again in similar situations were the evidence.

I'd seen other people act normal thousands of time. I'm reasonably intelligent, yet I couldn't pick it up or get myself to do it. I just didn't believe I could. My residual thoughts were like a third arm I had no control over. I was doing things that weren't appropriate for someone like me, and I knew it. I had to do something about it.

Steven believed he wasn't good with people, and this shut him off from the parts of himself that could make him good with people. He ended up limiting himself, feeling powerless, and doing things to push others away. The truth is that we are all good with people, but residual thoughts can have us believing we're not. Steven wasn't being himself; he was being who his residual thoughts were telling him he was. He decided to do the steps and go in a different direction.

Steven: First I wrote a letter to my dad confronting him. I can't believe how emotional that was for me. I was really glad my wife had taken the kids shopping for the day because I spent a good hour or two in my den crying and writing. This is what I wrote:

"Dad, I know you had a drinking problem. Although this was your problem, while I was growing up, you made it my problem, too. You embarrassed me, Mom, and the rest of the family. Now that I am an adult and I have my own family, I refuse to allow this to be my problem anymore. I am writing this letter so I don't have to put people off the way I've been doing or carry around these thoughts anymore.

"Maybe I never said anything about it or told you how I felt in a way that you could understand, but now I know I must tell you the truth. I hated you for humiliating me in front of my friends. I hated you for what everyone would say about our family, and I hated you for never doing anything about it, for making excuses, for doing the same thing over and over no matter how much pain you caused.

"I may hate what you did, but I've thought about this a lot and I don't hate you anymore. I want you to know that, even though you never asked to be forgiven, I understand that you're human like me, and I forgive you. I forgive you for all the things you did and for not doing what you needed to do to change.

"I want my family to have a normal life and not to have to go through what I went through with you or to have to suffer with the results of what carrying around this pain has caused me. I want them to have happy lives, free of the turmoil I experienced being your son, so I am telling you this, and I'm taking actions so that we can have the best lives possible. I know that if I had gone through some of the things you went through as a child, I may have had a similar reaction. I want you to know that I love you, but your life wasn't my responsibility, Mom's, my wife's, or my kids'. All I can be responsible for is my life and my family. I am determined from this day forward to intervene in my life, to make this the best life possible, to let go of these feelings and create the ones I want to replace them. Know that wherever you are, I forgive you. I forgive you. I forgive you."

When I was done writing, in my mind I saw my father smiling. I didn't consciously make the decision to see that. There were tears in his eyes, and he looked happy and proud of me, like he saw me as a bigger man than himself, and he was glad.

The following week I took a train to my old high school, went out to the field where we had our graduation ceremony, made sure no one was around, took a lighter, and burned my letter. When I got back home I went to my son's basketball practice, walked over to the coach, and asked him if he needed any help, something I never would have dreamed of doing before I started all of this. But for some reason, after burning my letter, it felt right. Three weeks later he handed me a whistle at practice and said, "Steven, you are now the new assistant coach. Congratulations." I have to tell you that felt really good. I talk with all the parents. I work with the kids. My son is getting better, and I thought he might be embarrassed having his dad around, but he isn't. One day as we were driving home in the car after practice, he said to me, "Dad, you're not like the other fathers. They can be kind of jerks."

I asked, "So you don't mind me being the assistant coach?" and he said, "No, I like it." He looked over at me and smiled, and at that moment I realized I had my new ending.

Using a letter to confront allowed Steven to put his thoughts together, take them out of his body, and begin the process of releasing them even though the person he was confronting was deceased. In the next example, using a letter allowed my client Charles to create a confrontation that he felt would not only help him, but would also have a much better chance of having a positive effect on the person he was confronting.

Charles: I grew up getting hit by my father. I never thought about forgiving him until this part of the Clearing came up for me. I didn't understand why that was even necessary, especially since he never even asked to be forgiven.

I didn't think I could feel better about what had happened, so I guess I accepted feeling bad and tried not to think about it. Still, I could see how what had happened affected me and everyone else in my family. You live through something like that, it's going to cause some problems.

When I started asking myself about the events that ended badly from my life, I started to realize just how much I was thinking about the things that had happened with my dad and how bad they were really making me feel. When you talk to most men and ask if their parents hit them and they did, they usually chuckle, then make a joke about it, and say something like, "Those were different times," or, "That was a long time ago." No one ever admits how bad it was. But it's horrible because the person who you love and who is supposed to protect you is coming at you in a rage and hitting you.

It's traumatic as an adult to be in a fight. When you are five years old, and someone three times the size of you is coming at you, and there's nothing you can do, and you're not allowed to hit back, it's even worse. That went on for me for over a decade. I would get hit and watch my brothers getting hit. Sometimes it was my fault they were getting hit. Sometimes it was their fault I was getting hit. I know now that we were just kids, and we weren't to blame.

I would get in trouble for something and have to go and wait in my room for hours until my father got home to punish me. Sometimes he would hit me in front of other people. I remember one time he knocked the shit out of me at a family party in front of my cousins and their friends. While it was happening, I looked up and saw my uncle's face. His expression was pure horror. I'll never forget that look because at that moment I felt sorry for him. Maybe I was eight or nine years old at the time, and I was in the process of getting my ass kicked, literally, but I felt worse for my uncle. It was obvious he had never seen anything like that before and he was reacting to it. He seemed traumatized by it. I don't think he ever came back to our house after that.

I remember getting punched in the leg and screamed at by my father on the way home from soccer matches that we lost and when my father didn't feel my performance was the best. I remember getting out of the car when I got home, going to the shed, and having to wait for my father to come in and knock me around. I learned later on that what was going on in my house and what I was experiencing wasn't normal and that this wasn't what was going on in everyone else's house. My friends weren't constantly afraid in their own homes. They weren't getting punched the entire ride home in the car after losing a game, and they didn't have to get out of the car when they got home to wait in the shed for their beating. They weren't getting hit like me and my siblings. They lived in an entirely different world.

Sometimes I get sad that I didn't live like my friends. I would go to their homes, and I wouldn't want to leave. When I got my driver's license, I would get in the car and just drive. Anything was better than what was going on at the house. It was unfortunate that my father was like this and that I could never seem to talk to my brothers about what happened, but that's the way it was.

I was angry, sure. It was frustrating that my father didn't understand that it was wrong and that he thought there was something wrong with me for not responding well to this and not wanting to be near him as an adult. My brothers suffered through the same upbringing, and everyone seemed to pretend like nothing happened.

My father did good things, too. There was life in between the hitting—vacations, private schools, and so on. Like the rest of my family, I tried to focus on that. I tried talking myself into believing that everything was OK, but it wasn't. My father was so screwed up and so used to everyone going along with him that he thought there was something wrong with me or anyone who disagreed with what he was doing.

In a way he was right. There was something different about me, and he didn't like it. I reacted differently than the other people in my family. I objected. I didn't want to be broken. I wanted to fight back but I didn't have a lot of options. It took a long time to realize how I was doing it, but eventually I did. I realized that I didn't want my father to be right or think that he was right. I didn't want him to think that he did a good job or that he did the right thing by hitting me. A part of me also wanted to get back at him, so I started the pattern of screwing things up at what I call "the precipice of success." I couldn't hit him the way he hit me, because he was enormous and it just wasn't an option, but it did upset him when I did things wrong or when it looked like I'd win when I was playing a sport, and I'd turn around and lose instead. I wanted to succeed because I liked it, but I realized that subconsciously I also wanted to get back at my dad for what he was doing. So I developed this pattern when I was very young, and I'd been screwing things up in my life over the years in various ways ever since, not realizing what I was doing.

I was born into a bad situation, and at the time there was nothing I could do about it. My dad had some major problems, and perhaps he'll never see it himself. Something bad must have happened to him, and he got stuck with this anger he couldn't let go of. So he tried to give it to me and the rest of my family. I'm sorry he's like this because his life could have been different, and my childhood much better. I thought about it a lot, maybe too much, before I made my move. I went through the steps hundreds of times. I didn't want any more bad feelings. I didn't want to be like my father or feel that influence. I wanted my life without his pain in me.

I spent half my life feeling like I was bad and there was something wrong with me, but there wasn't. I was a normal kid. I never did anything really bad. I was too scared to. There was something wrong with my dad, though. He was tortured by something he never dealt with, and so he ended up torturing the people closest to him because of it. Maybe he never said the things he needed to say to his own father, and he was never able to let go. I didn't want this to happen to me. More than anything else, I guess I just didn't want these thoughts from what he did popping up in my life. I had tried everything to let go of the bad feelings. Now I was going to try forgiveness.

I knew confronting him in person was useless. I had tried so many times in the past to raise my objections, but I would get shouted down or dismissed with a laugh or some sort of jokey comment. So I wrote out what I wanted to say in a letter and placed it where I knew he would find it. If it was going to do him any good, he was going to need time to think about the things I would tell him, and a letter would allow him to do that. I would talk to him after if he wanted, but if what I was doing was going to have any chance of repairing what he had done to our family, he needed that chance to think about things instead of trying to argue his side and continuing on the way he always has. I knew my Clearing was about me, but if I could actually help him and my family in the process, I thought it would be worth it. Here is what I wrote:

"You hit me when I was growing up, and I know you want me to believe that was a good thing and that a grown man is somehow justified in hitting a little kid, but I don't think it's justified. You hit me in front of other people, and you humiliated me. You may have tried to convince yourself that what you did was out of love, but it wasn't. I saw the look in your eyes and the veins bulging in your head, and it didn't look or feel like love to me.

"You were a very angry and violent person when we were growing up. I tried to believe you were right. I tried to go along and think there was something wrong with me, and I know you may think that I was the reason you were angry because of the things you think I did wrong, but it wasn't. It was you. You have something from your past that happened and that made you the way you are, and I want you to know that I know in your heart you are not a bad person; you just never dealt with these things or your feelings. I forgive you for this. I forgive you for never apologizing, and for trying to make me feel like there was something wrong with me all those years instead of dealing with the problems you had. I forgive you for making me feel like an outcast in my own family and for coloring the way my siblings looked at me from a very early age. I forgive you for making everyone believe that I needed help when it was you who needed help all along. I'm sorry that no one ever helped you and that you felt like you had no choice but to take your pain out on us, and I forgive you."

I realized that even though my father was older than me and he looked old, he never grew up. Because it was so important for him to feel like everything he did was right, he used religion and the people close to him to help him feel this way no matter what he did or who he hurt. He didn't realize what he was doing or how hard it was to be around him. People just put up with him, kept their mouths shut, telling themselves it was no use, and buried their bad feelings — something I decided since my Clearing to never do again.

Reading your letter in person, mailing, or even hand delivering it can work if your situation calls for it. Be honest with yourself and decide what is the powerful action to take. If it is possible to say what you need to say in person, reading a letter or otherwise, then do it. For this moment, let go of your fear, because if you let fear dictate your actions, you will invite more fear into your life, and you will keep experiencing the emotions and limitations it brings you. Show yourself how brave you are instead. You will enjoy your life so much more when you do.

Option #3: Confronting over the Phone

If you're confronting someone who lives far away from you, the phone can be a good way to decrease the distance and say what you need to say. Sometimes, like with my client Sophia, the phone can be an equally effective way to provide the opposite by giving you the space to say what you need to say.

Sophia: When I asked myself who I needed to confront, something that happened when I was seventeen came into my mind. I think I've spent most of my life not standing up for myself, and it all seemed to go back to this incident in high school.

When I was sixteen, I started dating one of the more popular boys at school. He was smart, good looking, and athletic. He was also very poor, and I had watched him charm people to get the things he couldn't afford. Teachers worked to get him scholarships. Our school counselor offered to give us money so we could go to the prom. A woman whose son he tutored gave him a car.

Like most girls my age, I was insecure and had almost no confidence. I remember when he first asked me for my phone number, I replied, "Why do you want that?" I never even considered he would want to go out with me. My friends and I could not believe I was dating him. Once he was studying at my house when one of my friends came over. She looked at him on my floor reading and whispered to me with glee, "I can't believe he's here." And I whispered back, "I know!"

Besides a couple of teachers, he was the first person to make me feel special. I remember him telling me how smart he thought I was and that I could go to any college I wanted. Attention-starved, I became addicted. And then suddenly he stopped calling and didn't return my phone calls. It was summer so I couldn't see him at school to ask what happened. I was crushed. My mother said that I spent days in bed not moving or eating, but my memory of that summer is mostly blank.

When school started, I was desperate to get him back. I wanted to have that feeling again of thinking I was special and worth someone's notice. He was elusive, though. I remember doing things like making him and his friends cookies to try to win him back. Finally, I thought, I will offer him sex and then he will pay attention to me again.

He accepted my offer and drove to my house late that night. I snuck out without waking my parents and met him in a nearby field. I was a virgin, and I was terrified. He told me to take off my clothes and lay down on the blanket. He began sticking his fingers in my vagina. It hurt, and I was scared. This was not what I wanted. I told him so and that I wanted him to stop. He looked at me and said, "If we don't do this now, I will never speak to you again." I protested, but then I gave up, and, in the end, he just did what he wanted.

It's so ridiculous to think about this now. He was a smart guy. He wouldn't have hit me or anything like that. All I had to do was get up and leave, but I didn't. I told him to stop, and then I stayed there. I didn't stand up for myself. I froze and just kept my mouth shut, which is what I would end up doing over and over again in difficult situations I encountered in the years to come.

I remember going into my bathroom afterward and looking at myself in the mirror. I wanted to know if I looked any different. I didn't. But I was different. I repeated what I did that night in countless other situations: I didn't stand up for myself at work, at college, in personal relationships. I did things I didn't want to do and kept my mouth shut because I was scared of confrontation.

For more than ten years after that night, he would continue to pop up in my life—an email or phone call, an unexpected visit. And while nothing like that ever happened again, we would always follow the same pattern. Once we went to a store together and while we were there, he saw a CD he thought I should listen to. He demanded that I buy it, and even though I didn't have a lot of money in my bank account and didn't want to spend it on something I didn't even want, he was insistent, and I finally gave in. Years later I still had that CD, and it was one of the first things I Cleared.

Once he asked me, "Do you remember that night?" I said yes. He said, "I've thought about that a lot. I basically raped you." Again, I said nothing.

During my work with John, I told him about what had happened and that I kept thinking about it. He was shocked that I was still in contact with this person. He suggested that I change my email address and phone number, and he counseled me to confront him and then to never contact him again. After all, allowing him to continue popping up in my life was only reinforcing my identity as someone who doesn't respect herself. There was no doubt in my mind that I needed to do something.

Changing my phone number and email address was easy. Calling him was not. Luckily, I had written down what I wanted to say and practiced role-playing the conversation with John. When the time came for my confrontation, I dialed the phone number, he answered the phone, and in the most confident voice I could muster, I went right to it. I said, "I'm calling to tell you not to contact me again or try to get in touch with me in any way. You did rape me that night, and if you ever contact me again, I will tell everyone we know about what you did."

He protested. He said he didn't know what I was talking about (despite what he had said years earlier). John had advised me not to engage in conversation but to reiterate my demands. I asked him if he understood, he said yes, and then I hung up.

He has never attempted to contact me since. After that call I was shaken, but as the months went by I found I was different too. I had always felt stupid for letting something like that happen, and now I didn't really feel that way anymore. I was seventeen when it happened. No one taught me how to handle day-to-day interactions at school, let alone what happened that night. I had no idea what I was doing back then, and it's OK. I'm not that person anymore.

After that call, I found it much easier to stand up for myself. Today people know that I'm not someone they can take advantage of. I recently said to John that I almost wish I could make that call now with all the experience and confidence I have. John smiled and asked, "Do you think you'd have this much confidence if you hadn't already made that phone call?" He's right. I just wish I had always felt the way I do now. It makes things so much easier.

Confronting makes your life easier because it changes the way you feel about yourself. It allows you to take an ending that was creating lasting negative feelings, continue the story, and change it to an ending that makes you feel good. If the phone is the best way to make that happen, then go for it. Reduce the distance or create more by picking up the phone and saying what you've prepared to say to create your new ending, and Clear your residual thoughts.

APOLOGIZING

Just like confrontations, keep your apologies simple and direct. Begin by briefly recalling the incident you want to apologize for: "Remember five years ago at your birthday party when I put that lampshade on my head, made a pass at your wife, and jumped in the pool with my clothes on?" Then follow with something like, "I'd like to apologize for what I did. Will you forgive me?" And that's it. You don't have to add anything.

Apologizing isn't complicated. What it comes down to is stating what you did wrong and then saying, "I'm sorry." It seems so simple, almost too simple to even be that important, yet it is one of the most powerful actions you can take. Nothing creates good feelings out of bad ones or has the ability to turn a contentious situation around and eliminate residual thoughts quite like a sincere apology. If you've never been big on apologizing, stop missing out. The effect is awesome and far-reaching, and it's easier to do than you may think.

Will it be comfortable? No, not likely, but the reward is something far more valuable compared to a minute or two of feeling uncomfortable.

Rachel: After I broke up with my boyfriend, I really hit bottom. My aunt was great. She gave me money and a place to live for a year so I could get back on my feet. While I was there, I screwed up the house and invited the wrong kind of people around. It ended badly, and I haven't spoken to her in years. I kept thinking about it and feeling terrible each time I did. I was able to turn things around for myself eventually, and a big part of making that happen was what my aunt did for me.

When this part of the Clearing came up, I was scared because I knew what I had to do. I was also glad because I wanted to do it. I wanted to apologize, but I didn't know how. I grew up in a house where no one really apologized for anything. I don't think I've ever heard my parents say those words. To me it just seemed like something other people did. I learned to defend and attack, that even when you were wrong it was best to argue until it looked like you could be right. Apologizing felt like the weak thing to do. I knew I was wrong this time, but thinking about calling my aunt and apologizing still made me sick to my stomach.

    I thought about what I would say, and then I wrote it down. I kept visualizing seeing myself smiling after hanging up the phone like John told me to. Although it felt ridiculous, I took his advice and exaggerated the outcome. No one could see what was going on in my mind so I figured, what the heck. I even imagined having the conversation with my aunt and then jumping into the air afterward, saying "Yes, I did it!" while raising my fist and smiling. I would sit in my living room with my eyes closed, laughing at this vision in my mind. Then one morning I woke up and made the call.

    By that time I was well rehearsed with what I had written to say, but I kept the piece of paper next to me anyway. My aunt listened, told me she was glad I called and how much she appreciated it, and we had a great conversation. With that phone call, I took that badness out of my life. This was something I had been carrying around for years, and it was gone in seconds. I was afraid, but I wanted to complete my Clearing. I wanted to feel better, so I practiced and I did it. Now I never think of the old ending. I only think of the new one and it feels good.

    I will admit that seeing myself happy with the successful conclusion to my apology was something I did not want to do. When I thought about it, every part of me was like, "There's no way I'm going to do that." The voice in my head immediately said that it was a waste of time, and I would think to myself, "It's not like you actually deserve to be forgiven." But why didn't I deserve it? Because I made some mistakes? What I was doing in my life to be happy wasn't working, and I couldn't think of any better options. I did have some pretty bad thoughts about myself surrounding this event and others like it and I knew I needed to do something about it. I was paying John, and I wanted to get my money's worth, so I forced myself to do what he said.

    Even if I was just pretending that things were working out, I think in the end seeing that it could turn out OK, rather than some kind of disaster, made the difference for me. In the past I never saw anything good coming out of doing something like this, and that's one of the reasons why I would always talk myself out of apologizing and just blame the other person instead. I would just keep it inside, think about it, and feel bad.

Saying I was sorry turned out to be one of the most powerful things I did during my Clearing. I think I was so scared because it was something I wasn't used to doing. It was just easier to think that someone else was wrong because it spared me the pain of having to look at myself. But the truth was that I wasn't saving myself from any pain. If anything, by not doing something to make things right, I increased it.

When you apologize, avoid the non-apology apology. You know what I'm talking about because you've probably heard a few of these before. You may even be guilty of whipping out one or two on occasion yourself:

"I'm sorry I said that, but I only did it because you..."

"I would have waited for you, and I'm sorry I didn't, but you were the one who..., and that's why I did what I did."

"I'm sorry you feel that way."

"I'm sorry you can't accept the fact that..."

"I'm sorry but if you had just... I would have never have..."

No one ever says things like, "Everything is going great for me in my life because I never admit when I'm wrong," or, "I attribute the success of my marriage to my stubbornness and a lack of sincere apologies. It's really made my spouse and me closer." And you've probably never heard anyone say anything like, "It's so sweet the way Jack never takes responsibility for anything he's done. God, I love that about him," or, "One time Katie apologized to me for something she did, and I'm glad because now I understand how the whole thing was my fault."

If you haven't already, it's important for you to learn right now that an apology isn't going to give you what you are looking for if you use it as a way to point out what the other person did wrong and to make excuses for your actions. Why rob yourself of the good feelings you could have by backhandedly blaming the other person for something you did? Why justify your actions when doing so isn't going to give you the resolution you're looking for?

Pursue this direction, and you will create more resentment, anger, and residual thoughts to slow you down, and the person you are trying to apologize to is just going to end up more upset and think even less of you. If you leave the "buts" and the excuses out of what you say, you can create a true apology, and you will release your bad feelings and change your thoughts. Remember, this is the reason you are apologizing in the first place — it isn't to create more bad feelings to live with and to make others feel like they are wrong. You do things wrong all the time, every day. It's the same for me and everyone else. It's time to accept this fact and get over it. You will do things wrong today, and you will do more things wrong in the future, and the worst thing you could do wrong is not to admit what you've done, that you could have done it better, and that you are sorry that what you did hurt someone else. Apologize and free yourself from these feelings and thoughts. Travel without their weight, and you will like your life so much more when you do.

James: Looking at life in terms of what made me happy or what made me feel powerful was very different for me. I was so completely focused on my problems and complaining about my ex-wife to whoever would listen that I never really thought about it. I remember what a woman I had dated after my divorce told me one night when we were out to dinner. She said, "You know, James, you're a good-looking guy, but you are kind of a downer." At the time I chose to focus on the first part of her comment and ignore the second. Now I realize she was right. In fact, I became a worse downer after she pointed that out.

When my divorce was final, I hurt my back and started watching more TV. Usually I watched sports, but now I was watching political TV shows. I was really angry about things and hadn't realized it until I asked myself if these shows made me feel powerful, and then

I understood what was going on. I kept bringing politics up in everyday conversations, and like with the wonderfully honest woman I had dated who tried to clue me in, I was oblivious to people's reactions. I was angry, and these shows made me even angrier.

After I Cleared my home, John talked about letting go of residual thoughts, and I definitely had more than a couple events with my ex-wife that I would rather not have to think about anymore. He talked about forgiving and moving on, and I didn't want to hear about it. She was wrong, I was right, end of story. But some of what he said stuck with me.

John took me through some visualizations that I started to do at home. I saw myself happy and moving on with my life. I started thinking about what had happened with my marriage, and I began to see things differently. Then it was like a door opened and I saw the truth. It just hit me: I wasn't mad at her, I was mad at myself. I knew she wasn't right for me at the start of our relationship, but I was stubborn and I blamed her for not being the person I wanted. It was me all along, but I couldn't see it because I wasn't letting myself. Instead of facing the truth, I was taking it out on her. We never should have gotten married in the first place, and I think we both knew it.

I ended up apologizing to one of my best friends who had just about had it with me. I apologized to my ex-wife, something I never thought I would do in a million years. I cut out the political shows, stopped pushing my opinions on everyone, and started being less angry. I even paid to put a new roof on my ex-wife's home. She thought I'd lost my mind, but I feel great. I figure she deserved something for all the torture I put her through.

I stopped thinking about myself and my problems so much and I met someone. I know that if she had come into my life earlier, I would have missed her. I'd have been chewing someone's ear off about what was wrong with this and that and would have let her go right by. This life is wonderful, and I forgot that for a while. I realize that now and that I'm not always right. I don't plan on ever forgetting those two things ever again.

How do you feel when someone you know makes a mistake and hurts you? How does it feel when that person apologizes? How does it feel when you don't get an apology, and you get blamed instead? Not being able to admit when you are wrong cuts you off from good feelings, from wisdom, closeness, and love. It separates you, isolates you, and creates resentment.

How do you feel when you say something like, "Yeah, but I'm right, and I only did what I did because..."? Be honest. Whether you want to admit it or not, it doesn't feel good, and this is your signal that you are not being you, that there's something you have to deal with from your past, or you will always feel like this during moments when you should be admitting that you are human, you made a mistake, and apologizing instead.

If you haven't sincerely apologized to someone during the past year, if you've never apologized to your kids, spouse, boyfriend, or girlfriend, if you can't remember the last time you used a sentence along the lines of, "You know I was wrong about that, and I'm sorry," or, "I shouldn't have done/said that, will you forgive me?" then you're being a jerk. You know you've made mistakes. It happens. We aren't always at our best. We get upset. Negative emotions come into play, and we don't always do and say things that display the truth about how wonderful we are. A few of these occasions are probably popping into your mind right now as you read this. Make today the day that you deal with them. If you apologize for just one thing you did wrong the way I've laid out in this book, you will like the feeling you get a hundred times more than the feelings you get from trying to ignore what happened or blaming someone else.

If there's a voice in your head saying, "I don't have to do this because I know I'm right," or, "They know I didn't mean it," or, "Everyone understands that's just how I am," or, "They know I'm sorry," you need to accept that these are all excuses. Maybe you've let this stop you before, but now you can do it differently. It's easier than you may think. I've seen little kids apologize with perfection—simple and direct. You can do the same no matter how unique your residual thoughts are telling you your situation is or what good reasons you may think you have for not doing anything.

You know the scene in the movies where the guy on his deathbed is suddenly apologizing to everyone for all the years he was being such a miserable bastard? At the end of your life, you will feel the same way about how you were with certain people and some of the things you did. You won't want to leave the earth without making it right. You won't want to bring these bad feelings with you wherever it is you're going. Even if you don't believe you are going anywhere, why have them with you now? Now, or at the end of your life, you will want to be forgiven. Why wait a second longer when you can enjoy this freedom today?

If you need to apologize to yourself or to someone who is deceased to create your new ending, you'll still need to complete your steps. Do this by finding a place where you can be by yourself undisturbed and read the apology you wrote under *What I Will Say*. Then, follow the instructions for "Taking a Second Action" coming up.

FORGIVING

Forgiveness is usually what you feel after someone sincerely apologizes to you. You can also feel forgiveness when you gain information that gives you a broader understanding of a situation or of the other person. But what if you never receive an apology? What if you don't have any information that would allow you to feel different? How do you feel forgiveness then? If you decide to walk up to the person you think has been acting like a creep and who hasn't expressed any remorse, and say, "I forgive you, buddy," it isn't going to go over big or create the new ending you want. So what are you supposed to do?

As much as you may wish you could just say the words, "I forgive you," or think them and be done with it, you aren't going to release your residual thoughts unless you get to the point where you truly mean it. To do this, you might need to get something off your mind and out into the air, and that means confronting.

Maybe you're thinking that you don't want to go through with a confrontation. Maybe you're thinking, "Enough already with these confrontations, I'm just going to forgive and be done with it." Maybe there's a voice inside you saying, "There's just no way this is going to happen. They aren't even worth it." While it's true that you don't want to feel the pain your event left you with and under normal circumstances you'd be very excited to say goodbye to it, your old identity may be telling you that it isn't that bad, that this is the way things should be, or that the way you feel isn't something you can do anything about.

Your old identity could have you thinking "What's done is done," or wondering, "Why should I let them off the hook when they should be paying for what they did?" keeping you blind to the fact that you're the one who's on the hook and you're the one continuing to pay by holding these bad feelings and thoughts inside.

Don't waste your time with any of this garbage! Forget about who's right and who's wrong and who did what. Always remember, this isn't about anyone else. It's about you and the way you feel. If you have thoughts that are stopping you from feeling forgiveness, you are having them because you've never said what you need to say. Remember that when you forgive you are letting go, and what you are letting go of is pain. If you have to confront to do this, then do it. Say what you need to say, and take the thoughts that have been swirling around inside you, distracting and weakening you, out of your body.

If after you confront you still don't feel forgiveness, consider the possibility that there is something that you need to apologize for. I know you may be thinking, "Apologize? What the heck do I have to apologize for?" You may be able to understand why you would need to confront before you can forgive, but why would you need to apologize in order to feel forgiveness? How does that even make sense? They should be apologizing to you, right?

I know how you feel: You're angry, irritated, frustrated. You don't want to go through all of this. You just want the other person to stop being an idiot. If you are feeling this way, it's your focus that's stopping you from connecting to what you need to be happy.

To change this, first consider that if you had a magic ball and could look back in time, you would most likely see that the same people who have hurt you have been tortured, misunderstood, and mistreated just like you, maybe worse, and just like you, they have reacted to people trying to steal their power. Consider also that under similar circumstances and with a similar background and experiences, you might act like the person who has wronged you. I know this isn't always the easiest thing to do. Believe me, I struggle with this myself, but do it nevertheless.

You know you've made some boneheaded moves in the past. You've hurt people you could have helped, taken advantage of others, and started your own fair share of fights. Yes, you. You've done these things and you know it. We all have. You've misunderstood situations and acted in ways that later, in calmer moments, you realized weren't the greatest. Just like the people around you, there are circumstances that have led to your shortcomings and the people who have hurt you have circumstances that led to theirs and if you knew their whole story, as you know your own, you would most likely understand and sympathize with their predicament. The truth is, you have no real way of knowing how you would react or even if you would do as well as those around you if you were in their shoes.

Consider all of these things, and then look at what happened at the original event again. Look at who was there and see if you may have hurt someone without realizing it. See if there is something you could have done differently. Ask yourself if the person you are mad at did you a favor in some way or if there is something that happened that you were responsible for that you haven't owned up to or been completely honest about. Ask yourself if what you don't like about this other person is really what you don't like about yourself.

Apologizing may seem out of the question for your new ending or like a really bad idea at first, especially when you originally thought the action you needed to take was to forgive, but consider it. Allow for the possibility that there may be something you missed, and then look for what that could be. Go back and review the previous two sections, and if you need to, confront or apologize first. You can do it! Say out loud what you've been holding inside. Give yourself this chance to feel forgiveness and for your residual thoughts to lose their hold.

To Clear some of your residual thoughts, you may need to forgive yourself for mistakes you've made. Do not discount the importance of this. Even if it feels a little strange to do, complete your event chart, decide what to say to yourself, go someplace where you can be alone, and read what you've written out loud. We all wish that during an event we had the knowledge that we gain once we look back on it. We each struggle with what to say and the best actions to take for the situations we find ourselves in. Sometimes our residual thoughts cause us to misunderstand, to take offense, and to get angry. The access we have to our best parts—our intelligence, talents, and abilities—gets blocked, and we end up doing things that are less than who we are. We all screw up. Understand this is part of the human condition. This is how we gain wisdom. We take steps, fall down, we get back up, learn from what has happened, maybe even seek counsel, and then we move forward. Learn what you need to by completing your event chart and taking action, and instead of continuing to weigh yourself down with pain and regret, forgive yourself just like you would other people. Feel good about the fact that instead of passively living with your bad feelings and making a bunch of excuses, you're doing something to make things right.

To feel forgiveness in situations where there is no interaction with other people, complete your event chart. Fill in *What I Will Say* even if the person you need to forgive is you, hasn't asked to be forgiven, or is deceased. Do it even if there is no one to speak your forgiveness to but yourself. Write what you will say, and then, when you are ready, go someplace where you can be alone and read what you've written out loud. Take your words of forgiveness out of your body and hear yourself saying them, and then prepare to take a Second Action.

TAKING A SECOND ACTION

A Second Action is an action you take that's related to your event in some way and shows you that you aren't who your residual thoughts said you were. If your new ending is missing an interaction, a Second Action is your chance to have one. It's an opportunity to create the emotion necessary for you to let go of who your original event made you believe you were, and see yourself as the person you truly are.

Let's face it, if your event is that you smashed your father's '69 Mustang into a tree when you were fifteen and then blamed it on a carjacker, your father has since died, and you did the steps and read your letter to the air, it isn't going to have the same effect on you as if you also took a Second Action by donating the book value of a '69 Mustang to your father's local veterans group and then apologizing to one person you've lied to in the last ten years.

A Second Action like this can give you a chance to experience the emotions needed to release your residual thoughts and truly move on, to see that you are truthful, that you do the right thing, and that you're an outstanding and generous person. Whereas without a Second Action, the truth would stay hidden, these really great parts of yourself would remain unused, and your new ending may lack what it needs to stand out over the old one in your mind. This is important because when similar events arise as you move forward with your life, you want your mind to access the truth of who you are instead of what the residual thoughts from your original ending had you believing about yourself.

For these instances where your new ending lacks that interaction, follow the same steps as you would for any event you're Clearing. Confront, apologize to, and forgive yourself and anyone from your five events who hasn't apologized, is deceased, or you are unable to locate by going somewhere you can be alone and reading out loud what you've written on your event chart under *What I Will Say*. Then, look at what you wrote under *The Truth* and figure out an action you can take that's related to your event and that demonstrates what you wrote about yourself there. Write down what you will do, prepare, repeat your three communications, and when the time comes, take your Second Action.

Diana: There was so much in my life that was negative. I had been trying forever to lose weight. I felt gross. I looked gross, and even though I would start a new diet each week, I was really doing zero about it. My social life consisted of going out with my friends, having too many drinks and way too much food, ragging about my life for a few hours, then going home, looking in the mirror at my stomach and my thighs, and crying.

I'd start a diet, have some alcohol, and everything would go out the window. My attitude was that life is hard and you have to live a little, but the thing was, with food I wasn't living a little, I was living a lot. I ate junk, and I ate too much of it. I was in a rut. I didn't like who I was. I was just trying to get away from things I didn't like about myself, and nothing was helping me. Something to eat, a few drinks—everything I did was to feel good temporarily. I hadn't really looked good since high school. Truthfully, I stopped looking like myself years ago.

I wanted to feel in control again, so I went to John and he told me that I was in control, that I was an expert at control, and that I was keeping things the way they were with what I was saying to myself and what I saw around me and in my mind. He said I was telling myself to have this life, and while I didn't want to believe it, he was right.

When I thought about who I needed to confront, apologize to, and forgive, there were people who came to my mind, but for many of my events it was also me. I needed to confront myself about what I was doing. I needed to apologize for wasting so much time, and I had to forgive myself for certain things that happened in my past.

Before I started writing, John told me I needed a new best friend, and that he was appointing me to that position. He told me to write what I needed to say to myself as if I were this best friend, so I started out talking about my good qualities because this is what a best friend would do. Then I got honest about what had been going on with my life, my friends, the eating and drinking. To finish my letter, I wrote, "I want you to have a great life. I forgive you for what you've done; now I want to help you. You are my best friend, and I love you."

The tears came when I was writing that last part. I'd been so busy treating myself like dirt for so long that I forgot that I was supposed to be on my side, that I was supposed to be looking out for me. I was treating myself like an enemy, not a best friend. Who would say, "You're fat. You can't do it. There's no use," to her best friend? I was saying these things to myself all the time, but it wasn't what I wanted or how I wanted to see myself.

When I started paying attention to what I was doing, it was all so depressing. I had been making my life hard, and I told myself that I couldn't do anything else, that the things I needed to do to change were too difficult. I had convinced myself that I couldn't have what I wanted, so I sat back and criticized anyone who came up in conversation or my field of vision. I'd melt into the background and turn everyone to dust with my thoughts. I criticized myself in my own head and to my friends. I cut myself down with the people at work. These things didn't make me feel good, yet I did it all the time.

For my Second Action I wanted to do the opposite. I didn't want to sit back and criticize anymore. I didn't want to be who my residual thoughts were saying I was—I wanted to participate. Since one of my biggest problems was without a doubt the things I was saying, I started thinking about joining Toastmasters. A part of me thought it would be interesting, while at the same time that negative voice in me was ripping the idea apart.

When I realized how this voice had been ruining things for me and keeping me from actually doing anything besides looking at my Facebook page and perfecting the art of pointing out assholes, it made me really mad. So, instead of standing in the background and criticizing everyone and pointing out how badly things sucked under my breath, I told the voice to shut up. I told myself I could do it, and I started going to the meetings.

I decided to devote myself to giving speeches where I pointed out things that were going right and the positive attributes of whatever

I was speaking about — nothing phony, just the truth with a positive focus. Whether I was giving a speech or making comments, I focused on the future and what had the potential to create good feelings or at least some sort of agreement. Instead of always criticizing, I talked about what I liked. I made these things my priority.

Taking this Second Action and joining Toastmasters has made me very aware of my old habits and that old negative voice. In my mind I keep a giant hammer, and when I start getting negative thoughts that I know aren't really me and that serve no purpose other than to make me feel bad and keep me from actually doing anything, I see the hammer come out and I start smashing. I actually laugh when it happens. Each time I get quicker and quicker. I even stop myself mid-sentence sometimes when I'm about to spew some useless negativity, and now the response I get from those around me is night and day compared to how it used to be. People actually smile when they come up to speak to me, and I smile too. I don't feel like complaining or pointing out what's wrong so much anymore. I just enjoy what I'm doing and the conversation I'm having. Now I feel better about so many things. Best of all, I feel better about me.

Charles: I ended up not liking sports too much because of what happened with me and my father. I guess there were just too many negative associations. I thought competition was bad because of what it brought out in people, but that was only what it brought out in some people. After I started Clearing my events, I realized that I didn't have to have these bad feelings or cut myself off from this part of life. I liked being on a team. I missed the camaraderie. I missed hanging out with people who shared the same interests as me. Allowing these old events to continue to cut off this part of my life didn't seem appropriate after what I'd been doing with my Clearing.

I don't know whether I wanted to show myself that those bad feelings weren't me, or if I just felt better after writing my letter, but I decided it was time to get involved in sports again. The thing was, none of the sports I used to play really interested me anymore, so I took up one I knew nothing about and had zero experience in. I researched it, got some instruction, and started practicing. I entered my first competition, came in close to last place, and had the time of my life. There wasn't a single part of it that wasn't fun. That hate I had wasn't me. Those bad feelings weren't mine. They were forced on to me by my circumstances. I was a little kid. I didn't really have any choices, but now I do, and doing this feels good to me.

My Second Action has spurred a whole new part of my life. I laugh and have fun when I compete now. I feel good whether I win or lose. It's crazy, but all those bad feelings are gone. When I notice my teammates getting upset about their performance or their score, I smile and I think to myself, "They need to Clear some residual thoughts." Then I quickly get back to having fun.

Danielle: One of my events was from when I was around seven years old and I had gone to Toys R Us with my dad and my three sisters. Somehow they all had gotten something and I didn't, so after we got to the car in the parking lot, I started to cry. My father ended up walking me back into the store, and I got to buy a My Little Pony toy. The residual thought was that I'm someone who makes people feel bad to get what they want, and when I look at my life, I can see how I've been manipulating people this way and how it hasn't been working out for me.

I knew I was bad with people. I knew I was doing something wrong, but I never really stopped to think about what that was. I never made a connection between how I acted and my lack of success with relationships. It was all just a big mystery to me. I'm pretty and I'm smart, so why is my life so terrible? I just thought life was like this, other people sucked, and I wasn't doing anything wrong. I didn't even consider that there was another way to do things.

This event at the toy store was part of several similar events that I needed to confront myself about and to forgive myself for. I had wasted so much of my life screwing things up in this way. For some reason, this event was the one that stood out to me the most and the one I knew I should do a Second Action for.

As I was thinking about what happened that day and what my action should be, an idea came to me: "Go back to that store and buy a My Little Pony." I ignored it at first because I thought it was dumb. What would that really tell me about myself anyway, that I have the means to buy a toy if I want to?

Then I thought about it some more and decided it wasn't dumb. When I wanted something and I wasn't getting it, I thought I had to immediately make people feel bad. I had to complain or make them feel sorry for me somehow or make them feel guilty. I thought that was part of the process of getting what could make me feel happy. I never considered the possibility of just directly asking for what I wanted.

I looked at my chart, and under *The Truth* it said, "I'm generous and kind. To get what I want, I treat people like royalty." I started thinking about what that meant and what a generous and kind person who treats people like royalty would do for a Second Action. There was something about buying a My Little Pony that made sense, and I liked it.

It just needed something more, something bigger. Buying one My Little Pony wasn't going to be bringing up any strong emotions, so I decided to go to the same toy store I went to with my father and sisters and buy ten cases of My Little Ponies, then go to ten different charities and drop off a case at each one for their holiday toy drives.

I didn't have money to burn like that, so there was definitely some significance there. The other thing was the giving aspect. Because I wasn't giving them to a specific person in order to manipulate them into doing something for me later or some other reason like that, because I had no connection with the end receiver and they didn't know the toys were from me, there was something pure about that and it felt like it fit.

At the last center I dropped off at, I talked to the director. She said they were looking for people to help with distribution the next day. I knew what she was going to ask me, and I was thinking, "God, please don't ask me to help." I wanted to get in and get out, do my Second Action, and complete my Clearing. I was worried that if I went back, something might happen that would mess things up.

I couldn't think of any way to turn her down, though, so I agreed to help. I went to the center the next day and spent a few hours handing out toys to families and watching everyone around me be incredibly happy. I saw a couple of girls get a My Little Pony, and I couldn't help but get a little emotional when I did. Really, they should have charged people to volunteer because knowing how much fun it was, I would have gladly paid to be there.

Making people feel bad really doesn't fit who I am now. It didn't really fit who I was back then. Seeing the girls at the center made me realize how ridiculous I was being with the way I was dealing with people. I wasn't a little girl anymore, and crying and making a scene to get what I wanted, even if it was done in a more adult way, wasn't the best way to have a good life.

When I got back home, I wrote a letter to myself for my closing ceremony. I felt bad for all the relationships I had spoiled because of the way that I acted, but I also realized that I was being hard on myself. No one really showed me how to do it the right way. My parents were totally dysfunctional when it came to personal relationships, and I did the best I could with what they taught me. I knew I didn't want to hurt people. I wanted to be loved like everyone else. After what happened at the center, I understood what I was doing. I still had regret, but it wasn't the same. It was OK. I have my whole life ahead of me now to treat people better. This is part of what I wrote in my letter: "I forgive you for all the times you manipulated people and ruined relationships. You are a good person, and now you know how to let that come out. You know how to do this better, and I promise to do this right from now on. And, if I don't, if I should slip up, I promise to go back and create a new ending that reflects who I am and not who my residual thoughts had me believing I was."

Roman: I had residual thoughts from an event that took place when I was about eleven. I was on a family vacation in Dallas. My mom, dad, my sister, and I were out getting something to eat. We turned a corner and there were two men kissing. As we walked by I heard my mother say, "Disgusting," under her breath. I didn't realize how much that had affected me, but that's what came to me when I asked myself what events ended badly from my life.

I barely even considered it an event, but I realized after I started to really think about it, that's how I thought of myself. I did feel like I was disgusting, but at the same time it felt good to be around men and to think about them. I was totally confused. That was a long time ago, and I feel better about myself today, but my mother's voice was still with me, and I knew why and what I had to do.

I had to confront my mother and come out to my parents. Everyone at work knew I was gay. Everyone in my life knew, except my parents. They were still asking if I was seeing any "nice girls" and trying to set me up. I was tired of thinking about it. It was too stressful not to be myself when I was around them. I didn't need this in my life. I didn't need the fear or bad feelings. This definitely wasn't making me feel powerful. When I visualized the destination I wanted and felt the relief of not having to think about it anymore, I knew it was time.

Really, it was what my mother said that day that was stopping me, so I knew that was the event that needed a new ending. First I focused on what I wanted to feel: on being free, on being myself around everyone and never having to hide. I practiced seeing it in my mind. I wrote down what I wanted to say to my mother, and it was three pages long. After I went over it a few more times, I shortened it to one. I started to feel better the moment I made the decision to tell them, and surprisingly, I wasn't that scared when I did—not as much as I thought I would be, anyway. I think I was excited more than anything else.

Before I went to their place, I spent a few days preparing. I would go to my bedroom, close my eyes, and see myself at my parents' house right after I told them. For some reason, I always saw my mother crying, but she was happy and we were all relieved, like a heavy burden we'd been carrying was suddenly gone. Then I would see myself at a big party with all my friends. I always looked really good in these visions, and everyone wanted to dance with me. I had no plans to have a party with all my friends, but it was a fun image and it made me feel good, so that's the one I chose. I also envisioned us further in the future. I saw my boyfriend and me having Thanksgiving dinner at my parents' home and everyone smiling and laughing.

I always thought that when I said, "Yeah, but they're my parents," it justified why I wasn't telling them I'm gay. John called me out on that, and I remember how mad I was at him, but then I thought about it. Why was I deciding to make myself feel this way? I thought I was doing the right thing and protecting them somehow, but then I saw how those feelings were affecting my life, and I knew I was wrong. I was afraid of their reaction, but I wasn't responsible for that. I was responsible for me and for being a good person; and that meant being true to myself, which meant not living my life with these thoughts dragging me down.

After going through the steps and doing my chart, I felt better than I did when I thought about doing this any other time. It happened pretty fast too. I started writing, and then practicing. Three days later I was at my parents' place confronting my mother. It hadn't been that long since I had seen her last, but for some reason this time my mother seemed so human to me, so fragile. Maybe it was because I was thinking of her from back when the event occurred, and now she was so much older.

I said all the things I had prepared to say. We cried, and she told me that was the way she was raised, but she had eventually adopted a more *"c'est la vie"* attitude, as she put it. She knew that how she used to think was wrong, and she was sorry about what she had said that day and for a few other things she'd said since. I told her that I forgave her, and I meant it. I had changed my attitudes in many ways too. I had evolved and become better, and so had she. I thought about it and realized we were both letting go of our residual thoughts. She asked me some more questions about my life, we talked for a while, and then I left.

In the end I think everyone was relieved by my revelation. Now it's like my parents are some kind of super gay activists and I get to be myself all the time. I didn't feel like I needed it because I felt so great after talking to my mother, but I decided to take a Second Action anyway. I got a group of friends together, and we made a float for this year's GLBT pride parade. It seemed like a fun way to show myself I was different now. I didn't feel proud back then. I wanted to hide, and I did for a long time. Driving down the middle of the street while standing on top of a giant wedding cake, dressed in a tuxedo and kissing my boyfriend that day, there was no place to hide. It was the opposite of what the first ending had me doing, and it turned out to be one of the most beautiful moments of my life. As it happened, we did go dancing afterward, it was very much a party, I looked great, and everyone did want to dance with me!

Your new endings can heal the old ones. They can deflate your bad feelings and allow you to see yourself differently. Taking an action where you're interacting with others or in some way with the outside world, is a big part of making that happen. Like Diana joining Toastmasters and giving her positive speeches, like Steven helping out his son's basketball coach, and Roman with his parade float, for your Second Action find an action related to your event that reveals the truth about who you are.

This is an opportunity to feel good right now. It's a chance to become accustomed to using the abilities inside of you that your old endings made you believe weren't there and a great start for creating your new habit of using them to feel good in your life today.

If your new ending has an interaction already, whether you complete a Second Action is up to you. Regardless of how triumphant a new ending makes you feel or whether there is an interaction, you can make what you are doing even more meaningful by showcasing the truth of who you are and increase the effect your Clearing has on your life with a Second Action.

22

CLEARING YOUR RESIDUAL THOUGHTS: THE DO'S

～

#1: DO BE A PART OF THIS

Any fight you keep going over again and again in your mind, any situation you keep analyzing that you can't seem to let go of, any unresolved moment from your past that has bad feelings attached to it—this is your chance to do something about it, let the bad feelings go, and move on. After you confront, apologize, and forgive, thoughts that have been irritating you, dragging you down, and keeping you from what you want to do become less than they once were.

You can wake up one day and feel as if your residual thoughts were never there. I know this not only because of the experiences of my clients, but also because of what has happened with my own residual thoughts. Situations that I had literally taken time every day to feel bad about were there one week and gone the next.

I want you to experience this. I want you to know that you have this power and to understand what it's like to use it. I want you to wake up in the morning free of the residual thoughts your five events have imparted onto your life. When you do, you will see what those before you have seen, and you will understand your life in a new way.

If you truly do it, Clearing residual thoughts changes you. I see it in my clients' eyes. There's something different. Sometimes I notice it after they Clear their first event. Sometimes I see it when they finish all five. Sometimes it's there when they come to me with new events that happen after their Clearings and they tell me how they behaved differently from how they would have in the past.

In subtle ways, and sometimes in obvious ones, the changes unfold as you go. Do be a part of this. Decide to make your life even better. If you follow the steps, create your new endings, and remain consistent with your new thoughts, your focus will change, and so will your life.

#2: DO SEE AN ARGUMENT-FREE DESTINATION

Maybe a few of the people you're going to be speaking to are used to engaging you in arguments. Maybe they like to yell and scream or provoke in an attempt to get a similar reaction from you. Maybe in the past when you approached them you were shouted down, and instead getting to say what you wanted, you found yourself being attacked and listening to a list of all your faults and the things you've done wrong. You may think that you don't have a choice and that there is only one way to go in these situations, that conflict is inevitable and disaster a foregone conclusion, but the truth is, there are hundreds of ways to create your new endings and make them turn out the way you want.

When you feel that there is potential for conflict, your three communications are going to be the key to creating the outcome you're looking for. Each time you go through them, you're repeating specific thoughts and emotions and training your mind to associate them with your new endings. You're creating a natural tendency to move in that direction and respond in a way that will create similar thoughts and emotions when you go to take action. Instead of walking into arguments, you're helping yourself avoid them or get out of them quickly should emotions flare.

Spend extra time doing your three communications, your fear will diminish, and the quality of your interactions will increase. But no matter how well you prepare, there could still be a difference of opinion, and things could get heated during a confrontation. Are you going to yell and become angry? Will the person you're confronting get upset?

Maybe, and that's OK.

Recover and keep moving forward. If some of the people you speak to have a bad reaction to what you're saying, if they become argumentative or try to provoke you, the preparation you do with the steps will help to get you through and complete what you've come to do.

You can prevent arguments and still have success even if the person you speak to insists on attempting to engage you in one. If you commit to the process, you will be prepared, and you will continue the story in a way that will give you the feelings you want. If things get tense or a little uncomfortable, that's OK. Do what you came to do, be awesome, and leave knowing that you stuck it out and honored your commitment.

#3: DO CONFRONT AFTER A PERIOD OF SILENCE

A period of silence isn't as ominous or absolute as it sounds. It's simply taking a break from the normal way you communicate with someone so you can create an atmosphere that will increase your ability to arrive at the outcome you want.

If you are going to confront someone who you would normally speak to on a regular basis, there may be ways you are used to interacting with each other that could make your confrontation more difficult than it has to be. Sometimes the people around you get used to treating you like they do because you're always there to treat that way. Sometimes you get used to acting a certain way because your residual thoughts keep you from believing you can act any differently. By cutting back on your communications before your confrontation, you can interrupt that old dynamic and lessen the chance that the inertia of the past will interfere with what you have to do when it comes time to take action.

Chelsea: After Clearing my home I felt great, but I had some leftover thoughts when it came to my mother. I never considered the impact she was having on me and the way I felt before, but it turns out I was letting her influence my life and not in a positive way.

Recently, I met an incredible guy. Up to this point in my life, I hadn't had much luck with boyfriends, or even with friends, and I really wanted our relationship to last. I felt genuinely happy for the first time in my life, but my happiness always seemed to cause the opposite reaction in my mother. I remember that one day I had come home to a closet full of dresses my new boyfriend had bought me. Before I finished my Clearing, I used to speak to my mother on the phone a few times a week, so I called her to tell her how excited I was, and she told me she thought it was suspicious. "Why would he do something like that?" she asked. I remember another time she made a joke about him losing his hair, and once when I told her how happy I was, with fear in her voice she said, "Don't be too happy."

When I thought about the events in my past that made me feel bad, events with my mother popped up one after the other. I looked back at our life together, and it was always the same. Whenever I was excited about something—a new project I was starting, a compliment someone made on the work I did at my job—I would tell my mother, and she would slowly suck the joy right out of me. I remember feeling exhausted after these conversations, like I needed to lie down and take a nap. I could be happy all day, talk to my mother for ten minutes, and then feel bad for weeks.

I didn't want to think about these things anymore. I didn't want my mother's thoughts in my head. When something was making me happy, I didn't want to interrupt it to think, "Don't be too happy," and be suspicious. I wanted to get rid of all of that doubt and fear from my life. Looking at life the way she did and thinking about the things that she shared with me wasn't powerful—it was depressing.

There are things you assume in your life, and I think most of us assume that our parents want us to be happy. We picture them smiling and cheering for us when good things happen, but that wasn't what it was like with me and my mom.

I sat down and took a long look at our relationship and I saw that she had been doing this to me my entire life. As painful as it was to admit, I realized that my mother was not on my side. I think she didn't really want my life to get better because that meant her life would change. Maybe she thought that if I had a good relationship with someone else, she would lose me, and then she wouldn't have anyone to tell about all the things she thought were wrong with everything. My father had never been a thoughtful or affectionate type of a person, and the stories of my boyfriend and all the things he did to make me happy probably made her feel a little sad about her own life. Maybe she was jealous and didn't like feeling that way or admitting that that's what was going on.

Chelsea needed to forgive her mother for the way she had acted during certain events from her past and forgive herself for what she had been doing or not doing with her life since. We talked about this, and she agreed that it was a "nice" idea, but that she didn't really feel like she could call up her mom and say, "I forgive you for being a terrible parent and trying to make me and everyone around you feel bad." Chelsea needed to confront before she could forgive, but before she did either one, she decided she needed some space.

I asked Chelsea to close her eyes and, after she did, I said, "See yourself confronting now, and see it going great. Your mom is crying. She can't believe how wonderful you are, and she is overcome with feelings of gratitude."

At this point Chelsea was smiling and chuckling a little.

"Now imagine how you want it to be with your mom. See in your mind the relationship you want to have. Now imagine yourself confronting some of the other people from your life today. Just let them flash in your mind. If there aren't any, that's OK. See the future you being calm, cool, and confident. See your life the way you want it to be after you make the changes you want to make.

Experience these feelings in your body. Let yourself feel good. You've done it. You've made your life better. See yourself looking good. You're comfortable in your own skin, and you're enjoying the full command of your abilities. You're confident now, and it shows."

Then I said, "Now, what would the you that you see in your vision tell you to do to get these same feelings from confronting your mom?"

I waited, and then I saw Chelsea smiling. I asked her what she saw, and here's what she said:

Chelsea: I thought about confronting my mother this weekend because I have to drop something off. Then as you were speaking, this scene from a movie popped into my mind. It was a cop waving people away from an accident, and I realized that if I confronted my mother this weekend, it wasn't going to turn out well. I need more time to prepare, and we both need to be ready. I thought that instead of going over there this weekend, maybe we could both take a break from each other.

That's something I've never done, so it would definitely be different. Once I started thinking of doing that, that's when I could feel myself smiling, and that's when you asked me what I saw just now.

Chelsea decided to take a break from her mother. After a few months of almost no communication, she felt the time was right to confront her.

Chelsea: At first I thought I would feel guilty about separating myself from my mother. Before all of this, I never would have even considered it was possible. I can say now, without hesitation, that I didn't miss her once. I know that may sound horrible, but it's true. I don't miss the things I used to think about and all the frustration I used to feel. I thought I didn't have a choice. But I did have a choice.

My mother was wrong about so many things. My boyfriend's behavior wasn't suspicious; he's just a great guy. The good things that happened at work were just that, and it was OK to be happy. I didn't have to ruin the way I felt by always worrying about something bad coming around the corner. I think I just needed to separate from her for a while to really see what was happening. I think that made it easier for me to go through with my confrontation and to live the way I am now.

When I confronted my mother, it ended up being very different from what I first thought it would be. I'd never spent that much time without speaking to her before. I can't remember a week ever going by when I didn't talk to her at least once. When I went to her house, I could tell things were different. I think she figured that since I was away so long, she must have done something wrong, or else she was just curious. Whatever it was, I felt very much in charge, and she was ready to listen. I know it never would have gone the way it did if I hadn't spent that time away.

Not every case is like Chelsea's, but in situations where there is a pattern of interaction that isn't conducive to the conversation you want to have, or where there is a lot of raw emotion and frustration, a period of silence can create the calm you need. By interrupting your normal patterns, a period of silence not only tells the person you will be speaking to that something is different, it tells you that something is different, and it can put everyone involved in a more receptive mood for what is about to take place.

It's important to understand that a period of silence isn't about punishing people or giving someone the "silent treatment." It's not about hurting others, and you don't need to cut people off to have a successful Clearing. This is about taking the time you need to prepare for what you are about to do. With a period of silence, you are temporarily decreasing your interactions so you can have better ones in the future. How much they decrease is up to you. It isn't necessary to ignore someone completely or instantly cut them out of your life. You are redirecting your focus, and if some of your friends and family notice that you are suddenly a lot less available, go ahead and let them know that you have something going on that needs your attention.

Avoid unnecessarily hurting anyone's feelings. If a little reassurance is needed, go ahead and give it. Why not? You can say, "Don't worry, you're still my friend. I just need some time to think a few things through." Or "I have a few things I need to deal with. There's no need for concern. We'll talk soon." You could add, "Thanks for being so understanding."

How long your period of silence lasts is up to you. Make it the duration that is appropriate and not a moment longer. It could be a few days or a few months. You will need to reflect on the time that is necessary for this stage in your Clearing. You don't want to drag things out, but you still want to do what you need to do to create the best feelings possible with your new ending. Remember, everyone needs time to think and to be away from their usual influences at some point in their lives. Take the time you need to prepare, and then move on to your confrontation. What is most important is for you to complete your event chart, go through the steps, and to get to your new ending. You want your new life. You don't want to sit around distracted by these remnants of the past. So, whether there is a period of silence or not, move swiftly.

If you live with the people you will be confronting, a free afternoon or two to work on your steps and what you will say might be more appropriate than a period of silence. Whatever you decide, don't let pursuing a period of silence keep you from taking the actions you need to confront, apologize, and forgive. Avoid creating more problems with your preparations or holding on to residual thoughts longer than you have to. If a period of silence seems like too much of an issue and a potential source of friction for you, get to the task at hand. Complete your steps and create your new endings.

#4: DO ASK THE PEOPLE YOU ARE CONFRONTING FOR HELP

Asking the people you are confronting for help is a great way to start. Why not? It's true, you do need their help. You are creating a new ending, and, even if they are only listening, they are playing a role. Most people will want to help if you ask them, and if you use this approach instead of immediately launching into a list of what you think they did wrong, you will find you get a better reception, and those you speak to will be much more accommodating.

Nancy: I started most of my conversations with, "I need your help," and then saying why I needed it before proceeding to the apology or confrontation. I think that maybe this worked because the people I spoke to got to feel benevolent. Instead of sitting there and getting accused of a bunch of stuff and feeling like they had to defend themselves, which was normally how these things would go with the people I confronted, when I presented myself as someone in sincere need, and they were the ones who could help me, they got to feel like they were doing me a favor and helping me out.

You can say something like, "I'm doing this process that changes the way I think about things that happened in the past; can you help me with it? All you have to do is listen," or, "There's something that's been on my mind, and I'd really appreciate your help with it," or, "I have something important I want to talk to you about, and I need your help. Do you have a minute?" Or you could say something as simple as, "Can you help me out with something?" and then go right into the event you want to talk about.

Putting those you want to talk to in a more receptive state to listen is a smart move. Even if you are angry at the person you are confronting, you have a much better chance of arriving at the destination you envision if you start off going down the right road. This doesn't mean that in all cases there won't be any negative emotions brought to the surface by what you're saying. Mistakes were made during the events on your list, misunderstandings happened, and some of the old feelings that were created could come out when you continue the story.

Start off by asking for help. Go in a different direction right from the beginning. Smooth the path, get the other person on your side, and make it easier to say what you need to say.

#5: DO STICK TO YOUR APOLOGY NO MATTER WHAT THE REACTION

Many times the people you're speaking to may not have heard a true apology in years, and when they hear yours, you could see angry exteriors melting away, and before the last words even have a chance to come out of your mouth, you could find yourself being enthusiastically embraced by your new number one fan. Sometimes when you apologize, the reaction you get may not be what you had hoped for. Some of the people you speak to may still be upset with you even after you've owned up to the things you've done, and that's OK. If, while pouring your heart out and being incredibly wonderful, you find that the other person isn't taking it well, keep going, and then give them the time they need afterward to deal with their new feelings.

Always remember, your apology isn't about the other person's response; it's about revealing the truth of who you are. It's about using the parts of yourself that you didn't use during the original event and showing yourself that they are there and that you can use them whenever you want to.

Another scenario that may come up when you sincerely apologize is that people may be so grateful that they will do everything in their power to make you feel better about what you've done and rationalize your actions for you: "You didn't really have a choice," or, "I probably would have done the same things if I were in your shoes," or, "You were under a lot of pressure at that time," or, "I didn't really give you a chance to do anything different." If this happens, and the people you apologize to try to come to your rescue by tossing out excuses for you, stick to making your apology and taking responsibility. Complete your ending according to the person you are. Thank them. Tell them that they are being kind, but let them know that you are responsible for the things you do and that you are truly sorry.

Stay focused on what you have prepared and on doing your part no matter what the reaction is, and make sure you're saying the words and performing the actions that are in line with who you really are and not who your residual thoughts may have had you thinking you were in the past. If after some consideration, you feel certain aspects of your apology didn't represent the true you and that's why you didn't get the ending you wanted, create another one. Put in what you left out the first time, show yourself the kind of person you truly are, and you will create the ending you need to move on.

#6: DO PAY ATTENTION TO YOUR THOUGHTS, AND USE THE "IS WHAT I USED TO SAY" TECHNIQUE

Those who are experiencing success and happiness are doing so because they aren't being cut off from what they have inside themselves that can help them attain it. They aren't knocking themselves down with their words and their thoughts, and they aren't seeing themselves as powerless or lacking what is necessary to affect their surroundings the way they want to.

You are powerful, and with each new ending you create, you will see that this is true. Even if you don't believe it yet, why think of yourself any other way? Why work against yourself with thoughts that aren't true and that hurt you when it feels so much better to be on your side and help yourself out? Think about it for a second, and then ask yourself this: Do you feel like you have more access to your abilities when you're thinking, "You know something, I am truly awesome, and I can do this," or when you're thinking, "You know, I really suck, and this probably won't work out"? Did it inspire you to pursue your dreams when in the past you called yourself a "fathead" or told yourself, "I am such a stupid ass"? When you said these things, did it improve your life in any way?

That sentence you throw out to the world that seems like nothing, that seems like no big deal, is part of what keeps your life from changing. If you are saying a bunch of negative, limiting things about yourself, you are stopping your life from happening the way you want, and that doesn't have to happen.

When you cut yourself down in your mind, when you say that you're no good and that you can't, when you keep picturing yourself failing, it feels bad because you're telling yourself that you are someone you're not and because you're stopping yourself. The thing is, you aren't meant to be stopped. You are meant to use the potential that's inside of you. Unused potential creates bad feelings and causes bad behavior. It's like a two-year-old puppy that never gets to go for walks or run around outside, and you're the owner wondering why your sweet little buddy is chewing the legs off all the furniture.

During your Clearing and each day after, pay attention to your thoughts. Pay attention to the negative things you're saying in your mind and out loud about yourself and change them. The quickest way is to use the "is what I used to say" technique. When what you're saying goes negative, it will help you turn things around in seconds, even to the point where what you are saying ends up helping you in the end.

If you've been declaring what you're terrible at or what you think you'll never get right, using sentences that start with phrases like "I can't," or, "I'm no good at…," or, "That's not me," or, "I suck at…," or, "I'm not someone who…," or calling yourself names like "dummy," "loser," or "idiot," that's OK, just keep talking. Continue these sentences like you are continuing the story with your events. Give them endings that make you think and feel the way you want to about yourself by simply adding, "is what I used to say," followed by, "and now I say…" and then finish by saying the opposite of what you started out saying.

If, for example, you caught yourself saying, "I'm terrible at this," immediately continue with, "is what I used to say, and now I say, I'm good at this," or, "I'm getting better each time I do this." If you find yourself saying something like, "I'll just screw it up, this isn't going to happen," add, "is what I used to say, and now I say, I'm going to make this right. This is going to happen." Keep it simple, or add something fun on the end if you like, such as, "Soon there will be parades in my honor to celebrate this day," or, "It's almost like I'm some kind of superhero."

Begin to pay attention to what the people around you are saying and how often they cut themselves down, and you will begin to notice the times you do it yourself. When you do, immediately move to interrupt the destruction and bad feelings you're about to inflict on yourself. Use the "is what I used to say" technique to help you stave off any old identity negativity that may crop up during your Clearing. It's simple, and it works. I teach this technique to all my clients, and I use it myself. With it, you can stop the habit of voluntarily adding bad feelings to your life and turn the messages you're sending that are dragging you down into messages that are going to help you instead.

Do you really want to be the one telling everyone else how shitty everything is? Do you really want to waste your time telling yourself what you can't do when doing so doesn't help you in any way? Do you really want to be that person and to have tendencies like these be part of your identity? Employ the "is what I used to say" technique (even if it feels odd or silly), and give up your position as the town crier—in your own head or otherwise. Be who you are, and feel a whole lot better instead.

Stop thinking you're someone you're not and using your words to command yourself to be someone you don't want to be. Never say another negative thing about yourself from this day forward. Be strict with yourself. For your Clearing you need to be a hundred percent on your side and break the habit of using your thoughts against yourself. Take the steps you need to take to crush it, employ the "is what I used to say" technique, and have some fun while you leave it in the past.

#7: DO CONGRATULATE YOURSELF AND INDULGE IN YOUR GOOD FEELINGS

When you create a successful new ending and good feelings come around, instead of saying, "That's great," and then moving on right away, ride the wave as far as it can go. Indulge in these feelings and really experience the emotions you've achieved. Curl up in them as if they were a warm blanket and allow yourself to feel the power of what you can do. Whether your good feelings are from seeing the destination, the actions you take, or something that randomly comes along, relish them. That's right, I said "relish." Spread them on your life like your favorite condiment and add a little of their flavor to everything you do.

You will go where your focus leads you, so as you Clear the events on your list, focus on your good feelings. Instead of downplaying your accomplishments, congratulate yourself. Each time you create a new ending, say to yourself, "Good job, Ashley," or, "Dave, you did it. You are an excellent dude!" and really feel it. Instead of immediately going back to letting problems or negative thoughts cloud your brain, dwell on your good feelings. Confronting, apologizing, and forgiving may not be something you came skipping into town all excited to do, but you are doing it anyway, and by doing so you're stepping into the land of awesomeness. The feelings you achieve are yours. Do everything you can to make the most of them and keep them in your life.

Congratulate yourself when you Clear an event and for everything you do during the day. I don't care what it is. Tell yourself you did a great job brushing your teeth, or parallel parking, or handling an interaction with a coworker, or calling the cops on the naked guy you found passed out in your garden the other morning. It doesn't matter what it is you do. Begin making yourself aware of what you are doing right, not just with your Clearing but with everything, and then indulge in the good feelings you create when you do.

#8: DO CLEAR ADDITIONAL EVENTS

While you were doing your steps, maybe you remembered another event, one that has affected the direction of your life and has you seeing yourself in a negative way. Maybe an event came up when you were making your list but didn't make it into your top five, and you still feel it's important to address. If you've created your five new endings and Cleared your list, and you're having these thoughts about an additional event or two, go ahead and Clear them. Complete an event chart for each, settle on your communications, and get right to it.

Remember that the point of the Clearing isn't to spend all your time searching around your past for everything that went wrong in your life. You want to Clear your five events and then move on using what you've learned here to help you be happy and succeed each day. But if there are additional events from your past that keep coming up that you feel are important to Clear, then go for it. Clear the way for new memories and then get busy making them.

23

CLEARING YOUR RESIDUAL THOUGHTS: THE DON'TS

#1: DON'T DELAY CLEARING YOUR RESIDUAL THOUGHTS

You've got a big project at work. Midterms are coming up at school. Your son just joined the baseball team. You're remodeling the house. If you look for them, you will always find reasons for not Clearing your residual thoughts, and when it comes to the things you don't want to do, the timing will always be wrong. You have to realize that Clearing residual thoughts is about you being happy and doing everything in your life better. That means doing better on that project at work. Doing better on your midterms. Doing better at being a parent, and even creating a better remodel when it comes to your home.

It's always a good time to get rid of thoughts that are making you unhappy and your life much harder than it has to be, so don't delay. Take care of what you need to take care of to Clear your list. This is something that needs to be completed as soon as possible, and as soon as possible is right now. Don't plan on getting to it next summer or when you think you may have more time. This is your moment to take action.

Putting off Clearing your residual thoughts isn't like putting off cleaning out your refrigerator. This is much more important than some old vegetables and spilled juice, and it's going to have a much greater impact on your life. Once you've listed your five events and identified your residual thoughts, you know they are there and what they are doing. Continuing to live with them would give these thoughts an even more prominent position in your life, shifting your focus to the past, increasing the potential for more problems, and putting off what your life could be. These events need new endings, and your residual thoughts need to go now. Life moves quickly, and it's time to live yours as who you are meant to be instead of the person your residual thoughts have had you masquerading as.

#2: DON'T LET FEAR STOP YOU

Maybe when you were a kid you stuck your hand into the lit burner of a stovetop. You hurt yourself, and for some time after you were afraid, but you got some instructions, learned a few things, and moved forward. You didn't let fear stop you, and today you aren't afraid of the lit burner of a stove anymore. In fact you probably use it to create delicious food and to make yourself happy. You learned that it isn't necessary to be afraid and that if you follow instructions you can take something that once scared you and use it to enhance your life.

Don't let fear stop you from creating your new endings. Use what you're learning here to move forward and replace painful experiences with good ones. You may not realize it yet, but *the only thing your fear is protecting you from is feeling good.* If you are afraid of some of the things you have to do to confront, apologize, and forgive, get yourself accustomed to your destination and prepare with your three communications. The more you tell yourself where you want to go, the more you see yourself at the destination you want and as the kind of person who is successful, the more your surroundings tell you that this person is you, the greater your connection will be to the potential inside of you.

Your destination images are especially helpful in these situations because the emotions of success they inspire work to calm your fears. Repeating these communications is like continually flicking on the light in a dark room that you're convinced is filled with monsters. If you keep doing it, you will realize that those monsters were never really there, that they were just something you made up because of the thoughts and emotions your residual thoughts had you experiencing.

You are brave. Don't kid yourself. There are a lot of people who would never even consider attempting to do anything like what you've done so far with your Clearing. You can be brave and at the same time still be scared of some of the things you have to do. If you are, it's OK. We all have times when we feel this way, but being afraid doesn't stop everyone, and it doesn't have to stop you. If you follow the steps and repeat your communications, the light will stay on and you will gain confidence. You will move past your fear and on to the destination you've envisioned.

#3: DON'T ALLOW YOURSELF TO BELIEVE WHAT HAPPENED IS SOMEONE ELSE'S FAULT

If you are resisting taking action to Clear an event, you're probably sure that what happened was the other person's fault. But you must forget dishing out blame because that doesn't work. Blaming others only forces you to hold on to negative feelings much longer than you have to. I know it seems easier to think the problems you're having are because of what someone else did and that they're the ones who need to change and not you, and maybe they do, but when you think this way you take away your options and give the responsibility for how you feel to the person you're having a conflict with and how often does that work out? If you want to continue to feel bad and allow those feelings into the projects you have at work, the time you spend with your kids, or the things you do with your significant other, then blame those around you. If you want your power back and to have resolution and good feelings, don't waste your time going down that road.

Always remember that you want to get rid of your anger and resentment or any other negative feelings you have. You want to release yourself from their weight and distraction. Sure, other people screw up sometimes. They act as less than the people they are. They can be mean, vindictive, and awful. But focusing on what others have done isn't going to get you what you want.

If you're skeptical, pick one of your events where you want resolution, think about the things the other person did wrong for a few moments, really dwell on it, and then immediately try coming up with a solution. What you will discover is that all the solutions you arrive at in this frame of mind will produce much the same feelings and results as your original event. That's not what you are after with the Clearing.

Focus on the part you played in what happened, and reclaim your power. When you do, you will free yourself to take the actions necessary to let these feelings go and create the outcomes you're after.

#4: DON'T SKIP ANY PART OF THE PROCESS

If I have clients who are Clearing their residual thoughts and they aren't getting the results they want from a new ending, I ask them about the steps and the things they did to prepare. I'll say something like, "Tell me about the destination image you used in step 3," or, "What did you say to yourself for your three communications in step 4?" For those having trouble, I get responses like "Well, I didn't really have a destination image for this one," or, "I didn't think I needed to do that this time because…," or, "I decided doing all three communications wasn't really necessary for this event since I…" Whenever there were problems, it was because someone had gone off the path, stopped following the steps, and let the old identity call the shots.

Clearing your residual thoughts can be a bit of a battle with your old identity. You may be so used to what it's been telling you and how you've been seeing the world that excuses for skipping steps, doing things halfway, or dismissing parts of the process you don't like could seem perfectly reasonable to you. But let this be understood now: If you are not completing steps 1–6 for each of your events and step 7 after you've Cleared all five, you are falling prey to your old identity and dooming yourself to more of the same problems and a life that won't be much different from the one you're having now.

If you are not experiencing the feelings you want from a new ending, then take a look at the steps. Were there any you missed, did halfway, or decided to modify? Your old identity wants you to do things the way you are used to doing them because that's all it knows and what it's comfortable with. It wants to sit in the back seat, tell you how to drive, get you to take the wrong turns, and then blame the Clearing and say it doesn't work when you don't end up where you want to go.

If your old identity crashes your Clearing and starts blabbing about what isn't worth doing and what steps to skip, telling you that maybe you should take a break and get back to this at some later date, realize what is happening and be prepared to get tough. Take swift and decisive action in the other direction. Your choices are either listening to the old identity and repeating the problems it brings into your life or Clearing your residual thoughts and giving yourself this chance to be free. Knowing what you know now, which option do you really want to choose?

Decide before you even begin not to let anything stand in your way, especially not an old identity that isn't making you happy or helping you have what you want. This is your life! Instead of being tricked into skipping certain parts of the Clearing by an identity that's trying to sabotage you, put everything you have into doing your absolute best with each step. Honor your commitment, and experience the rewards of revealing your true nature when you do.

#5: DON'T RELY ON THE OTHER PERSON'S RESPONSE TO FEEL GOOD

What's important isn't the other person's response. What's important is that you reveal the truth about who you are to yourself with the actions you take and the words you say to create your new endings. Give the people you speak to the time they need to let the emotions of the moment dissipate and to see the truth for themselves. The ending you've envisioned and the emotions you want may come at a more gradual pace than you've anticipated, so accept this possibility. Remember, *you don't need to talk anyone into seeing your side of things*, and your three communications aren't a failure if you don't end up getting the response you wanted. Your three communications are designed to help you take the actions and say the words that will reveal the truth about you, not about the other person. If what you say has a positive effect right from the start, that's wonderful. If it doesn't, that's OK too. While those you've spoken with figure things out, get busy with your own life and your plans.

Will your new endings be like the ones you envisioned when you practiced seeing the destination? Sometimes they end up being exactly like them. Other times the responses you get when you confront, apologize, and forgive turn out to be quite different from what you were expecting. You may picture a big hug and get a smile instead. You may envision a wonderful ending full of laughter and joy, only to get yelled at and told what an ass you are. The people you speak to are choosing between acceptance or denial. They could quickly see themselves in your words and accept the truth, or what you've said may go so strongly against the way their residual thoughts have them seeing themselves that the truth could end up becoming a part of their lives at a much slower pace.

No matter what happens, stick to moving toward your destination and finish saying what you've come to say. As you create your endings and Clear your residual thoughts, don't allow the emotions of the moment to take you off course, and don't rely on the other person's response to feel good. Rely only on what you can control by focusing on what you are doing and on your own reactions, and create your good feelings with what you do.

#6: DON'T MAKE YOUR GOAL CONVINCING OTHERS THEY ARE WRONG

If you're holding out on feeling good until the people you talk to admit they are wrong, you could find yourself waiting a long time. Why wait? Why live with bad feelings when you don't have to? If your goal is to make sure that other people are contrite and embracing their wrongness, or if you become distracted by the sudden appeal of setting someone straight during your interaction, you could end up feeling frustrated and angry and creating additional residual thoughts to feel bad about. If you make your goal saying what you need to say so you can move on and revealing the person you wrote about in your event charts under *The Truth*, you will create much better endings.

Your Clearing is about you. Why risk your feelings by focusing on influencing someone else's? When you take action to create your new endings, forget presenting your case and going for a conviction. That's not what's important. Instead of criticizing, talk about how what happened made you feel. Instead of using the words that your residual thoughts would have you use and saying them in the way your old identity would have you say them, say what you've prepared in a way that the real you would. Put your best into your words and actions, and you will have what you want instead of what your residual thoughts would usually have you stuck with in the end.

24

Q&A

1. I don't think I have any events I need to Clear. Am I doing this right, or am I missing something?

Everyone has leftover negative feelings that they need to let go of from past events. Everyone has been hurt or has hurt someone else and carries residual thoughts because of it. Maybe you lied or in some way hid the truth. Maybe you feel guilty about something you did. Maybe someone did something to you during a situation where you didn't have much control and your only choice at the time was to survive and carry the pain. You've made mistakes dealing with other people, and other people have made mistakes dealing with you. It's called being alive.

If you aren't feeling powerful, if things aren't going the way you want them to, if you are dissatisfied with what you've been able to accomplish up to this point in your life, if you're overweight and struggling without success to do something about it, or if you've simply been drawn to this book, there are events you need to Clear and feel different about, and you need to confront, apologize, forgive, and maybe even take a few Second Actions to do it.

Think of the things you do that have been getting you in trouble. Recall any recent situations that went wrong or any problems that have been repeating in your life. Think of how you felt, and then ask yourself if there is another time in your past when you remember feeling this way. Take what memories come to you and get started.

This is your chance to be honest with yourself, to find the moments that have been affecting your life in negative ways, give them new endings, and change the thoughts and feelings that come from them.

2. I've Cleared my possessions, and now I just want to move on with my life. Do I really need to Clear residual thoughts too?

I want you to experience what those who have completed their Clearings have experienced. I want you to be happy, consistently happy, with the old ideas of who you were, the ones that used to come in and ruin your good feelings, gone forever. I want you experience life without any events from your past coming along to slow you down. This is why I want you to Clear your residual thoughts.

Doing the Clearing is a two-part deal. If you stop now, you risk sliding backwards and undoing your good work; you risk letting your residual thoughts dictate your life and having more bad memories attached to the things around you. When you step up, when you do what needs to be done to relieve yourself of residual thoughts, when you have that difficult conversation you've been putting off, when you apologize to a friend or forgive someone, you show yourself what you are capable of. You show yourself that you can do the hard thing, and the benefits come through in all areas of your life.

Sure, there will be moments when you are uncomfortable, but when have you ever done something new and different and not felt that way? What if you had let that stop you from things like learning to drive or asking someone to the school dance? What if you had let that stop you from going off to college or moving to someplace new?

As with many of the other wonderful things in life, there may be times when doing what you need to do to Clear your residual thoughts could be a little awkward, and just like when you faced these challenges in the past, working your way through these moments can result in some wonderful benefits. Many times, doing only what is comfortable leads to feeling uncomfortable and will have you hanging on to problems much longer than you have to. Look at your life, examine the times you took the easy way, and understand the truth: *Doing only what seems easy makes things harder in the long run.*

When you hold on to residual thoughts, the bad feelings they create don't go away. They are there in the similar situations you find yourself in today. They are the raw nerve, the overreaction, the bruise that never heals. You can medicate yourself, drink too much, overeat, have affairs, avoid going home by staying late at the office night after night, lie, steal, run away, act passive-aggressively, or give up, but none of these things works. None of them will give you the feelings you really want.

Religion, philosophy, traveling the world looking for answers — it doesn't matter what you try. In the end, to move on with your life and be happy, it will always come down to using your three communications and confronting, apologizing, and forgiving.

Do what you may believe is the hard thing. Do the uncomfortable thing. Out of all the choices you have, you will find that, in the long run, Clearing your residual thoughts is without a doubt the easiest. You are almost there. What you have now from Clearing your home is wonderful, but it can't compare to what you will have when you take this final step and Clear your residual thoughts.

3. **Can I bring someone with me as backup support when I confront, apologize, or forgive?**

If you bring someone along, the people you speak to could feel like they are being ganged up on, and that might cause them to become defensive. Besides, you aren't always going to have someone with you as you go through life, and confronting, apologizing, and forgiving are things you will continually have to do. One of the biggest benefits of Clearing your residual thoughts is showing yourself that you are strong and capable and that you can do these things on your own. Forget about pausing to listen to your old identity tell you differently. Repeat the steps, and really focus when it comes time to do your three communications; your confidence will grow, and you will find that you are perfectly capable of confronting, apologizing, and forgiving on your own.

4. **Should I talk to my family members separately or together?**

There are advantages to both. You have to look at your family dynamic. Are your parents even-tempered people? Will they listen objectively when you speak to them, or are they more likely to come to each other's defense and join together for an attack on you? Is your sister's husband going to give you the space you need when you go to apologize to her, or will he interrupt and add his own thoughts into the mix? Are you going to be able to confront your brother if your mother is hovering in the background? You have to make a judgment.

Create a situation where you can say what you need to say. If you confront a friend or relative around others, some of those present may feel like they need to come to the rescue of the person you're addressing. You could also find yourself in a situation where the people you are speaking to may not feel as though they can be completely honest in front of the others present. Some could hear your conversation and see an opportunity to make their opinions heard or to air their own resentments, and you could find your new ending quickly being derailed. The truth is that you don't always know what kind of residual thoughts the people around you have.

You have both options. If you are still unsure after thinking about it, picture the successful destination for the event in your mind, and see who is there. If this doesn't give you the answer you're looking for, you can also create a visualization where you're speaking to your family as a group and another one where you're speaking to them separately, and ask yourself which will most likely give you the thoughts and feelings you want. Once you have your answer, make it a part of your three communications and pursue your new ending.

5. **I have to be truthful: I have a very busy life, and I'm not sure I'm going to have the time to go through my three communications or even remember to do them. I guess I should just do what I can, right?**

How well have things turned out for you those times when, instead of doing things all the way, you just did what you could? Is that how you've been able to create success in the past? Think of how much time you spend being unhappy or dealing with mistakes you've made. Think of how much time you spend thinking about what you did wrong or fearing it will happen again or being upset when things don't go the way you want them to. The time it takes to repeat these patterns of the past and suffer their consequences is much greater than the time it would take to Clear your residual thoughts. It can't compare.

When you find yourself thinking you don't have time for this, realize it's your residual thoughts talking. It's fear and powerlessness knee-jerking their way in there to try to keep you from doing anything that could change what's going on in your life. Sure, it could appear easier to believe your old identity than to actually do this, but you've come too far now to let this voice start calling the shots again. Why give the mugger back his gun after you've wrestled it away and then be upset when you end up with a bullet in your back? Instead of slowing down, or stepping back into your old life and giving up your power, move on, really do your communications, and put everything you have into making this turn out the way you want. It feels good to see inspiring things. It feels good to see yourself being successful and reaching your destination. It feels good to tell yourself you can, and it's very satisfying to use new communications to get what you want instead of using old ones and getting what you don't all over again.

Lie in bed before you start your day. Turn on your light. Look at your picture, close your eyes, see the destination for whatever event or situation you are working on, and then recite your sentence or sentences. Do the same thing at night after you've brushed your teeth and you are ready to go to sleep. All that's left is one more time during the day. Your old identity may make it seem like doing things like your three communications will take you a long time, but it will probably only take a minute or two to go through them. Believing you don't have time for this simply isn't true.

Don't let your old identity talk you out of the good things that could be in your life by telling you that you don't have time or that you are beyond this, that you don't need to do your three communication, or that you can create your new endings your own way. If you are going to do this, then really do this. You can believe you don't have time and be unhappy, or you can embrace the truth, connect with your powerful feelings, and have plenty of time to lose weight, fall in love, make more money, and be happy.

6. I don't think I can visualize. How am I going to be able to do this?

Memories are constantly flowing in and out of your focus. You see images in your mind all the time. If you have a date, for instance, you picture what you will wear. You envision yourself going out to dinner and talking. You create images of what could happen. If you have an important meeting at work, you imagine who will be there. You see yourself asking questions and the way your coworkers may react. If it's your week with the kids, you may picture the different dinners you need to prepare, the places you will drive to, and maybe a few images from movie trailers you've seen recently to help you decide what to do for entertainment. All through the day, and each night when you dream, whether you are paying attention or not, you are visualizing.

When I say, "Picture a red ball or your child's smiling face," or I mention your wedding photos, you get some sense of these things in your mind. This is visualization. Look around the room you are in right now. Maybe there's a table with books stacked on top or a chair with your jacket draped over it or a painting on the wall. Pick something out, look at it, then close your eyes and see if you can still picture it. Pick something with a lot of bright color and do it again. What you see doesn't have to be perfect and include every single detail as if you were watching a movie. No matter what level of detail, when you see images in your mind, it's visualization.

You can do this. You are good at visualizing—better than you thought you were. You are an expert. You've been doing this your whole life to get the things you have now, even the things that you don't want. Don't be fooled into believing otherwise. You control the images you see in your mind, and you can replace the old ones that got you the things you don't want with images of what you do want, and move in a different direction. This is the car you've been driving all along, and you know how to work the controls. Take the wheel, turn it toward your new destination by changing the images you see, then put your foot on the gas, and go.

7. Do I really need to write down what I want to say and practice saying it out loud before I confront, apologize, and forgive?

Have you ever rolled around an idea in your head that you thought was good, and then when you said it out loud you realized how ridiculous it was or how far off you were? That's because the idea only existed in your interior world. When you take it outside of your body your other senses can process it. There's more light and more surfaces to reflect off of, giving you a broader perspective and making it easier for you to see the truth. This is why doing things like writing down what you will say and then practicing saying what you've written out loud a few times before you take action is so important to your success.

Becoming good at confronting, apologizing, and forgiving is like developing any skill. Whether it's ballroom dancing or playing the guitar or mastering a software program, you repeat new actions, and in time they become something natural for you to do. With practice, you're spinning across the dance floor, playing your favorite songs, and impressing everyone at the office with your new Photoshop skills. You're using different parts of your brain and getting different results from those you had before.

It's the same with the steps. You learn new actions, you repeat them, and before you know it, you're using your skills to create the endings you want. Once you've had enough practice, you will be able to complete an event chart in minutes and then eventually without having to write anything down at all.

The more you do this, the closer you move to the point where you will be so aware of who you are and what you can do that, even during conflicts and upsetting situations, when the threat of acquiring residual thoughts arises, you will apply what you've learned in the moment.

For now, complete your event charts and write out what you want to say for each of your five events. Spend some time focusing on making sure that what you've written says what you want it to say and represents the truth of who you are. Say it out loud. Send it out of your mouth and into the air and ask yourself if these words will create the ending you want. If the answer is yes, you are ready to move on to the next step.

8. **If I have a bunch of similar events, which one do I create the new ending for? Should I go with the earliest one?**

When I started doing the Clearing with my clients, I thought that if there were more than one related event, creating a new ending for what had happened first would be the best option. As things progressed, I discovered that choosing the earliest event wasn't as important as choosing the event that comes to you the strongest. While the first event started the ball rolling, creating a new ending for an event that came after can sometimes offer a greater opportunity to reveal the truth of who you are.

To choose which event to create your new ending for, go ahead now and think of your similar events. Just close your eyes and think about each event one after the other, and take notice of your emotions as you do. When you've gone through all of them, ask yourself, "Which one of these events is standing out over the others?" and then see what comes to you. In most cases your mind will quickly give you the answer. It may be with an image or a sudden idea. If you are still unsure, you can ask yourself, "Out of all these events, which event do I least want to deal with?"

It isn't important to struggle with this. Let your mind show you what it wants to, and accept what comes to you when it does. Your subconscious knows your residual thoughts don't belong, and it knows which events they come from. Talk to yourself, give yourself a chance to realize the truth, and you will find the answers you're looking for.

9. I feel bad confronting. I don't want to hurt anyone. What should I do?

No matter what the reaction is from the people you speak to, if you say what you need to say, you will change the story and free yourself from your residual thoughts. The people you confront will have the opportunity to see themselves and to grow, an opportunity you'd be denying them if you decided to do nothing.

Don't let old habits win or let the past ruin the things you want to do today. Refuse to simply go through the motions of your life. Take action to feel different. Be understanding when you confront because it's powerful, but keep in mind that understanding stops being powerful when you turn away from saying what needs to be said, whether it is pleasant to say or not. Be kind to those you speak to while remembering that being kind doesn't mean acting like some kind of meek creature scurrying about for scraps. If you bow down and let someone step all over you or hold back on the things you truly want to say, you aren't protecting your power — you're decreasing it, and the person you end up hurting the most is you.

Any momentary pain, embarrassment, or humiliation you believe you might feel when you confront someone cannot compare to the waste of your talents and abilities that will occur if you do nothing and continue to maintain these thoughts and feelings in your life. Some of the people you speak to may be hurt by what you say, but not as hurt as they would be in other ways if things were left unsaid. The truth is no one wants to be confronted. No one ends up saying things like, "Boy, I really enjoyed that confrontation," and that's OK. The results that come afterward are where the benefits can be found. Sometimes you have to take a few challenging steps to get there, but it's always worth the effort when you do.

10. What's the best way to end my conversations with the people I'm confronting and apologizing to?

Simply saying, "Thank you for listening," works great. Regardless of what has occurred, the people you speak to are helping you out by listening. Saying thank you is an excellent choice; it's polite, it gives your interaction a verbal ending, and it provides an opportunity for you to make an exit or move on to something else. If you are thinking that saying thank you in this situation could come across as weak or subservient, it isn't so. Said with confidence or simply in a normal tone of voice, "Thank you for listening," can be an excellent way to end your interaction smoothly and potentially increase the good thoughts and feelings you create in the process.

11. What if someone I'm confronting, apologizing to, or forgiving from my past wants to re-establish our relationship and I'm not sure that's something I want to do?

When Clearing residual thoughts, make every effort to get in and out gracefully. Do what needs to be done, say what needs to be said, and then move on. This isn't about re-establishing old relationships; it's about feeling powerful and moving forward. Ask yourself if the relationship will allow you to do these two things. If it doesn't, be prepared to move briskly toward what does.

Maybe someone you were involved with romantically feels so good after your talk that he or she suggests getting together sometime and you know that isn't a great idea. You could say something like, "We've had our time together, and I think you are a good person, but now it's time to move on. I know you will have a great life. I wish you the best." You could say, "I'm glad we had a chance to talk like this, and now it's time for us both to move on. I feel better than I did, and I believe you do too. Let's leave it like this and continue with our lives."

Whether it's an old romantic relationship, a friendship, or someone in your family, keep it simple. Be direct, honest, and sincere. See the destination to put you in touch with the parts of yourself that will help you find the words that work the best and practice what you will say to move forward gracefully before you make contact.

If you speak to people from your past and they suggest re-establishing relationships by reconnecting through social media, and you're thinking, "That sounds like a truly powerful idea that will enrich and improve my life," then go for it. If that isn't the way you feel, then don't fall into the trap of holding on to bad feelings in this way. When you decline someone's invitation or when you remove certain people from your contacts, you are protecting your new life. Instead of giving your power away, you're using it to help yourself, and this is what you are supposed to do. Ask yourself where you really want to put your time and your focus: with someone you've let go of from the past or with the people in your life now and those you will meet in the future? Your old identity may come up with excuses for why you should stay connected, "at least online," like maybe they're a good business contact, or you want to keep your numbers of friends and connections high, or you want them to stick around so they can be jealous of your amazing life, or because you don't want to hurt their feelings. But all that matters is whether keeping them in your life makes you feel powerful. Why trap yourself into having to think about someone you would rather not be reminded of? If you've determined a relationship isn't powerful, it isn't powerful, online or otherwise.

Why dance around the rim of a volcano if you know you are going to get burned? Take the steps necessary to make a clean break. Then put some more attractive options in your focus, and begin to pursue them.

12. To Clear one of my residual thoughts, I have to tell my friend something that may affect her marriage. Should I still do it?

You are out to dinner with your husband. You are having a wonderful time. Before the last course you decide to go to the restroom. On your way you spot your best friend's husband out with another woman. No big deal, right? After all, she could be a relative or it could be a business dinner. Wrong. Before you can continue on your way, he leans in toward her and kisses her passionately on the lips. You are too shocked to move and end up standing there, staring at them from across the room with your mouth open.

As he pulls away, he looks up and notices you. He recognizes you, and a look of guilt flashes across his face. You regain your composure and continue on to the bathroom. You look in the mirror, feeling sick and confused. After you wash your hands and take a deep breath, you head out the door to return your table. Before you can take more than two steps, your friend's husband is there. He wants to talk. He makes excuses. He tries to explain. He says the affair is over and that if his wife, your best friend, finds out what's been going on, she will be devastated and the marriage won't survive. He pleads. He promises. He requests that you give him a chance to make it right. You walk back to your table stunned and with the weight of the world on your shoulders.

Are you feeling powerful? No way. A minute earlier, you were laughing and having a good time. Now you feel like someone has kicked you in the stomach. Time goes by: one month and then another. The bad feeling grows. Each time you see your friend, you are reminded of what you saw and that you are keeping it from her. You are angry. It's unfair. This shouldn't have anything to do with you, but now it does. You try to rationalize the situation by telling yourself that your best friend and her husband will work things out and that what goes on between them is none of your business. But you are stuck with these terrible thoughts, and they are putting a damper on all the good feelings you usually have. You used to think about fun things: what you get to do throughout the day, your kids, and plans with friends. Now your thoughts are of cheating, affairs, secrets, betrayal, and lies, and it's affecting you and those around you.

What will make you feel powerful? Will you feel powerful knowing that telling your friend what you saw was the impetus for the demise of her marriage? Maybe she will be depressed and lonely after she hears what you have to say, or maybe she will end up leaving her husband, meeting the person of her dreams, and being blissfully happy because of what you've done.

Several more months go by and you find yourself avoiding your best friend and doing without the closeness and good feelings your relationship brings to your life. You have residual thoughts about yourself now from keeping this secret. You can leave things as they are, or you can continue the story in a way that will allow you to remove these thoughts and emotions, replace them with new ones, and get on with your life.

What's really important in this scenario is the way you feel. One thing is for sure: Keeping something ugly like this inside and leaving the story as it is isn't going to create the feelings you want in your life. It isn't going to help you be patient with your kids or talk to your husband at the end of the day. It isn't going to help you deal with the people you meet or have to work with at your job. It isn't going to help you be happy.

Maybe there's a different route to consider, one where you make yourself feel powerful and get the ending you want while creating the least harm possible. Focus on your event chart and your three communications and you will access the talents and abilities you need to create the best possible outcome. Let go of your fear. Allow yourself to do things differently, to think differently, and the answers will come.

As you move through your list and begin Clearing residual thoughts, some ethical dilemmas might surface. No matter what situations arise, follow the Seven Steps and take action. If an event needs a new ending, then it needs a new ending. Do it in a way that causes the least harm possible and that allows you to let go of your residual thoughts. The steps will help you to arrive at the best course of action and, when the time comes, to do what needs to be done. They will help you get these thoughts and emotions out of your body, continue the story, and create a new ending that reveals the truth about who you are.

13. **I'm really angry at the person I want to confront. How can I avoid this getting the best of me and making a mess out of my new ending?**

Sure, you're angry. I completely understand. This person did something to steal your power, and it worked. You ended up thinking about what happened. You focused on things like what the other person did and what you wish you had done. You took these thoughts and the feelings they created in you, you added them into what you were doing in your life, and the things you did suffered because of it.

You don't want to feel worse when you create a new ending. You want to feel better. You want to feel powerful. You want to take away thoughts that will show you the truth of who you are and help you with your life. You don't want an ending that will have you feeling a similar way or creating more residual thoughts that limit you. You want to feel different and to come out of this on top.

If you know you have anger and think that it might get in the way, use Option #2 and have what you want to say written down and with you so you can read it to the person you're confronting. Reading a letter will help you feel more in control and stay on track. It also has the added bonus of making it less likely that you'll be interrupted. When you have something with you to read, there's a start and a finish, and even if your emotions get raised in the moment, it's easier to get through to the end. Once you've written your letter, practice reading it out loud, then practice some more. The better you know your material, the more used to it all the different parts inside you will become, and the more comfortable you will be saying what you need to say to create the ending you want.

Along with your letter, nothing will help you deal with anger like your three communications. Right now, if you are angry and thinking about your new ending, you're probably imagining things going wrong and telling yourself it isn't going to work out. You may be picturing similar events from your past that ended terribly and saturating yourself with bad feelings. Instead of sending yourself messages that you want more anger and failure, tell yourself that you want to create a new ending that makes you feel good and where things work out. Replace the old messages, then prepare what you will say and practice. The successful ending will feel right to you, and you will move toward having it.

If you follow the Seven Steps, you can get past any roadblocks your old identity has set up for you and decrease the role negative emotions play in your confrontation. You don't have to let anger ruin your new endings. There are more choices and tremendous power inside you. Allow the steps to direct the flow of that power toward the destination you want, and you will find yourself reaching it.

14. **I want to confront my father, but for as long as I've known him he has never admitted he's ever done anything wrong. If he does this again after I confront him this time, do I still need to forgive him?**

Maybe the people you need to forgive have never owned up to doing anything wrong in the past. Maybe now you think they would be getting away with something if you did forgive them. But they're not getting away with anything. By not admitting they're wrong, they're carrying around residual thoughts from what happened, and those thoughts are affecting everything they do. It's happening to them the same way it's happening to you.

Understand that you don't have to receive an apology or be asked for forgiveness to forgive. Some of the people you approach may not be at a point in their lives where they are ready to take that step, and it's not your responsibility to get them to take it. Forgiving isn't something you do for other people anyway; it's something you do for yourself. It isn't about those around you admitting they're wrong; it's about you feeling good and not having to think about the things that are bothering you anymore. It's about you living without the negative influence of your residual thoughts in your life.

Take actions that define the type of person you are instead of actions that reflect a focus on someone else's shortcomings. Confront, if that's what needs to take place, and then, regardless of the response you get, forgive. If you say what you want to say during your confrontation, you will find the old thoughts going away. You won't care so much about what happened because there will be a new and much better ending to occupy your mind, one where you were strong, stood up for yourself, and said some things that may not have been particularly easy to say. You will find that you've let go, and in letting go you've forgiven.

Think of all the people you know who are good at admitting when they've done something wrong or hurt someone else. Is anyone coming to mind? Most of us aren't particularly fond of taking responsibility for causing others pain or playing a role in things turning out poorly. Some people can't stand the thought of it and will immediately launch an attack or become defensive no matter what approach you use. Some may behave this way because they think it would make them look weak to admit when they are wrong and that it somehow gives others an advantage over them if they do. What is the truth? Not admitting when you are wrong is the love destroyer. It sows the seeds of resentment, and what ends up growing are bad relationships, disappointments, and frustrations.

Forgive because you are compassionate and strong. Forgive because you are worth too much to waste another second of your life holding on to thoughts and feelings that have you believing you are less than you are. Forgive because of what it does for you. No matter how the other person responds, forgive and take the influence of the thoughts you associate with this person and these events from your life and replace them with ones that display the truth of who you are.

Whatever the situation, say what you need to say. Be concise and to the point. Confront, forgive, and if the relationship isn't powerful, move on. What the people you've confronted do after you speak to them is up to them. If they choose to continue feeling bad and avoid admitting to any wrongdoing, forgive them for falling short and not being able to do what you can, and then go in a different direction. Take a Second Action, create a better ending, and make this event an even greater source of good feelings.

15. I want to apologize, but I'm afraid that a few of the people I want to apologize to are still too upset. What do I do if they have a bad reaction or don't want to talk to me in the first place?

Take a moment to think about it. The last few times you approached these people, were you expecting the worst? Were you telling yourself it wouldn't work out and rehearsing your own failure in your mind? Maybe you envisioned them getting upset or lashing out at you in some way. Maybe you never got that far because your residual thoughts stopped you from even considering doing anything at all. Maybe you said to yourself, "There's just no way this will work," and this became the internal command—don't make this work—and the parts of you that could have created your success did as you requested and remained unused.

When you engage your negative emotions and then say to yourself, "Now come up with something that will help me succeed and make me feel good," you're probably not going to get what you are looking for. Your negative emotions block you from the really good answers, so give yourself an advantage right from the start. Engage your joy, self-confidence, generosity, and ingenuity. Open yourself up to these things instead of your fear. It's OK to be afraid, but it's not OK to run back and do things the same old way that doesn't work or to ignore what needs to be done because of your fear. Give yourself the advantage. Use your good feelings to determine the actions you will take and then take them.

16. I feel like a baby and a little embarrassed for being upset about the things I'm upset about, and I'm worried that the people I need to speak with will probably feel the same way about me and might get mad. Is this really going to help? What should I do?

If you don't confront because you are afraid of the reaction you will get or you're worried that you will look foolish, you are making excuses and letting your residual thoughts run the show. You may think you have really good reasons for not saying anything and for keeping your bad feelings and unresolved thoughts inside, but they're not good reasons. They never are. Using what you think may be the other person's potential reaction as an excuse for not taking action is giving away your power, and giving away your power is lame.

No matter how scared you are or how embarrassing you believe what you have to say is, no matter what reactions you've gotten in the past, what's inside of you needs to come out. If it doesn't, you're setting yourself up for more problems. *Holding these thoughts and feelings inside doesn't work because they never stay inside.* They come out in ways that can make you feel confused and cause others to question your sanity. Remember my client who blew up at her brother-in-law because of the Harry Potter joke he told at her birthday party? She was really mad about his inappropriate behavior from years earlier, but no one else at the table knew that (and at first, neither did she). They just thought she had serious anger issues.

Your feelings have to come out. Let them come out in a way that is direct and honest and save everyone, especially yourself, from the confusion and frustration that happens when you attempt to bury them and blame someone else for why you are keeping them inside. Confront, apologize, and forgive no matter who the people you're going to speak with are or what they're like.

This isn't about being a baby or not being a baby or what anyone thinks. This is about you Clearing your events and you determining the course of your life. If someone is mad or thinks less of you when you do this, so be it. Follow the steps and take action, and then none of that will matter because, instead of living with the lingering pain and the negative emotions you'd be left with if you did nothing, you'll be busy enjoying your life and living as the person you truly are.

17. **How can I confront my spouse? Things haven't been going well lately. Every time we talk, we just end up fighting. I'm just afraid that nothing I say is going to be right. I don't see how this is going to work out.**

That's really the key right there. You have to see things working out to help them work out. You have to use your communication system to tell yourself what you want.

Maybe for one of your events you have to confront your husband, and maybe in the past when you did something like this you approached him when you were angry. Maybe instead of getting the feelings you wanted, you ended up yelling and saying something like: "You never do anything nice for me anymore, but I always seem to be doing things for you. Why do you have to be such an ass all the time? I wish you were more like you were when we first met. Now you are just a selfish turd!"

This time, avoid allowing your confrontation to be directed by your anger or fear by following the steps and using your three communications. If you access different parts of yourself from the ones you've become used to accessing in these situations, that same confrontation can turn out something like, "Remember when we first got married and you used to fill up my car with gas? That really made me feel special. Whenever I would get in my car and see that the tank was full, I'd be reminded of what a great person you are, and I'd think about how much I love you. You do such a great job for our family. I know you get busy, and that's why a part of me feels like I shouldn't even be asking, but I would really love it if you did that again, and maybe there's something you like that I could do for you."

You don't have to come up with what to do and say on your own, because you have the steps. Instead of using your anger or some other negative emotion to decide what to say, the steps will help inspire emotions that will allow you to create different outcomes and get the most you can from your Clearing. With good feelings in your body from seeing the destination, you will find your generosity and understanding, your empathy, your kindness and cleverness (Yes, you are kind and clever!) coming through in the words you use, and instead of the old things you used to say that didn't work, compliments and comments about the things you appreciate will start coming to you.

Maybe, for example, Clearing one of your events involves confronting your wife. Maybe she'd been complaining about your going out with your friends, and it built up to the point where one day when she approached you about it you blew up at her and said, "Get off my back! Why do you have to be such a clingy bitch? I'll do what I want, and not you or anyone else is going to stop me."

As a result, the sex dried up, the laughter stopped, and the good feelings went out the window. You ended up resenting each other, and things got worse. Maybe you started to become short with your children or the people at work. Maybe you stopped caring about how you looked or what your wife thought, and you put on some weight. Maybe you started having more fights and going out more often, even though you would much rather stay home and have things the way they were. Now you want to Clear this event from your list. To create the ending you're after, see the destination, follow the steps, and then your confrontation could sound something like this: "Remember when we were dating and you were so cool about my going out with my friends? Now that we're married, I'd like to be able to go out with them without upsetting you. I don't want you to feel bad. I want you to know that I love you and that I still love you when I'm with my friends. In fact, I love you more because, when I hear about how everyone else has it, I'm reminded of how good things are for you and me. I honestly feel that no one compares to you, but not having a chance to hang out with my friends like I used to without feeling guilty or like I'm somehow hurting you takes away those feelings and hurts us. I want to be the man you fell in love with, not the man you think you want me to be when you tell me you don't want me to go out. Having fun with my friends doesn't take away from all the fun I have with you. I love you, and all I want you to do is think about this. Let's go out to dinner this Friday, just me and you. I was thinking you deserve a night out for all the hard work you've been doing.

I know this sounds almost too wonderful, and life would truly be grand if you could always confront without anger or frustration getting the best of you. The point is that you can. Use the steps, get your good emotions going, show yourself where you truly want to go, tell yourself you can get there, and you will see.

18. I feel funny apologizing to my kid. It seems like every part of me is rejecting this idea. It just isn't how I was raised. How can I do this? Is there another way?

What do you want to teach your children? What skills do you want them to have to help them with their lives? Do you want your kids to have the experience necessary to confront, apologize, and forgive as soon as the need arises? Do you want them to be able to quickly take action toward resolution and avoid carrying bad thoughts? The effect of creating new endings and releasing residual thoughts doesn't exclude your children. Children learn from watching their parents, and if you never apologize, you're not only depriving yourself of a great relationship with your kids, you're depriving them of valuable skills they could be learning from you.

Maybe you're thinking, "If I admit when I do something wrong, I'll lose all credibility, and they'll never listen to me again." But the truth is that your kids know when you've screwed up, and by not apologizing you're missing an opportunity to get your credibility back and teach your children how to do the same should they find themselves in similar circumstances. Maybe a part of you is thinking, "I'm the parent. That makes me right." There can be some frustrating moments when raising children, but if that is your attitude, what has it really gotten you? When you were a child, did it make you happy when, instead of teaching you some skills that could help you handle situations where you were frustrated, your parents did nothing or took actions that ended up hurting you, and then told you it was tough and that's the way the world is, so live with it?

Teaching your children that someone's position automatically makes them right will set them up for a lot of unnecessary hardships and bad feelings in the future. If you teach them to confront, apologize, and forgive, then when they are out on their own they will be better able to negotiate the situations they find themselves in and have successful relationships in business and their personal lives. Just imagine if you were taught by your parents how to let bad thoughts go and change the way you feel. Maybe you were, and that's wonderful, but if that wasn't your experience, what if it had been? What if your parents had shown you how to do this when they interacted with other people? What if they had talked to you about how it was done and taught you how to confront, apologize, and forgive in a way that created the greatest possibility of things turning out the way you want them to? Do you think you would have liked something like that? Do you think your life would be easier if you had grown up developing those skills?

If this wasn't how you were raised, start your own way of doing things. Apologize to your kids when you've done something wrong. Forget the excuses and the explanations. State what you did wrong, say, "I'm sorry," and move on. Increase the love in your life, and do your part as a parent. You win in every way when you do.

19. When I tried to confront my mother about something, she wouldn't listen to me. She told me that was all in the past and I should get over it. Other things she denied even happened. What should I do?

You know it can be uncomfortable to be faced with the truth, especially if you've been behaving badly. If the people you confront aren't ready to accept what they've done, and if you think that saying something is going to help give you the feelings you're looking for, go ahead and acknowledge it. You could say, "I understand why you wouldn't be so eager to accept what I'm saying. If I were in your position and I had done the same things, I might feel the same way, but your denial doesn't change what happened and the part you played. One day you may take responsibility for these things, and on that day you will have the opportunity to feel different and to let your bad feelings go. It is only important to me that you've heard the truth. Thank you for listening."

Show yourself the real you. Leave out the anger and other negative emotions, avoid saying what you need to say with an accusatory tone (the three communications will help you), and you will create the ending you're looking for.

20. **My parents have never been too good of an influence on my life. I confronted them, and I forgave them. I feel different, but they're still the same, and now they just make me sad. I feel like I shouldn't be around them. What should I do?**

There is going to be a little dysfunction in everyone's family. We are human. We make mistakes, and we each struggle to come up with ways to deal with what we've done and the emotions we experience. While you can accept other people's faults and forgive the pain they caused you, that doesn't mean you need to spend every Sunday having a family dinner and bearing witness to their unique way of squashing happiness. Whether you are preparing to confront them or have already gone through the process, you might be in a situation with your parents, or with some of the other people in your life, that could benefit from some distance.

It's OK to take a break from your family or other people who make you miserable if you need to. It's OK to move on. You don't have to resign yourself to situations that don't make you feel good or give you what you want in life. Part of the reason the people who treat you badly do so is because you let them. Why should they change if you keep coming back for more?

You could have been raised in a wonderful, supportive, understanding environment, or you could have spent a good portion of the first part of your life with people who were, whether they were aware of it or not, putting their problems and unresolved feelings from their own past into you under the guise of parenting. Guess what? There are things you've spent enough time feeling bad about during the earlier years of your life when you didn't have a choice of who you were around. Now you do. As an adult, this is something you really don't have to make a part of your life anymore. You're free, and you're not responsible for these problems. You didn't create them. You don't control them, and it isn't your job to make the people who have them understand or resolve them.

You have to be smart about the atmosphere you place yourself in. If being near your family is like stepping into a quicksand of bad feelings, taking a break could be the right move. You don't have to be with people who make you miserable or have you feeling powerless, no matter who they are or what they tell you is right. Decide to feel powerful and put yourself in situations that maintain and increase this feeling.

There is an entire world out there for you. The bad feelings aren't you. They're only something you've become used to and may have been living with for so long that you think this is the only reality, but it isn't. Culture, religion, and society may all be telling you to stick it out and that's just the way it is, but that isn't the way it is. The way it is is however you make it and not how those around you are telling you it has to be.

21. **I apologized to my sister about a fight we had, and it didn't turn out well. In fact, she just got angry with me all over again. What should I do now?**

Your sister may need a little more time, or there may be a few of the steps that could use a little more attention from you. If you aren't ready to make a sincere apology, if you aren't at the point where you feel remorse, if you haven't yet admitted to yourself that there was something you could have done differently during the original event, if you are just going through the motions to get it over with or doing this only because it's what you have to do to complete your Clearing, the person you are apologizing to will feel it, and you will end up creating more residual thoughts and increasing their influence in your life.

If you are still thinking about all the things that are wrong with the people you need to apologize to, and if you are focusing more on what they should change about themselves than on your new endings, you will be holding on to feelings that aren't going to let you release your residual thoughts. You have to do your three communications, so that instead of feeling anger and frustration when you try to find a solution, you can feel positive emotions and allow them to influence the decisions you make. When you connect with these positive emotions, you will see the truth of the part you played and increase your ability to produce similar emotions with your new endings. You will find the words you need, and when you go to take action, you will say what you came to say in a way that will create the ending you want.

When something goes wrong in your life, you may become disappointed in yourself. You may feel like you failed and find yourself lashing out because you don't like the way you feel. You may be frustrated that despite your best efforts and intentions, you did something wrong and hurt people. You may be scared that you won't be forgiven if you admit what you've done, that maybe they will give up on you and want you out of their life. You may think that if you apologize, then they get to feel like they are right and that it's all your fault. You may be so angry that you find you are unable to let what happened go long enough to do your three communications. Whatever it is, if these thoughts and emotions are blocking you, you need to see things in a different way if you're going to create a different outcome.

This was the situation my client Amy found herself in when she was preparing to apologize to her boyfriend for the second time. The first time it went horribly wrong. When I asked her what she had said, she told me, "I said that I was sorry about the way he said I acted." I asked her if that's the way she phrased it, and she told me that it was.

"So you were sorry about the way he said you acted and not about the way you actually acted?" Amy laughed when I asked her this, but it was obvious that she was angry and that her anger was getting in the way. To get to the ending she wanted, she needed to get to her residual thoughts and then to the truth, but her negative emotions were stopping her and she was stuck repeating the thoughts that maintained them.

When I asked her about what she did to prepare for her apology, Amy admitted that she had done only one of the three communications. She had looked at her picture but hadn't used her destination image or her sentences. She confessed to me that she thought it was "unfair" that she should have to apologize. Even with the prospect of feeling great and letting go, she didn't care. She said that he "could have avoided the whole incident," and that it was partially his fault for "overreacting." She told me, "If his threshold for being angry and annoyed was higher, we wouldn't have to feel bad."

I gave Amy a pen and a piece of paper and asked her to write down the thoughts she was having about her boyfriend and about what happened immediately after the event occurred. Here's what she wrote:

Amy: I'm sick of apologizing to him. Why can't he let it go this one time? Why can't he think of all the things I've done that were right and let this go? He doesn't apologize for every time he hurts my feelings or treats me badly, so why should I apologize to him? Why am I expected to do that when he isn't? He is blowing this way out of proportion, and now I have to apologize because he's letting a little thing get to him. Do I have to be perfect to survive in this relationship? It seems like that's the only thing that will make him happy.

Amy was in love with her boyfriend, but she was hurt and angry, and her anger was limiting access to her abilities and stopping her. She needed to feel different if she was going to apologize in a way that would get her the feelings she wanted. I gave Amy another piece of paper and asked her to write each sentence separately, leaving spaces between them. I then had her write what she felt was the opposite of each. I told her not to be concerned about what she was writing or what it meant to her life, only to make sure that she followed these instructions. Here's what she ended up writing:

Amy:
I'm sick of apologizing to him.
　　—*I'm sick of not apologizing to him.*

Why can't he let it go this one time?
　　—*Why can't I let it go this one time?*

Why can't he think of all the things I've done that were right and let this go?
　　—*Why can't I think of all the things he's done that were right and let this go?*

He doesn't apologize for every time he hurts my feelings or treats me badly, so why should I apologize to him? Why am I expected to do that when he isn't?
—*I don't apologize for every time I hurt his feelings or treat him badly, so why should he apologize to me? Why is he expected to do that when I'm not?*

He is blowing this way out of proportion, and now I have to apologize because he's letting a little thing get to him.
—*I'm blowing this way out of proportion, and now he has to apologize because I'm letting a little thing get to me.*

Do I have to be perfect to survive in this relationship? It seems like that's the only thing that will make him happy.
—*Does he have to be perfect to survive in this relationship? It seems like that's the only thing that will make me happy.*

When Amy was through writing, I told her to read only the sentences she had written that were the opposite of her originals. When she was done, we talked about each one, and she admitted they were all true. She told me, "He even apologizes when he knows he's hurt my feelings."

It's amazing how much what she had written told Amy about herself and how much she found herself agreeing with each statement. We even started laughing about it, and I think for Amy it was a relief. Her perspective changed. She saw what her anger had been keeping her from seeing. After that, the new ending happened quickly. She apologized to her boyfriend. She got the feelings she wanted and inspired him to apologize to her and say that he could have handled the whole thing better, which gave her even more good feelings. She was able to put love and understanding into her second apology, and she ended up getting love and understanding in return.

Nice.

Be honest with yourself from the start. If you want the other person to feel bad more than you want to feel good, you are going to screw yourself out of being happy and create more of the same bad feelings. To get past your anger and other negative emotions, use your three communications. If you are so angry that you can't see any sort of successful conclusion, then go with it and let your anger out. Get out a pen and some paper. Take everything you hate or can't stand about this person and everything you are angry about surrounding the event and write it down. Go ahead and point your finger and get it all out. Then take each sentence and write down the opposite. When you're done, read through what you wrote for your opposites only. Really look at them and consider if what you wrote contains some truth.

Even if you don't want to do it, even if you think this is a fine thing for other people and just isn't for you, write the opposite. Don't even think about it. Just do it and then look at what you wrote. I know that truly seeing yourself can sometimes suck. I've felt the sting of self-realization myself, and I won't say it's my favorite feeling, but like receiving a shot from the doctor when you were a kid, it's a moment of pain in exchange for a lifetime of possibilities.

If you love the sensation of anger and you just have to have it at all costs, then don't do this exercise. If you want to feel in control and powerful, if you'd rather not spend your time thinking about people you aren't particularly fond of and the things they do that you hate, then do this instead. Get your anger and bad feelings out of your body and down on paper. Then write the opposite, and determine what is the truth.

I love this exercise because it helps you to see yourself, and if you use what you see, you will find what you need to get past your anger and create a successful new ending for your event. Use what you've written to help determine what your residual thoughts are and then to find the truth about yourself and the abilities you possess. Once you do, put them to use creating your new endings.

22. **Now that I'm done Clearing my residual thoughts, I'm doing my three communications to ensure that I have positive interactions with my coworkers so I don't rack up any more residual thoughts. However, things don't always go great at work. I'm telling myself I can do this, but sometimes it doesn't work. How can I feel like I'm not lying to myself when I try to do the three communications now?**

I don't know anyone who started doing this and could instantly achieve a hundred percent success rate. You still have to get back on the bike though. If you don't like an ending, keep going and create a new one. This goes for every ending you create in your life. There are no exceptions. If you are using your three communications to have positive interactions with your coworkers and something goes wrong, create a new ending. Confront, apologize, or forgive — it's always going to be one of the three — and then move on.

Don't waste time demanding that your three communications work exactly the way you want them to for each ending you create or being upset when other people don't respond like you think they should. Focus on continuing forward until you create a new ending that gives you the thoughts you want to have about yourself. Never just take away bad thoughts and think you're done with it because those thoughts will stay with you. You aren't lying to yourself when you say you are awesome and that you can do it. But you are living a lie if you don't go back when things go wrong and make things right by continuing the story and creating an ending that reflects the truth of who you are.

In the past when you thought you were a failure, you were simply giving up too soon. Keep going, and you will find that when you tell yourself you can do it, you're telling yourself the truth. Things may not always go the way you planned at work, but if you are consistent with your three communications, you will find they're working out the way you want them to a lot more often.

25

YOUR CLEARING AND AFTER

FORGET ABOUT HOW you think you should feel about an event, and deal with how you actually do feel. Even if you think it's immature to be upset about how your friend from work treated you at the company picnic last summer or what your brother did with the money you lent him, even if you think it's silly that you are still angry about what your husband said to you two years ago when you were out to dinner and discussing having another child, even if you think you are too old or too much time has passed and you shouldn't still be thinking about what happened between you and your parents when you were in high school, even if you believe it isn't right to feel the way you do, don't talk yourself out of confronting, apologizing, and forgiving. Deal with the truth of your feelings, and free yourself from what's holding you back.

The residual thoughts you have and the emotions that go with them aren't just in the past. They are here in the situations you're struggling with and feeling bad about in your life today. Like ghosts, they hang around and haunt you until you take action to let them go.

You had momentum before your residual thoughts became a part of your life. You had speed. You were going somewhere until they came in and changed you, until they took up residence inside you and told you that you aren't capable or that the things you want aren't worth it. That happiness is just something you get to feel every once in a while (like on your birthday maybe, or when you take a vacation) and not something you can expect to have happen too often or with any consistency. Before these events, you were you, you had hope, you had good feelings, you saw possibilities, and you were different.

Whether you realize it or not, it's your residual thoughts that are telling you that you're too fat to date, that you don't have the will to end the affair, or that you'll never have the money or guts to make your dream of attending culinary school in Paris a reality. They're what's telling you that you shouldn't say anything at the dinner party next Friday because it will probably come out wrong or sound stupid, and that having a crummy marriage is just the way life is and the best someone like you can hope for. Your residual thoughts are what's telling you that you can't, while others who don't appear to have half as many advantages, who don't display nearly the amount of spark, drive, good looks, style, or intelligence as you, are passing you by, and the only reason they're doing so is that they don't have the same residual thoughts as you standing in their way.

Your residual thoughts are like a stone in your shoe. You may try to convince yourself that you don't have the time right now to stop what you are doing, take your shoe off, find the stone, and fling it away. You may think that the stone really isn't that big of a deal and that you can just live with it for now. But that stone is a big deal. It's keeping you from losing weight and getting along with the people at work. It's keeping you from enjoying sex, having happy relationships, and pursuing all the things you want and are totally capable of having. It's causing you to put pain from your past into the things you do and then sticking you with the problems that creates.

Is it worth it to remove something from your life that causes you pain and affects every move you make? You better believe it is. Create new endings, no matter how accustomed to the pain you've become, no matter how many excuses and good reasons come into your mind not to, no matter how embarrassed it may make you feel to do so, or what you fear other people may think of you when you do.

You have a way to do this now. Follow the steps, prepare, and make your move. You could run before that stone was there, and you still can. If you keep what needs to be said inside, if you pretend like you are past it, that what happened wasn't that bad or important, if you try to continue your life with these words, these thoughts and emotions left unexpressed inside of you, you will suffer, the people you love will suffer, and all the things you want to accomplish, all your efforts, your happiness and everything you are capable of contributing to the world will be lessened in some way.

If you're feeling fear right now, ask yourself what you are really afraid of. Consider the possibility that what you think is fear may simply be the feeling of being anxious about doing something new. Think about it. Is living as a trim and fit person really scary? Do you picture yourself looking sexy in your swimsuit and walking down the beach with someone you love and then instantly have to run to your bedroom and hide under the covers? Are things like playing golf every weekend at the country club you've always dreamed of joining and living with someone you feel passionate about really that scary? Which is more frightening to you: spending the next twenty years working at a job you hate, being overweight, and dreading going home at night because your relationship sucks, or making the move to pursue what will actually make you happy in your career, being in shape, and truly feeling good about the person you're sleeping next to at night?

Get on your side. I mean really get on your side. Don't let the excuses rise to the surface, and don't ever let a single sentence of doubt and discouragement complete itself. Instead, go in your new direction each day and allow what no longer belongs in your life to fade from existence.

Be aware that as you continue forward your old identity may try to come around for a visit (usually when you're feeling down for some reason). Maybe, for example, you'll be trying to lose weight. Maybe you will lose ten pounds. Everything is going great. But then one morning you get on the scale and find that instead of losing more weight, the numbers have gone up and you've gained two pounds. The old identity could be more than halfway out the door, but it could seize this opportunity to try to regain control by feeding you the old lines and good reasons it used in the past to get you to give up. It will have you suddenly seeing pictures in your mind of yourself failing and focusing on the things you hate and the people you don't like. There will be a familiar voice telling you that you "can't" and that it "won't work," and anything else that will make it easy for you to quit and then blame something or someone else for choosing not to follow through. What it will say will seem legitimate. You should feel powerless. You should feel bad. After all, you gained two pounds. That's a good reason to get down on yourself, right?

Wrong. You've lost eight pounds. You are doing great, but even though this is true, your old identity can warp your perception. It can turn your focus toward the negative so much that it will seem to you that the two pounds you gained are actually much more than the eight you lost.

Don't let it! Instead of pausing to give these distractions from your past some thought, instead of opening the door to your old identity and allowing it to spoil your good feelings and conjure excuses to quit, increase your speed in the other direction and create some distance. When you're at the beach and the waves are crashing down on top of you, you don't set out your towel, lie down, and expect to stay dry. When your old identity comes around with images of failure and thoughts of you being "no good" and throwing out all sorts of good reasons why you should quit instead of reaching your goals, move! Treat what comes to you like waves filled with hungry sharks that are about to rain down on you, and move with extreme speed in the other direction.

The Clearing is a process, and it's also a lifestyle philosophy. It's a way to live, to move on, and to be happy every day. You want something better, and within you is the potential to have it. The ability to be awesome and happy in all situations is there inside you. You can be the life of the party, you can be brilliant and articulate in business meetings, you can dazzle the beautiful girl or attract the hot guy, and you can even lose the extra weight. Apply the Clearing to your life and realize the truth. Change doesn't have to be as hard as you may have imagined it to be, and it doesn't have to feel bad while it's happening. It may feel strange to do some of the things you are beginning to do now, but don't let feeling different stop you from what your life could be.

When you're doing something new and it feels different, it doesn't necessarily mean that it isn't working or that there's something wrong. It usually just means that you aren't used to what you're doing yet. Even if it feels funny for a while, you will adapt and enjoy the new things you do once you've given yourself the chance to get used to them.

Take a second and give it some thought. Do you really want to go back to letting unresolved issues pile up when you know how they affect your life? Of course not—you want to feel good. You want to move forward without any new bad feelings or thoughts weighing you down. So deal with situations that need new endings as they come up. Make confronting, apologizing, and forgiving what you do whenever you're faced with a less-than-satisfactory outcome, and transition from Clearing the major events in your life to Clearing what comes up as you go about your day.

If things don't work out, if something happens that makes you feel bad, if you find yourself with lingering negative thoughts over a situation, don't wait. Complete an event chart and continue the story. Figure out what your residual thoughts are, fill out *The Truth*, and then write out what you will do:

"Tomorrow I will apologize to Patty for missing her art show."

"In the morning I will confront my husband about leaving his underwear in the bathroom sink and using my deodorant as his jock itch medication."

"This weekend I will confront and forgive my mother-in-law for coming over unannounced at any time of the day or night and then set clear parameters for her to follow."

Decide what you will say, do your three communications, and when the time comes, take action and create your new ending.

As you move forward, don't be put off by temporary failures or missteps. Don't let the old identity back in so it can start calling the shots. Don't let it push you around. Be prepared instead. You have the tools in your hands, and because you've completed the steps, you know that they work.

Maybe in the past when things went wrong and you wanted your bad feelings to go away and you didn't know what to do, you ate too much junk food and candy, wasted too much time on the Internet, and had sex with anyone who was around just to try to feel different. Maybe you ended up taking a few wrong turns, letting the people into your life distract you, and holding back on your dreams. Maybe you kept feeling bad and failing, so you started to believe you were powerless to do what it takes to change your life and make yourself happy. If these feelings should resurface, Clear away what makes you think that this person is you. Keep creating new endings with the steps. Expose the truth, free yourself to discover other options, and then pursue the ones that make you feel powerful.

If things go wrong or don't work out exactly as planned, it's OK. Making mistakes means you are on your way. You're being brave and taking action. If you look into the stories of successful people, if you scratch just below the surface and do some research, you'll see it was much the same for them as they made their way toward success. Most failed miserably, but even when they were embarrassed or humiliated, even when things went horribly wrong, they kept going. This is how it is for everyone who succeeds no matter what they're trying to achieve. So if things go wrong, if you make some mistakes, don't worry about it, keep going, and you'll be in great company. Even if you've failed a hundred times before, it doesn't make a difference. You can still be successful at the things you want to accomplish.

Realize that as you figure things out and gain knowledge, your identity is supposed to change and you're supposed to feel different. When people are trapped in identities that are too confining, they act out, they lie, they have affairs, they create problems and drama, they put on weight and point their finger at what's around them instead of taking responsibility and using their power to make themselves happy. You don't have to do these things. You can change yourself and inspire those around you. You can improve your relationships or find new people to be with as you begin to redefine yourself.

Everything is moving forward. Everything is evolving. This means you have to evolve too. If you try to stop the process, you will never feel right. Growing up isn't just something you do when you are young or something that stops after high school. You do it your whole life. There will always be challenges to face. You could wrestle with the human condition or embrace it. What choice do you really have?

You want to have peace of mind. You want to maintain these new feelings and continue to go in this new direction. So commit to this new way of doing things until it becomes a pattern, until it is simply the way you live your happy and successful life. Become an expert at creating new endings. Become a grand master at using your three communications. What you've learned here works, and it will continue to work for the rest of your life *if you use it*. If in the past you've gone from book to book, from method to method, gotten inspired, and then moved on to something else without following through or making permanent changes, do this differently. Commit to practicing what you've learned and using it in your life each day. Instead of jumping right into the next new thing that comes around, keep doing the Clearing. You've found what works, so work it.

Why treat yourself as less than who you actually are just because someone from your past treated you like dirt? Why rob yourself of the life you could have because of the way you interpreted something that happened to you when you were twelve? Practice what you've learned instead. Continue to do periodic Clearings of your home. Make sure your new possessions pass the Power Question and that you aren't acquiring any new residual thoughts as you go about your life. Set a reminder to go off on your phone or computer the same time each day or once a week with the question, "Who do I need to confront, apologize, or forgive?" Make sure you're always creating the thoughts and feelings you want and letting go of the ones you don't.

This isn't the time to drift back into your old life. You have to get used to the idea that you don't have to be who your residual thoughts said you were anymore. To remind you of this, and to keep moving in your new direction, look at the situations you regularly encounter, and instead of just doing things the same old way, focus on what you can do differently each day.

Now is the time to learn a new sport or join a different club. If you used to go to spin class, switch to swimming or weight training. If you used to try to get in shape on your own, hire a trainer, work out specific goals, and get started. Go to a different grocery store, gas station, department store, gym, nail salon, hairstylist, dentist, chiropractor, massage therapist. Take a different route to work. Let go of the old repertoire and responses. If someone asks you about your job, talk about it in a different way. If you are used to meeting others for food and drinks, get together to do things that are more active. If you are out on a date, say something other than what you are used to saying. Discuss a different aspect of your life or something you've never discussed before. If you never reveal anything about yourself, then open up and reveal something. If you are an open book to every new person you meet, exposing your vulnerabilities right at the start, then hold back a little, take it slower, create a little mystery, and allow people to get to know you at a more gradual pace. If in the past you used to regale those around you with your views on everything that's wrong with the world, complain about the people at work, and dump every bad feeling or thought you have on your friends, start pointing out the things that are going right and the things you see that are beautiful.

Instead of unconsciously going through the motions and using the same areas of your brain and the same motor functions as before, when you do what is different you are activating different parts inside of you. You're helping free yourself from the old patterns, and this makes it easier for you to think the thoughts and say the words that will help you live your life in a different way. Doing things differently will help keep you from thinking that your life is the same and that you should just carry on as usual — because it's not the same and you shouldn't carry on as usual. This is one of the most important things for you to realize and understand: *If you continue doing the same things, your life will be the same no matter what events you Cleared.* Go back to doing what you used to do and all your effort will have been wasted.

It's time to start behaving differently, to take yourself out of your old patterns, and to continue to use of the parts of yourself you revealed when you Cleared your five events. Will taking a different route to work or talking about different things when you are on a date accomplish this? On their own, probably not. But as part of your efforts to bring what you've learned from your Clearing into your life? Definitely.

Prepare for the things you will do — the meetings you will have at work, the big date, the holidays with your spouse's family — by using your three communications. Use them to access your cleverness, your talents, gifts, and abilities (They are there. Don't doubt it for a second because it's true.), and to let yourself know, in a language that can be understood by all the parts inside of you, what you want and which way to go. Remember, you are always creating your life. You are continually moving toward something whether you recognize this or not. Devote yourself now to making what you've learned in the steps a part of each day, and continue moving in the direction you truly want to go.

Your life can be a lot of fun — it really can. From this moment on, tell yourself what you want the same way you did with your five new endings. Never let any one person or thing blind you to the awesomeness you possess, and if some of the events in your life don't turn out the way you planned, keep going, create new endings, and never stop making this the life you want.

26

MOVING FORWARD, SETTING GOALS, AND TAKING ACTION

YOU'VE CLEARED YOUR home. You've taken five events that gave you residual thoughts and weighed you down, followed the Seven Steps, and gave them new endings. You created new thoughts and feelings to replace the old ones and made some discoveries about who you are. This is major stuff, and you're probably feeling pretty good, and you should. So what's next?

Maybe there's a certain way you want your body to look, maybe there's an amount of money you want to earn, maybe there's a relationship you want to be in or a certain lifestyle you want to have. Regardless of what it is, there is something you want, and it's good to get serious about this now because if your mind isn't occupied with specific goals, if you leave it idle, if you just kick back for a while after your Clearing and let things happen as they may, you will become occupied with whatever strays into your line of sight and you could quickly find yourself covering the same old ground and getting sucked into problems and other distractions.

To keep moving past the life you had with your old identity, you need something to move toward. Pursuing goals will prevent you from backsliding into old tendencies. Goals will engage the talents and abilities you used during your Clearing and help make them a part of your life every day.

You may have goals that you failed to reach in the past or goals you never allowed yourself to go after because you were too afraid, because you didn't believe you had what it takes, because you thought it wouldn't work out and you didn't want to deal with the pain you believed you would feel when that happened. Now that you've finished your Clearing, you're realizing that you're capable of more than you thought, that these goals you've been falling short on achieving or that you held off on pursuing are actually possible, and now you're ready to do something about it. Or maybe your old goals aren't as interesting to you as they once were, and you've set your sights on something new. Whether it's new or old, whether it's starting your own company, traveling the world, owning your own horse ranch, racing cars, getting an MBA, learning how to swim, stopping yourself from biting your nails, becoming a real estate agent, pro athlete, or a fashion designer: To reach your goal, get specific about what it is you want and when you want to have it by, decide on the actions you will take to reach it, start using your three communications, and begin pursuing it.

> Three steps for reaching your goals:
> Step 1: Clearly define your destination.
> Step 2: List the actions you will take to reach it.
> Step 3: Do your three communications and begin.

For step 1, get specific about what it is you want and write it down. If you make your goal something like, "I want to be happy," the communication is unclear. There are parts of your mind that won't be able to recognize what "to be happy" is or to know where to go, unless you clearly define it. While being happy is terrific to pursue, using it as your destination is too vague. There is no "X marks the spot." What entails "to be happy"? How do you call it up in your mind and picture it? If it's having two healthy kids and a loving spouse who enjoys giving you massages, a top-of-the-line Mercedes in silver with a tan interior, a ten-acre estate on the beach in the Hamptons with a helicopter pad, and having it all within the next four years, then there is something to grab hold of and focus on—you have a clearly defined destination.

For step 2, write out the actions you will take to reach your goal. The best way to decide what you will do is to see the destination first.

Picture yourself successfully reaching your goal and loving it. See yourself there at your destination, enjoying what you've achieved and feeling good about yourself. Bring up all the wonderful emotions you can, and then ask yourself, "What would the successful me I see in my vision do to achieve this goal?" Show yourself visions of what you truly want and a future where things go your way, then use the good feelings you create and the parts of yourself you've accessed with these images to help you decide what you will do.

Be specific when writing out the actions you will take. If your goal is to have a new job with a twenty-five percent pay increase, move into a home with a swimming pool and a garden, and do it by your thirty-second birthday. For the actions you will take, you could write, "In order to achieve my goal, I will ask for a raise at my annual review in two weeks, send my resume out to twenty-five of the top companies in my field and follow up with a phone call, reach out to five of my work contacts each week to see what opportunities are available and get the word out that I'm interested. I will also work on improving my interview skills through online training, and I will practice for a minimum of one hour each week."

Maybe you have a side project you've been thinking about doing, something related to your job but more personal, and for your destination you've written, "It is my goal to publish a book on the history of American architecture, have my own website to promote it, and sell over 10,000 copies by three years from today." For the actions you will take, you could write something like, "In order to do this, I will wake up forty-five minutes earlier each morning so I can write before work. I will join my local writers group to get feedback and hone my craft, and instead of traveling this year for my vacation, I will use that time to devote myself to writing and reaching this goal."

If you want to lose weight, and your goal is to weigh 125 pounds by October 15th of next year, for the actions you will take, you could write, "To do this, I will jog one mile a day, seven days a week for six months and then a minimum of two miles each day for another six months. During this time I will cut out all soda and replace it with water, and I will no longer eat after 7:30 p.m."

Make your actions ones that you can maintain. Engage your intelligence, repeat your three communications, and move at a pace that allows you to sustain your forward motion consistently. Your enthusiasm is precious. Spread it out. Don't crush it with a death blow by trying to create change overnight and beating yourself up when it doesn't happen. If you want to change your body, avoid trying to do it all in one day. If, for instance, you used to eat a bag of pretzels after dinner while watching TV and then followed it with a pint of ice cream ten minutes before you went to bed, and now you want to change what this has done to your body and you believe that means suddenly jogging five miles every morning and doing a hundred sit-ups every night when you haven't done either in years, realize that this is your old identity trying to come in and sabotage your efforts.

When it comes to your body and changing the way it looks, devote yourself to the long term and to keeping a steady pace. Those who try to lose weight and get in shape overnight just get frustrated. They get sore, injure themselves, and end up quitting. You are much too clever to get involved in these actions. Be smart and accept that your physical form will change gradually over time. This is actually a good thing. Imagine if you skipped lunch one day and woke up the next emaciated or had five slices of pizza one night and found yourself covered in blubber the following day. Accept the reality that physical changes take time, appreciate it, and be steady and consistent.

With all your goals, pursue actions that you can maintain as time goes on. Avoid trying to do too much from the start. If you find that you are sabotaging yourself in this way, ask yourself if there is an event from your past that's making you think you're someone who has to do everything all at once or who doesn't deserve to reach his or her goals, fill out an event chart, and create a new ending. Then look at your goal again, make adjustments to your actions, and keep going.

For Step 3, start using your three communications just like you did for your five events. Find an object or picture that gives you good feelings. Make it a new one that has no history or relationship to your life so that you can associate it only with your destination. Create an image in your mind of you successfully reaching your goal and having what you want. Tell yourself you can do it, and add a sentence or two if you like about yourself, about your skills, something that will make you feel really good and that will help you to hear before you make your move. Then begin repeating your three communications three times a day and taking action toward your destination.

Print the three steps for reaching your goals, and put them up on your wall, or keep them on a small piece of paper in your wallet or purse. Use them for whatever you want to have success with. Use them for your date tomorrow night. Use them to help you pass the bar exam or to get along with your ex-wife's new husband at your son's baseball game and the team picnic afterward.

As you move toward your goals, pay attention to what you are seeing with your eyes and the feelings your surroundings are creating in you. Keep the photo you've chosen handy, and use it to feel good and refocus throughout your day. If an old image of defeat crops up, visualize a big red X going through it or get out a giant mental eraser and erase it away. Put it in a box, throw in some imaginary dynamite, and watch it explode, or tie it to a rocket ship that's blasting off to the sun and see it disintegrate into dust. If you find that you are knocking yourself down with your words, employ the "is what I used to say" technique and immediately tell yourself the opposite. If your attitude gets tested along the way and you start thinking that maybe this is a waste of time, or if you find yourself asking, "Haven't I done enough of this already?" take a moment and remember how you lived before you started your Clearing. Remember how you felt, remember what brought you to this point, and acknowledge that you never want to go back to the way things were.

You could be living a much different life a year from now. You could have a much different life tomorrow. Keep going. Give yourself a chance to realize the truth of what I'm saying. Through whatever course of events, you found me and this book. Now is the time to use what you've found to continue to create the life you want. Set your goals, decide on the actions you will take to reach them, communicate to yourself what you want with your three communications, and begin.

27

CONCLUSION

AFTER THEIR CLEARINGS, my clients' lives began looking different. They saw that they weren't really overweight or lazy and that they didn't always fail. They saw that they weren't who their old thoughts had been convincing them they were. They realized why it felt bad to live the way they'd been living, that it didn't have to be that way anymore, and they started to change.

Some moved, some switched jobs, some asked for raises and received them, some got in shape, some found new relationships, and some made the ones they were in work again. Without the thoughts that were attached to their possessions and their old endings, my clients could see the truth and begin using more of what they had inside of themselves. Once they did, they started to experience much different lives.

It's easy to see how your possessions can influence you, especially if they have strong emotions and associations attached to them, and it's easy to see how the residual thoughts from the events in your past that ended badly could be showing up in your life today and causing problems. It is my greatest hope that by reading this book you will understand the value of your life and realize your capacity to create change.

No matter what has happened in the past—even if you've been disappointed over and over or chosen denial over change, even if you've become jaded and cynical, even if you gave up a long time ago—you can do the Clearing and make your life better. You have an opportunity right now to say goodbye to what's been slowing you down and causing you and others to perceive you as less than who you are, so take it.

The Clearing is like anything worthwhile: You have to do it. You have to ask the questions. You have to answer, and you have to take the actions that will change your life. If you are consistently getting bad feelings from any part of your life, it's a sign that you need to grow in some way. Until you take different actions and stick with them, the behavior won't change, the bad feelings will stick around, and you will always go back to the way you were.

Without guilt or obligation interfering, or allowing what other people think to get in your way, look at your surroundings and inside of yourself and decide what needs to stay, what needs to go, and who you're going to be. This is what you have. This is what you know is yours. It's your life. At conception you were the one who made it ahead of all the others. You won a race against millions, and that's why you are here on earth right now. Inside of you there is an incredible will to live. There is tremendous drive and ambition.

Can you be rich? Can you lose the weight? Can you make yourself and the people you love happy? Absolutely. How could there be any doubt? I don't care how old you are; you've only begun to do things. You are powerful. Seriously powerful. I've never met you, but I know it's true. Don't let any of the bullshit you grew up with or any mistakes you made in the past tell you differently. They are so small in comparison to your true potential. They are a tiny crumb, too tiny for even a mouse, compared to what you are capable of.

Doing the Clearing is your chance to change your life and reinvent yourself. If things aren't working, then you are right to want to do something about it. This is where you begin. Remember the race you won to get here and embrace what you will do next with that same passion. That passion is you. The fact that you are breathing and reading this book is proof. You've made it. Now that you're here, what are you going to do?

*One of my greatest joys is helping people with their Clearings.
If you are interested in scheduling a Clearing,
please contact me through my website at
www.johnbenz.com*

Made in the USA
Middletown, DE
04 April 2015